THE SILENT TRAVELLER
IN NEW YORK

THE SILENT TRAVELLER
IN NEW YORK

記 畫 約 紐

Written and Illustrated by Chiang Yee

With a Preface by Van Wyck Brooks

APPLEWOOD BOOKS
Carlisle, Massachusetts

ALSO AVAILABLE

The Silent Traveller in Boston
The Silent Traveller in San Francisco

First published in 1950

Copyright © 1950 by Chiang Yee

978-1-4290-9387-3

Thank you for purchasing an Applewood book. Applewood reprints America's lively classics—books from the past that are still of interest to modern readers. Our mission is to build a picture of America's past through its primary sources.

To inquire about this edition or to request a free copy of our current catalog featuring our best-selling books, write to:

Applewood Books
P.O. Box 27
Carlisle, MA 01741

For more complete listings, visit us on the web at: www.awb.com

10 9 8 7 6 5 4 3 2 1

Printed in China

TO

STELLA AND PAUL

PREFACE

About a dozen years ago a book appeared in England that was called *The Silent Traveller in Lakeland*. It was the work of a Chinese painter and writer who had been for nearly five years a magistrate and district governor in his native city of Kiukiang on the Yangtse river. With an added interest of his own in scenery and animals, Mr. Chiang Yee followed in the footsteps of his father, an able amateur painter of flowers and birds, and he and his friends on walking-trips had sketched and improvised poems as well at picturesque and legendary spots in the mountains. He had watched the sunrise from various peaks, especially Lu mountain near Kiukiang, renowned for its wild waterfalls and rocky scenes which the great Chinese poets and artists had sung and painted. The " Silent Traveller," the title that Mr. Chiang Yee adopted, was a translation of his Chinese pen-name, which might have been literally rendered as "Dumb Walking Man." His work as a civil servant had kept him talking day and night, and, glad enough to escape from this, he had chosen a name that was not unlike the common phrase for a roaming Buddhist monk. Mr. Chiang Yee arrived in England in 1933, where he has lived ever since, appearing in a series of illustrated books as the "Silent Traveller" in London, Oxford, Edinburgh and the Yorkshire dales. He had explored first, as Mr. Herbert Read said in his preface to *The Silent Traveller in Lakeland*, the "very holy of holies" of the English nature poets.

The English lake district was a happy field for a Chinese artist with an inborn love of mountains, streams, trees and flowers, and, while he wrote about this region with a singular freshness and lightness of touch, he interpreted it also in pictures and ideograms. Unaccustomed, as he said, to occidental media and techniques, he used his Chinese brushes, inks and colours, following his own native method in painting, and in this and his subsequent travel-books, dealing with English and Scottish themes, he produced effects that were equally novel and charming. He was especially fortunate perhaps because England was a land of mists and fogs, like those one saw in so many of the great Chinese paintings, and the fickle English weather pleased him by constantly changing the aspects of scenes while it stirred him to record the changes in his own feelings. With a veil of rain familiar scenes passed through enchanting variations, and even his affection for sunshine increased because it arrived unexpectedly and because, like the objects themselves, it was elusive. He delighted in the soft fresh English green that had, as he remarked, both life in itself and the power of blending other colours, and at every turn the simple things of this countryside that was foreign to him carried his imagination back to China. A group of oaks with twisted trunks or a waterfall on a rugged cliff recalled to his mind's eye some old Sung painting, so that sometimes he followed the Sung style in a picture of his own, and, remembering the poets, hermits and scholars who had meditated in scenes like these, he was prompted to repeat their sayings and anecdotes about them. He was charmed by a cluster of horses in a meadow, by a heathery hillock, green and blue, fading into grey, melting into the dove-coloured sky, by dragonflies clinging to the tops of reeds, a knot of water-lily leaves and buds, a robin or a rose-tree in full bloom. Composing a poem now and then, he interspersed his observations with delightful examples of Chinese calligraphy also, with notes on characters whom he had met, wayfaring folk in city streets, old buildings and the customs of the country. Mr. Chiang Yee shared Wordsworth's pleasure in the meanest flower that blows. With none of the clichés of travel-writing, his books possessed the companionable charm of a mind of great natural distinction that was willing to be pleased.

When I heard that the "Silent Traveller" was writing a book about New York, I wondered if he would find this a happy subject. With his fondness for dull rainy days and the misty-moisty English scene, would he like the hard dry light of our stone and steel? In New York he would have for mountain peaks only metallic skyscrapers, and instead of the soft English rain he would have our thoroughly business-like rain that comes down as if it was also made of steel. I half wished that he had chosen first the luxuriant New England countryside, the valley of the Housatonic, the Franconia mountains,

she green hills of Vermont and the foggy rocky coast of Maine
that appears in John Marin's water-colours. What would he
not be able to do with the autumn foliage along the rivers
or the neatly winning Palladian villages and towns that are
surely little known in China? But I had not fully realized the
depth of Mr. Chiang Yee's interest in the urban and human
as well as the natural scene; and, besides, there were days in
New York when clouds enveloped the tall buildings, suggesting
for him a Sung painting of high Chinese peaks. In the six
months that he spent in the city, he made discoveries in
Greenwich Village that will surprise even the oldest New
Yorkers, and he made discoveries in Chinatown that surprised
a Chinese, for almost everything he heard there was invented
for tourists. He was alertly curious enough to get up at five
on Sunday morning to see what was left of Times Square
after Saturday night; he walked across the George Washington
bridge; he sailed up the Hudson to Poughkeepsie; he inves-
tigated the Bowery, Broadway, Wall Street, Harlem. He found
children everywhere who were lovable and playful. He
delighted in the ballet-like gestures of the hands and arms of
a crowd of girls at the summit of the Empire State building,
from which Central Park looked like a small lacquer tea-tray
inlaid with jade to represent trees and lakes, Seen from this
height, the other buildings were like infinitesimal bamboo-
shoots in a Chinese grove in early spring. Mr. Chiang Yee's
pen-and-ink drawings of street scenes suggest the omnivorous
and humorous eye with which he absorbed the multitudinous
life of the city, while the parks and botanical gardens of
Manhattan and Brooklyn provided for the landscape artist
a variety of themes. There he found cherry-trees in blossom
and willows with branches tossing in the wind that stirred him
to write poems as he painted and drew them, and even the
natural rock-formations, the waterfalls, thickets and gorges
that were immemorial subjects of Chinese painters. There were
the squirrels with sparkling eyes that were also cherished in
Chinese art, and he found birds in every corner of the city.
Almost every one of his pictures contains a pigeon, a swan,
a crane, or wild geese, ducks or seagulls flying aloft.

The fact is that Mr. Chiang Yee is a true citizen of the
world, like Goldsmith's observer from China, everywhere at
home, interested in all things human as well as in animals,

trees and birds, who has given us a fresh New York that is different from all others. An American admirer can only hope that he will visit other regions—Concord, perhaps, and Walden pond where Confucius and Mencius found wise readers who had the Chinese feeling for Shan-Shui also. Mr. Chiang Yee recalls Thoreau when he says that "winter clears the head," and a Chinese painter in monochrome would find he had much in common with Thoreau, who loved the winter colours of the scrub-oak and the rabbit. There are the Carolinas too where Audubon spent happy months among the scenes of William Bartram's *Travels*, the charming book that suggested to Wordsworth and Coleridge some of the famous images that appeared in their poems. Mr. Chiang Yee would find there the azaleas that "set the hills on fire" in *Ruth*, the rhododendrons he always associates with China and the flowering magnolia trees that he knew as a child; and if he went to the Southwest he would find the American Indians who were anciently connected, as he remarks, with his own honourable race. If Mr. Chiang Yee were to read Mrs. Mabel Dodge Luhan's *Winter in Taos*, he might well wish to fly or even walk there. Taos was the "only place that actually realized" for Leo Stein "the vision of the great Chinese landscape painters."

Since I am quoting Leo Stein, I may add what he said of appreciation, which had, he felt, a great role to play in the world. He saw society at the end of a road with only two alternatives, universal war or more appreciation—the appreciation of life and men that would lead people to give up the resistances and repressions that must otherwise lead them to fight. This, as it seems to me, is Mr. Chiang Yee's counsel too, and perhaps the general counsel of Chinese wisdom, one that we should welcome in America, where sanity is the last thing that anyone looks for at present. Mr. Chiang Yee repeats the saying of Mencius that a wise man should retain his childlike mind,— a rebuke to our tiresome ideal of "sophistication"; and he says that in securing the freedoms from ignorance and want we should also plan for a "freedom from too many desires." That might be his reply to our foolish cult of advertising, which exists for the breeding of desires, the more the better. In saying that man is a greedy creature, greedy for wealth, food, clothes or fame, he suggests that he himself is more often greedy for things that delight the eye or delight the mind—that he is appreciative, in short, as he kindles in others the appreciative feeling that alone perhaps can keep the world at peace.

VAN WYCK BROOKS.

CONTENTS

		PAGE
I	LEAVING ENGLAND	1
II	ON BOARD	6
III	APPROACHING NEW YORK	14
IV	ALONG WALL STREET	25
V	NON-OBJECTIVE SKETCHINGS	34
VI	ROUND TIMES SQUARE	48
VII	ALONG PARK AVENUE	60
VIII	IN CENTRAL PARK	72
IX	ALONG FIFTH AVENUE	93
X	AT BRONX ZOO	116
XI	ON BEDLOE'S ISLAND	125
XII	ALONG EAST RIVER	132
XIII	IN BROOKLYN BOTANICAL GARDENS	144
XIV	APPOINTMENTS WITH ART	151
XV	IN WASHINGTON SQUARE	164
XVI	AMONG THE LIGHTS OF BROADWAY	175
XVII	IN CHINATOWN	187
XVIII	IN GREENWICH VILLAGE	202
XIX	ON GEORGE WASHINGTON BRIDGE	216
XX	IN HARLEM	224
XXI	ALONG RIVERSIDE DRIVE	231
XXII	IN THE BOWERY	238
XXIII	ON THE HUDSON RIVER	249
XXIV	AT INNISFREE	260
XXV	TSAI CHIEN, NEW YORK	276

ILLUSTRATIONS IN COLOUR

APPROACHING NEW YORK AT DAWN   *Frontispiece*

FACING PAGE

WALL STREET AT TWILIGHT	32
WATERFALL NEAR BRONX ZOO	48
SKYSCRAPERS ABOVE EVENING CLOUD AND MIST	68
SPRING COMES TO CENTRAL PARK	76
THE MORNING LOOK OF THE CIVIL SERVICE BUILDING	100
FORT TRYON UNDER THE MOON	108
RUBY-THROATED HUMMING-BIRDS	122
THE WIND IN THE WILLOWS IN BROOKLYN BOTANICAL GARDENS	144
SUNSET OVER WASHINGTON SQUARE	160
THE UPPER HUDSON RIVER NEAR NEWBURGH	192
MUNICIPAL BUILDING IN SUMMER HAZE	208
RIVERSIDE PARK IN SNOW	234
SITTING BY THE LAKE IN CENTRAL PARK	240
MORNING MIST OVER THE PALISADES	256
THE LAKE AT INNISFREE	274
AN AFTERNOON STORM OVER TIMES SQUARE	282

I

LEAVING ENGLAND

CONFUCIUS once said that after he had reached forty years of age he had no more perplexities. I am now well over the halfway point of my life-span and yet introspection makes me more bewildered every day. In saying this, I am by no means seeking to compare my mind with that of Confucius, or in any way ranking myself with the great sage. But I do wonder whether if Confucius were alive now and my age, he would still say that he had no more perplexities.

Confucius

Confucius lived more than two thousand four hundred years before me, and even then he deplored the complications of human affairs and evolved a system of moral laws to regulate human relations. In those far-off days he would sit upright on a well-placed mat in a long-haired fox coat, pondering a problem for days on end without interruption. None of his disciples dared raise his voice in contradiction.

Suppose *I* tried to do that—tried, for example, to question why I should respect my elders and worship my ancestors—I would first have to find evidence to disprove Darwin's theory

that man and monkey had a common origin, or ask some fol-
lower of Freud whether the operative power of my parents'
mental apparatus was definitely superior to mine. At one
moment I read that 'man is a singular unit of all political
implications according to the different ideological interpreta-
tions.' At another I become aware that 'man is a minute
particle of a mass rolling along in the political and social
revolution under the principle of collectivism.' Then from the
B.B.C. each Brains Truster tells me what a man is, and no two
think alike. In the end I don't know what I think myself.

Although I can sink into a comfortable armchair in front

The Silent Traveller at Home

of a nice fire instead of sitting upright on a well-placed mat in
a long-haired fox coat, I have to jump up to answer phone-
calls or to attend to the postman, the laundryman, the milkman,
the coalman and others. In the act of eating cornflakes for
breakfast, I am told by the morning paper that cornflakes can
be made of old coats and rugs. If I indulge myself in doing a
bit of cooking, I am soon reminded that some cooking fat is
derived from coal tar. The thought that artificial rain can be
produced spoils my enjoyment of the freshness of a rainy scene.
My possession of a small store of knowledge of Chinese art
once caused me to be bombarded with questions as to 'the
source of variety of aesthetic expression in the inner spiritual

identity of culture,' which made me ask myself if I really knew anything about Chinese art at all. One view of a thing is sure to be met with another and contrasting one. One side denies what the other affirms, and vice versa. I seem to be constantly walking in turn on four square pieces of ground, marked respectively with the words Right, Wrong, True and False. How can I prevent my perplexity growing every day? I still doubt if Confucius could have prevented it himself. He said: "In a cultured world, we have flowery conduct, and in an uncultured world, we have flowery speeches." Could he now decide which world it is, cultured or uncultured ?

Perhaps I should have been less bewildered had I not been living in England since 1933. It is the life that I have led in England which has made me turn back in search of my simple self. And I have found that many fellow beings are doing the same, despite the invisible forces of modern thought entangling their minds. Before I left China, I was young and unassuming; I questioned almost nothing, though new ideas must have been seeping into my head. In England I have been brought into contact with a host of new and unfamiliar things, and my mind has had to imbibe a tremendous variety of mental food whether I could digest it or not. Many of my acquaintance presented themselves to me as substitutes for Confucius, until I was no longer sure who was the really wise man among them. Ultimately I had to push these perplexities aside and try to get back to where I used to be. An extra finger on a hand may grow naturally even though it is superfluous, and to cut it off entails temporary if not permanent discomfort. Many of the complications of modern life are superfluous, but I could not cut them all off, so I decided to turn back in search of my original simple self, and then to try to adjust that to my new surroundings. In the process, I started my series of 'silent travels' in England.

And now, as I was about to start silent travelling in New York, I experienced an unexpectedly poignant feeling at leaving England. It was not exactly 'parting sorrow' for I was only leaving for six months; but I had a sudden realisation of the hold which England had gained on me. Through my silent travelling in England, I had come to know the simple things of the country-side—birds, flowers, trees, streams, animals, the weather in its every aspect, and also the English folk.

Strangeness had vanished and affinities multiplied, until now I felt that England was my second home.

When I first read Mark Twain's marginal note in one of his books, 'What a man sees in the human race is merely himself in the deep and honest privacy of his own heart,' I doubted if he could be including every human race. This doubt vanished when I found in my silent travels in England that there is no fundamental difference between the human race of the English and that of the Chinese. In fact, there are no fundamental differences between any of the human races in the world. This discovery enabled me to go to New York with a much easier mind than that with which I had arrived in England in 1933. I was fully aware that in New York my limited mental apparatus would be more severely taxed, but I could resolve to take no notice of those who played Confucius. There must be simplicity in all complications. After all, what is life fundamentally? It is its simplicity that I seek.

Su Tung P'o (A.D. 1036-1101) wrote the following poem*

> Suddenly rubbing my sleepy eyes,
> I saw the brilliant lights of Hotang,
> The milling people were clapping their hands,
> And frolicking like young deer in the wilds.
> I realised then that the simple joys of life
> Could be enjoyed only by the simple man.
> What is happiness in human life?
> My ways, I fear, are all wrong.

I think that he would have asked the same thing of the Judge after death as did the spirit of the dead man in this old Chinese story :

A spirit entered the Infernal Regions, and was ordered by the Judge of Purgatory to return to earth as a rich man. "But I don't want to be a rich man," cried the spirit. "What I ask for is to return as an ordinary man with a regular supply of food and no worries; that I may enjoy drinking fragrant wine and bitter tea, and thus pass through my new life again". "Money I can provide, to any amount", replied the Judge, "but this simple, peaceful life you desire is not in my power to give".

Before I face the Judge, I intend to pursue the simple life in whatever ways I can. It is my belief that every creature under Heaven desires a simple, peaceful life. A ferocious lion is docile

* translated by Lin Yutang

when he has been well-fed. Only mischievous and greedy monkeys land themselves in troubles and traps. Such a desire for the simple, peaceful life is what I take to be 'The little that is Good' in Walt Whitman's thought when he says :

Roaming in thought over the Universe, I saw the little that is
    Good steadily hastening towards immortality,
And the vast all that is call'd Evil I saw hastening to merge
    Itself and become lost and dead.

I agree with Whitman fervently. Many of my fellow beings are at present more afraid than ever before of the vast all that is called Evil, but I think that if we humans of every race cling to the little that is Good, striving untiringly for joint peace and happiness, we have no need to be pessimistic. My experience in England has assured me that I can find the simple joys of life there. Whitman's words strengthened my happy anticipation of similar experiences in New York!

Hot-dog Push-cart

II

ON BOARD

I KNOW that luck cannot be found by seeking. I was getting things ready for the *Mauretania* on 5th February when a telegram came from Dr. Sze saying that I had been transferred to the *Queen Mary*, which was scheduled to sail on 3rd February. I was torn between joy at this unexpected good fortune and worry over the reduced time for preparation. But when I got down to it there was not really much to take—no more than would go into two small suitcases—and I reached Waterloo Station in time for the Southampton boat train.

The staff of the Cunard White Star office won my admiration by their perfect organisation. Everything went according to schedule. Members of the staff even came to the train and shook hands with travellers for whom they had helped to arrange passages. One of them whispered to me: "You must be Mr. Chiang Yee. Would you like to know your cabin number? You have a single cabin. Number 36M." I thanked him, feeling quite dazed at this unexpected stroke of luck.

In the boat train the passenger sitting opposite me was going to Australia via New York, and two others in the compartment were in the leather and wool trades respectively. All three had many little cases and hand bags which filled the two vacant seats. They talked anxiously about trunks and other luggage. My *vis-à-vis* commented that I obviously preferred to travel light.

No friends were allowed to see passengers off at Southampton. The hundred or so passengers, from the train, mostly men, were directed to pass along to the immigration officer and Custom House in single file. When I got on board, my two suitcases and a few telegrams were waiting in my cabin. I still felt a trifle dazed at the thought of having a cabin to myself.

It was then 5 p.m. and the boat was not due to sail until 6 a.m. next morning, so I thought that I would have a little rest before beginning a tour of the boat from stern to bow.

But immediately the peaceful atmosphere was shattered by a

6

noise in front of the purser's office, just below my cabin. I peered out. Two thousand G.I. brides were streaming on board, about seven hundred of them with babies. They invaded every corner of the boat, keeping up an incessant variety of sound—shouting, laughing, babies crying. Sometimes it reminded me of an orchestra, sometimes of cockerels in the early morning or the parrot house at the London Zoo. With all the men passengers, I watched them with great interest. One man, much older than myself, exclaimed: "What a sight!" Another remarked: "By Jove! I have never heard so many babies crying together in my life!" He was about seventy and probably a bachelor.

Just before dinner the mail service was opened. I thought I would send a few words to some of my friends, but the crowd was several layers deep and I could not get near the door. The young man who was dealing with the post and myself were the only males. Suddenly a loud-speaker called the war-brides to dinner, in two sittings. It seemed odd that we mere men on the boat should not even be mentioned. But it was then that I managed to post my letters and wires.

When it was our turn to dine, I told the steward that he could put me at any table. I was given a table for two, but the other guest did not turn up. Seated as we were in the main dining hall, we were out of sight of the brides and babies. My table was quite near some others and I could not help overhearing various conversations. There were only two topics: one was the unimaginable and unbelievable amount and variety of the food by comparison with the war-time austerity to which we were all accustomed, the other was the brides and babies. Could there be any better subjects for men to discuss? I felt I was missing much fun sitting by myself.

After dinner it was possible to buy sweets, cigarettes, and many other little things unobtainable freely in London. There were long queues at the two shops. Nearly all the brides seemed to be there and every one came away with a handful of bars of chocolate and other things. I was amazed. After a very long while, a few men joined the end of the queue to buy cigars and cigarettes. I managed to get a few bars of chocolate. There was to be another mail service in the early morning, so I squeezed two bars into a small envelope for Rita Keene, the little girl of the family with whom I live, at Oxford. I slipped this into the pillar box and hoped the chocolate would not melt and spoil important letters of other passengers.

Early next morning the loud speaker announced the time and urged the brides to get up for breakfast. The ship's sailing time was considerably delayed. Presently all the brides and babies were assembled on the left side of the promenade deck. The Mayor of Southampton had come aboard to bid them farewell. I heard him say that each of them was an 'unofficial ambassador' for England. Whether they felt proud or not I don't know. I felt happy at being able to travel with so many unofficial ambassadresses!

A tremendous blast on the ship's siren announced that the boat was moving. A band had played on the quay the day before but owing to the delay in sailing, it was not there for our departure. Even bandsmen must eat and sleep, I suppose. Men were busy attending to ropes, tug-boats were pulling, and uproarious cheers burst from the brides who were leaning all along the railings. Many held their babies. Some of the babies were crying while their mothers cheered. There was nowhere for the men, and we stood in the background. There was no danger of tears among the adults because no relations or friends had been allowed on the quay. One very young bride suddenly jumped on the railing; gripping an upright with one hand she waved the other as she cried "Goodbye England! Goodbye!" A chorus echoed her. They all looked very happy indeed. Just a few were silent. One bride shouted, "See you again England, in two years' time." A voice from below asked "Why?" "Oh, I want to come and see my mother!" "You may be back earlier than that," said the voice from below. "Don't be so silly," was the rejoinder.

Southampton, Portsmouth, the Isle of Wight, Bournemouth, faded from sight. I know these places because I have a good friend teaching in Portsmouth and another living in Bournemouth. So I waved as we sailed by. The uproar on deck gradually died down. A few men passengers were now strolling round at ease. I was one of them. Presently the dinner bell rang. I had to walk down a long corridor from my cabin to the lift which would take me to the dining hall. All along this corridor were cabins occupied by brides, and now and then a small child dashed out or a mother with a baby. To me, all children are lovable and playful. A little girl offered me a sweet and I bent down to talk to her. As I did so I bumped into an old steward who was sweeping the corridor and did not realise that I was there. We both apologised. But he did not smile at the little girl. He looked at me solemnly, shook his head several times, then exploded : "By God, I have never seen so many *wild* women in my life!" When I came back through the corridor after dinner, the steward was still there leaning against the wall of a cabin. He obviously thought I sympathised with his point of view, for he nodded to me, then grasped my arm confidentially and said: "You should get away from these wild women. There is a quiet little library above this deck in the right hand corner. None of them will go there." I wondered why he should be so concerned about me, but I went to find the library. It was a very cosy little room with many comfortable sofas and deep armchairs. A number of men passengers were already there, reading, writing letters and looking at magazines. I could not help wondering whether they had all been advised by that steward to come here in order to escape the wild women. However, I was grateful to him for letting me know about this library where I could sit in comfort and write a few letters and notes. I noticed one of my own books, *Men of the Burma Road*, lying among many others on the long table in the centre of the library, and the sight warmed my self-esteem !

All the deck-chairs were occupied by the brides and babies wrapped in blankets, and all the chairs and sofas in the main lounge had similar occupants. Some brides were playing table tennis in the recreation room, some were playing with their babies in the nursery, some were sitting on the steps of the stairs or standing watching the sea. I could find nowhere to seat myself so I just walked round and round the promenade deck. Most of the men passengers were walking in twos or threes. I was alone. Some people may enjoy being watched by bright eyes peeping from out of blankets in deck-chairs, but I found it rather embarrassing. The boat rocked a little, in spite of being so big. We were in the English Channel, and there was rain and a strong wind. We were evidently still enjoying English weather.

The loud-speaker wakened the brides next morning as before. But a good many were seasick and the doctors and nurses had a busy time. The Captain decided to slacken speed. There were fewer signs of jollity than on the first day. Perhaps, now that the excitement was over, the brides were beginning to taste again the troubled surface of life as well as that of the ocean. Certainly life on board was much quieter. Babies had to be attended to, and afterwards there were cards, and writing letters, chattering and gossiping. I marvelled at the amount they had to say to each other, especially since they had not met before. After three days the ocean was quite calm again, which pleased all on board including the staff and crew.

My favourite 'beat' was near the bow. It was refreshing to draw deep breaths of the salty and stimulating air. The strong wind probably prevented other passengers from joining me. There was nothing to be seen but sky and water. Even the seagulls, which had followed us for a long way, had disappeared. I had not realised there was so much water separating the land masses! But the *Queen Mary* went on her way in a steady and stately fashion, carrying her own little world with her.

On the third day after dinner, returning to my cabin through the long corridor, I met again the steward who had spoken of the wild women. He was holding a baby in his arms while the mother looked on. He nodded to me again but this time did not shake his head. I stopped to touch the soft young face, and the baby smiled and gurgled. Both the steward and the mother laughed too. Eventually the steward said: "I'm beginning to get used to it. Every kid now calls me 'Dad'." " 'e's such a good Dad, too," a voice added.

Every Kid now calls me 'Dad'

I still often retreated to the little library when I could not find a place anywhere else. There were still some of my fellow passengers there, but their numbers decreased daily. Man-like, they sought female company! Some sat on deck-chairs among the brides, no doubt relating wonderful stories of their adventures. Some played cards with them in the main lounge. Others

accompanied them in long walks round and round the promenade decks.

I heard that there was one 'angel' among the brides. She
was certainly different from the rest and I could not help
being infected by the general opinion. She never wore brightly
coloured dresses but simple, plain ones in mauve or blue. Her
face was fresh, her expression tranquil, her air innocent and
the movements of her arms and hands very graceful. She
looked entirely happy surrounded by her admirers. Later I was
urged to meet her; in fact I was more or less dragged in front
of her and given no alternative. I did not find it very comfortable
being introduced to an angel! However, the good fellow who
performed the introduction was not interested in my feelings.

By the fifth day I had begun to know a number of my fellow
passengers. One told me that he had met one of our delegates
at the first conference of UNESCO in London. Another gave
me his card with his home address in Trinidad and said he had
met many of my fellow countrymen there. A third wished he
could show me photographs which he had taken in Peking,
Shanghai and Canton some forty or fifty years ago. They were
extremely friendly and tried hard to convince me of their
great interest in my country. Two others I talked to, who were
going to America on business, never mentioned China but
gossiped, in the most natural way, of the trivial happenings
on board.

The *Queen Mary* was 'dry' on our trip. No one could get any
kind of drink except water. Even tea was not served. Once
I remarked to these two acquaintances that I longed for a cup
of hot tea. This started a discussion on drinks. They thought it
a pity that no drinks were served to the passengers, and told
me privately that they could introduce me to someone from
whom I could get any drink I liked. Suddenly one of the two
was called away by a bride. The other remarked with a shake
of his head that the whole of his friend's life had been devoted
to wine and women, women and wine. I was touched by his
confidence. Afterwards he invited me to come to his cabin,
where he opened a bottle and gave me a glass of Scotch. I was
amazed. I enjoy a little whisky but it must be a little; I emerged
with a red face and a feeling that the deck was much further
off than I had noticed before.

One of the passengers I came to know well was Mr. J.

Rufino Barrios, Vice-Consul for Guatemala at Liverpool. He took me to his cabin and showed me photographs of beautiful Guatemalan scenery and pictures of early South American sculpture and stone carving. I knew very little about them but remarked that they showed in design and decoration a great deal of resemblance to some forms of ancient Chinese art.

One afternoon, meeting Mr. Barrios coming out of the main lounge, he surprised me by remarking that he had sung a Guatemalan folk song in the entertainment of the previous night. I regretted that I had not listened to it, whereupon he said that he would be singing again in the main lounge that evening and urged me not to forget to be there. There was to be a gala dance and other forms of amusement. The brides all dressed in their best, and some put on paper hats. Not being able to dance, I hesitated to go, but having made my promise to Mr. Barrios I presented myself at the main lounge. There was not a seat to be seen. Gradually I was pushed back to the entrance. Two men were standing there already. We could not see a thing. Before I could find a better position, one of the ship's nurses smiled at me and pointed to a notice on the door: 'FOR WAR BRIDES ONLY'. I glanced at the other men, and we immediately turned to go.

"Men certainly don't count in this company", I said to myself. I had never been asked a single question by any of the ship's officers, and we men were not included in any of the broadcast announcements, which were all for the war-brides. (Incidentally, why war-brides? I thought G.I. Brides a better name.) We just conformed to what the brides were told to do. There was the matter of boat-drill, for instance. This was exciting, if only for the sight it afforded of so many young ladies putting on life-belts. Some tried fancy styles. Each of the seven hundred babies had a small life-belt. I must leave it to be imagined how they wore them. It was an unique experience to me.

It brought back to my mind a Chinese classic I had read in my youth called *Chin-Hua-Yuan* or *The Union of Flowers in a Mirror*, in which are related the travels of a Chinese scholar who, tired of public life, voyaged across the seas to visit different lands with two of his friends. In time they reached Nü-Jen-Kuo, the Country of Women, where women held all the important positions in every walk of life. The travellers saw men with long whiskers and beards and small bound feet, wearing women's clothes, doing needle work, looking after babies, and so on. One of the scholar's friends was a relation of his, a prosperous merchant who had travelled widely. He was always eager to sell his goods, so directly after they landed in this Country of Women he went off on business. Unfortunately he was seen by the King of the country, who was of course a woman. The King thought him the most beautiful lady she had ever seen, in spite of his long whiskers and beard, and she decided to make him *her* Queen. So he was taken captive by the King's 'men' and conducted to the palace. There he was surrounded by court 'ladies', all whiskered and bearded men, who were ordered by the King to bind his big feet till they were small, when the King would announce a day for the Royal Wedding. The book describes at length the agony this friend of the scholar had to endure from his bound feet; he had never suffered so much before. All who hear or read the story are torn between tears and laughter. The author obviously meant to attack the evil Chinese custom of binding women's feet. He described all kinds of other pains and difficulties which his hero had to endure on becoming Queen of the Country of Women. It is a strikingly ironical study of Chinese women's life at that time. But I had never dreamt before of this story being true. Now I had myself lived in the Country of Women for a week. I did not fear that my feet would be bound but I was always on the alert lest I should be chosen to be Queen of this country. Fortunately I have neither whiskers nor beard, yet I might well have been summoned to act as maid to one of the whiskered and bearded court-ladies. I was on tenterhooks until I landed at New York.

Oyster Push-cart

III

APPROACHING NEW YORK

生 日 舟 襟 風 接 一
未 如 裡 裾 浩 太 片
見 讀 看 大 浩 盡 混
書 平 初 洋 拂 天 茫

A mysterious whole unites the vast emptiness.
The wholesome wind of heaven tosses and twitches my coat.
I watch the early sun rising from the ship
And feel as if I were reading an unfamiliar book.

This is a rough translation of a poem I wrote while crossing the Pacific Ocean on my way from Shanghai to Europe in 1933. I thought then that nothing could be more wonderful than to watch the sunrise from a boat in mid-ocean.

I had watched the sunrise from the peaks of Lu mountain in my native Kiukiang, and from other mountains in China. On those occasions as I stood waiting, in contemplation of the vast expanse of the sky and of the fullness of the earth around, I always felt refreshed mentally. The first rays of the sun seemed to lift the dark shroud from the earth, bringing light and life to every growing thing and living creature, and I felt, as it were, the pulse of trees, flowers, birds, beasts and men quicken to begin once again the daily round of struggle, pleasure, joy and difficulty. My perceptions seemed to be sharpened by the penetrating sunbeams; even my own humble life took on more significance. Our ancient thinkers used to watch the sunrise in this way and perhaps their experiences contributed to the creation of the Chinese philosophy of rationalism and endurance.

Seeing the sunrise in mid-ocean for the first time had brought me a similar feeling of refreshment, but with certain differences. I did not see the sun from above but more or less from its own level. The sun's rays did not illumine the earth's fullness, but only the flat emptiness of the sea. Beyond that emptiness, however, I was aware of something which my eyes could not yet see. The boat seemed to be propelled not by her own engine but by a force drawn from the sun and by my own urgent desire to reach what lay ahead of me. A new philosophy was born in me at that moment. Adventure, progress and practicability were its watchwords. Perhaps western philosophy is as it is because western people are so used to the sight of the sea and to watching the sunrise over the ocean. This may be an absurd generalisation, yet I feel there is some truth in it. Being a Chinese who was born far inland on a continent this first unusual experience has guided me in the understanding of the western way of living ever since.

Now I was on a big ocean-going liner again. This time I was crossing the Atlantic instead of the Pacific Ocean. Recalling my experience of seeing the sunrise in mid-ocean, I wanted to repeat it, so I got up very early one morning long before the loud-speakers began their announcements to the war-brides. It was very cold when I reached the open deck near the bows. It was very dark too. Sky and ocean mingled without distinction. I could see nothing but the part of the deck on which I stood, under some electric lights from the masts. Two or three members of the crew were about, but they were negligible in the absolute stillness of the vast darkness. So must I have been to them. The lights above were very feeble, as if their rays could not penetrate far beyond the deck. I actually had the feeling that I was being carried along under an oil-lamp on a very small raft on the Yangtse river instead of by a world-renowned ocean liner. The intermittent noises of the waves against the steel body of the vessel, however, restored my sense of reality, and the flapping of the boat's flags told me how strong the wind was; yet the sea was in no sense rough and I was able to stand absolutely still.

As I stood there awaiting the sun, gradually individual waves became distinguishable and at the same time I felt that something had moved away to leave more space above my head. The sky had become darkish grey and visible. A clear line showed up between the sky and the ocean at the horizon. The day had broken. It did not take long for the sky to turn to a fish-white colour, while near the horizon a kind of yellowish glowing ray spread upwards brighter and warmer each second.

It was a fascinating spectacle of nature turning night into day. I gazed hard ahead with the happy feeling that I was getting near to the horizon before the sun rose, for the boat seemed to move more swiftly against the backward-pushing waves. Now the curved edge of the scarlet sun appeared; then half of it came out; eventually the whole circle cleared the horizon to bathe me and the whole ocean world in gold. In spite of the cold February wind, I was dazzled by the radiation of red, yellow and purple. My belief that adventure, progress and practicability should now be my watchwords was confirmed. I repeated to myself the little poem which I have roughly translated at the head of this chapter and also the following poem *Morning Light* by a T'ang poet, Shih Chien-wu:

吾唐　湯霧為門方羲日
絕施　無四戎開一和輪
句肩　塵海掃風軋推浮
　　埃蕩煙神天東動

The wheel of sun moves up at the push of the harmonious
    generator;
A creak in the East has opened the gate of Heaven.
The Goddess of Wind has swept away mist and fog for me,
All is spotless on the spacious moving surface of the sea.

A radiant feeling of immortality rose within me: the sun never fails to rise from the darkness of night and life perpetually renews itself.

From the start there had been a more or less perpetual commotion on board from the 2,000 G.I. brides and their 700 babies. On this particular morning it reached a peak. Every possible space along the rails of each deck was occupied and many brides shouted that they had seen land. This magical word has a perennial significance even for occasional 'sailors'. I found myself wondering, as many other passengers have probably done before, how Columbus and his crew felt when they first saw the land they were hoping for. The excitement among the brides was obviously due to the longing to see their husbands and sweethearts and to enter upon a new life. The *degree* of their excitement, at least, must have matched Columbus's. I did not allow myself to think too long of Columbus and his men, but fell to wondering about my own status. I could not put myself in the same category as the brides and babies, nor did I fit into the group of passengers travelling to the U.S.A. on business. I was making the journey solely to see America. Now that it lay before me in the distance, how could I fail to be a little sentimental about it?

I was roused from my thoughts by a young bride slipping off a lifeboat with a thud. In China I had never heard ladies make so much noise. With the few other men on board, I scanned the horizon for land through the spaces between the brides' arms.

Fortunately I knew of a spot near one of the funnels where very few passengers went, so I moved up there and could see clearly towards the point where we all thought land lay. I seemed to be far from the commotion below, because a strong wind was blowing noisily through the flags and was also carrying the other noises away on the lower level. As I watched, the sun became obscured by thick clouds. A heavy morning mist hid the distance and all I could see of land was a dark blob above the water, like the back of a whale. Gradually the sunbeams penetrated the mist and then land was truly revealed. Owing, however, to the swiftly-moving clouds the sunbeams seemed to shift hither and thither like a magic searchlight. It was wonderful to watch. The ocean surface was a mosaic of colours—blue, green, silver, and gold. Looking up for a moment, I noticed that some stretches of the sky, from which clouds had just moved away, were very blue indeed. This led me to think of colour formation and of the inter-relation of colours. It is one of Nature's mysteries which is always a delight to the eye.

The stretch of land I had just seen grew larger, and soon I could detect objects on it. Presently a gust of wind bore the faint sound of music. The *Queen Mary* moved more slowly. I stepped down to find out what was going on below, but could see no band. The commotion was bigger than ever. Speech was impossible. We were now in the bay. Someone shouted: "There's Liberty! The Statue of Liberty!" Everybody turned as if at a word of command. I could see only a faint thin column suspended in the air, for the morning mist over the water was still very thick. Beyond this column could be seen a few thicker ones joined together like dark clouds. The brides ran from side to side of the ship. I felt quite overcome. How many human creatures have longed for liberty since the beginning of time. Many shout at the sight of the Statue of Liberty, but liberty itself is elusive.

The invisible band began to play again and they all began to sing in chorus. I could not understand what they were singing about. Then, through their arms, I noticed a small steamer, decorated with American flags and a large strip of cloth bearing the words 'Welcome Home' in red letters. The band was on the steamer. One attractive young woman of nineteen or so, who must have noticed me standing near and not singing, turned her head to tell me that they were playing 'Here comes the bride'. "That is for you, not for me," I said and we laughed.

Soon I went back to my perch. The emerald-green Statue of Liberty now stood out from the misty background. Had it been a clear morning, other structures, masts and cranes, might have distracted the spectator's eye and obscured the statue to some extent. It was conspicuous from a long distance, and the sculptor, I thought, must have intended it to turn this beautiful colour with time. I have a passion for emerald-green and always introduce it into my paintings, because it can stand out even among other shades of green. It is, I think, the right colour for the Statue of Liberty. As the boat drew nearer the statue passed suddenly away from me to the other side. I was facing in a different direction, where, I supposed, my destination lay and where I might hope to encounter the realisation of liberty of the human spirit.

The mist was very dense in the distance but through it I could faintly perceive two or three big dark objects. For a time these did not seem to move or change, but gradually their outline became more distinct. Their lower half was still shrouded in mist and they reminded me of distant mountain peaks piercing the clouds as depicted in some old Chinese painting by an artist of the Sung period such as Ma Yuan. But there are no mountains near New York, and soon the 'mountain peaks' were revealed as three tall dark columns. I knew then that they must be some of the skyscrapers of which I had heard so much; but I was still reluctant to accept them as man-made structures because of the similar natural formations I had seen in my own country. In the Kweiling District of Kwangsi Province in southwest China there are a number of rocky mountains, standing apart from one another along the riverside and rising straight from the plain. The dark columns now in front of my eyes looked almost the same shape in the mist, and

Approaching New York

as more and more of them appeared, I was increasingly reminded of that particular bit of China. We have a well-known saying: 'The Kweiling landscape excels all others under heaven'. Now that I was facing a similar landscape I thought that 'New York' could take the place of 'Kweiling' in this phrase. I felt more grateful than ever to those who had transferred me from the *Mauretania* to the *Queen Mary*, so that I was able to approach New York in this way.

The ship moved very slowly as she entered the Hudson River. Buildings of all sizes were now clearly visible. I was particularly interested to see so many docks in a line. Some were brightly decorated with the Stars and Stripes and with 'Welcome Home' painted in large red letters. I doubted if these preparations could have been specially made for the arrival of the two thousand brides and seven hundred babies whom I had the pleasure of accompanying. They were more probably meant for returning G.I.'s themselves some time before.

Now I made my way to the rear of the ship. Most of the brides were still clinging to the railings, singing and shouting. Occasionally an answering cheer came from the quays. Outwardly, the brides all seemed joyously happy, but some of their hearts, I thought, might be hiding misgivings.

Shaking off my untimely thought, I watched the tall buildings sliding by. They were not far away from me now, and did not look so very high as I was standing high above the water-surface. I now found these tall buildings, with their regular lines of structure and their myriad tiny rectangular windows, rather like the toy houses I have often watched and helped children to build with rubber or wooden bricks; and I felt now a childish desire to move bricks from one building to another so as to level them off at the top. Then it struck me that their varying heights made a step formation similar to the Giant's Causeway in Ireland, composed of great cubes of limestone. I was struck once more by the fact that these man-made buildings should borrow shapes and forms from Nature. The human mind is often unconsciously influenced by natural formations. It has frequently been said that there is nothing like the buildings of New York in any other part of the world. This is true as far as height is concerned, but this mass of masonry reminded me of an old line-engraving of Venice in the XVIIIth Century by Peter Schenk. The many campaniles were not unlike the skyscrapers. One sure thing is that the buildings of New York look much brighter and cleaner than those of perhaps any other city in the world.

A boy of about ten came up to me and asked about the many ice-blocks floating on the river. I was grateful to him for drawing my attention to them. I don't think I have ever seen so many big ones before; not in the Yangtse river anyway. I began to realise how cold the winter could be in New York, though I was temporarily exhilarated by the sight of a new place and did not feel cold at that moment. The boy and I talked for a while. He asked if I were English or French and was surprised when I said that I was neither! It seemed absurd that he did not recognise me as a Chinese, but perhaps he was indifferent to appearances. It is only grown-ups who complicate matters by unnecessary discrimination. This boy then told me that he was travelling with his mother to live with his 'new' father!

Lunch was served one hour earlier than usual, and immediately afterwards all of us got ready to go ashore. The steward told me that my luggage would be taken to the office on the dock at which the *Queen Mary* was berthing. While the boat was still moving, press photographers came on board in search of copy. This created a new commotion. Brides swarmed round them making the photographers look like judges in a beauty contest. The men had a definite aim in mind, and were not slow to discriminate among the girls. In a few minutes a picked group of brides was assembled. But just as a photographer was about to take his picture he suddenly changed his mind, told one girl to stand out and put another in her place. A second photographer wanted a group of babies. Those he chose were very young indeed, and some of the mothers stood protectingly behind their babies, but a voice shouted: "I only want war-*babies*, not war brides. Move away." The order was obeyed. A very pretty and lovable little girl about one year old, smiled and laughed all the time after being chosen for the group. She looked at her mother, who smiled back, apparently delighted to have her baby in the group. Just as the photograph was about to be taken the little girl ran with both hands outstretched towards her mother. The photo was spoiled and had to be taken again without her. I found the process rather irritating and moved away. It was beyond me to understand whence these photographers derived their unquestioned authority. What captions would appear in the next day's papers under the photographs?

At last it was time for us to land. I expected a bigger commotion than ever, but that did not occur. The brides had to watch us menfolk go down the gangways first. I felt a glow of amused satisfaction at this masculine preference! A Rubenesque lady standing close to me in the queue told me that they could not go ashore until next day, as they had to wait for transport to their respective destinations. She added that her husband lived in Texas and could not come to meet her, and that she might not be able to go ashore for another two days. Then folding her soft, baby-like hands in front of her bosom and looking up at the roof of the deck on which we were standing, she said: "I wish you could take me ashore with you. Oh I do envy you! I have always wanted to see New York and I was terribly excited as the ship approached. Now we are here and I can't go and see it. Oh, I do wish you could take me ashore with you!" I could not think of a suitable reply so I just smiled.

Before I reached the queue for customs inspection, an elderly gentleman stepped up and gave me his card. He was Mr. Joseph Brennan of the Canadian Pacific Railway Company office on Madison Avenue, New York. He said he had come on business and that Mr. Paul Standard of the same company had asked him to give me some help. He was the first American I met on American soil. I cannot sufficiently express my gratitude for his help to me at that moment. He got me through the Customs, then got me a porter whom personally I could not distinguish from the travellers, and put me into a brightly painted yellow taxi. In a flash, as it seemed, while sirens were blowing all around, I found myself in the hotel room which Paul Standard had booked for me. I thanked Mr. Brennan before driving off and remembered his smiling face as he added that he feared these English girls were all expecting to live in castles and did not realise that there were no castles in America.

While I was still looking round my room, from the windows of which I could see no sky and where I had to keep on the electric light, the telephone bell rang and I heard the voice of Paul Standard for the first time. We had been corresponding for about three years but had never met. He is a typographer and a very fine calligrapher, and after reading my book *Chinese Calligraphy*, he wrote me a long letter care of my publishers, Methuen of London, asking if I could send him three copies of the book because none could be got in New York. That was in 1942, when the war was at its worst. From then on we corresponded nearly every month. When in 1946 it was possible for me to visit New York, I wrote and asked him if it would be possible for me to go on being 'silent' in America for three months or so, as many of my acquaintances, who had been in America had warned me to be prepared for noise and had suggested that I should have turned into *The Noisy Traveller* by the time I came back. However, he wrote encouragingly to say that I could be entirely silent for six months if I wished. Later I asked if he could find me a place to stay. This was a big problem at the time. He replied that he had tried every possible place in and around New York and no hotel would take any visitor for more than five consecutive days, because the housing shortage there was so acute. One can easily understand why there is a housing shortage in London: but why in New York? Eventually a wireless message reached me on the *Queen Mary* in the middle of the ocean informing me, to my great relief, that he had found a room. I was most touched by this act of friendship by one whom I had not even met, an act which I discovered later to be characteristic of Americans. He said now that he would come and fetch me for dinner.

When I went down in the lift, I greeted the lift-boy with "Good Evening" but received no answer. On getting out, I said "Thank you" but still received no response. I concluded that being a lift-boy day after day, he had grown tired of replying to his passengers' greetings. Before we met, I thought that after three years of correspondence Mr. Standard and I would have a lot to say to each other. But at first we had very little. I had some excuse, being a 'silent traveller', but Paul was rather silent too, perhaps out of courtesy to my name. He took me straight out of the hotel into a street-car and we subsequently changed on to a bus. I had had a full day. My mind had been fully occupied; now my eyes were dazzled by the street lights everywhere and my head vibrated with the movement of the street-car and the bus. Soon we reached Paul's house and were greeted by Stella Standard as well as by an irresistible fragrance from her kitchen. Stella is the author of a successful cookery book, *More than Cooking*, so I entertained great expectations as we sat down to dinner, and I was far from disappointed. It was a delicious meal, with turkey and all kinds of things making an unusally warm welcome for a long distance traveller.

I was so tired when I got back to the hotel that I went to bed at once. But I could not sleep and had to take off all the bed-clothes. I thought that even the warmth of the welcome I had received from my friends could scarcely have made me boil like this, particularly as I had felt icy cold in the February night after leaving their house. I discovered my discomfort

to be due to the central heating, which I had not turned off.
In the end I dozed, with the memorable first view of New York
hovering in my mind.

Peanut Push-cart

IV

ALONG WALL STREET

It was odd that I should find myself in Wall Street the day after my arrival in New York, for I am no financier nor does my way of living necessitate frequent contact with bankers; but it was necessary for me immediately to present my letter of credit. I had been lucky enough to find, staying in the same hotel, a fellow-countryman who told me where to find the Bank of Manhattan and the New York office of the Bank of China. As he was going in the same direction himself, I followed him into the subway at 103rd Street, where my hotel was situated. I had wondered beforehand whether to travel by taxi or by underground tube; London experience prompted me to choose the latter. But when I talked to my compatriot about 'undergrounds' and 'tubes', he did not know what I meant, and when we reached the entrance to the subway, I understood why.

There are many weak points in man's nature. I seem to possess them all. Having someone to direct me, I depended on him entirely. He was Dr. H. C. Yü, Professor of Chemistry in the National College of Agriculture, Peking, who had recently come to the States on some research work. I learned much from him of present conditions in my country from which I have been absent so long. We talked a little while descending the stairs to the train. Then, telling me to go on ahead, Dr. Yü put two nickels in a machine, and we emerged on the platform. A train came in and many people dashed for it, so I did too, but Dr. Yü stopped me because it was an *uptown* train, not the *downtown* one we wanted. Then came another train called *Local*, not the Express we wanted. The only indication of this, on the front of the train, was easily overlooked. Dr. Yü explained that the three different kinds of trains were distinguished by the head lamps, two white ones, one red and one green, and two red ones. It struck me as a good idea to have both Express and Local trains for underground transport.

Presently I was pushed into a train on which I had failed

to notice the lamps. We both had to stand and hold on to
straps. It was impossible to stand still and involuntarily we
were all rejuvenated into naughty boys and girls. I put out my
hand to keep Dr. Yü's body from swaying too much on to a
lady, of whom we could see only her hat; then I myself nearly
lost my grip when someone with the figure of the late G. K.
Chesterton fell against me. Before I could say "excuse me"
my body had suddenly swung in the opposite direction. My
face must have looked comical with my mouth open and eyes
staring and Dr. Yü kept smiling at me. I spoke to him, but
he seemed not to hear me. Then he told me not to be so
English. I was amazed. How could I be taken for English by
my own countryman? I began to argue with him, but just then
the train stopped, and he got out saying this was Times
Square and that I had to go on further.

I got a corner seat from which it was difficult to see which
station had been reached when the train stopped. Eventually
I overheard two young girls talking of getting out at Wall
Street, so I followed them. When I emerged from the subway,
I was bewildered by the strange surroundings. I held my
breath for a moment, feeling like an ant among the high buildings. As I moved slowly along, my body seemed to be pressed
hard from both sides and to be rapidly thinning out and
increasing in height till I felt like a figure being elongated
in an El Greco painting.

I was reminded of the so appropriately named Needle's Lane
near the Royal Exchange in London, and other narrow streets
around that banking centre. Wall Street is much wider than
those, but seems narrow because of the surrounding skyscrapers.
I wondered whether it was fitting that a street full of banks
should always be narrow. There was hardly any sky to be
seen. The little that there was reminded me of 'I-Hsien-Tien'
or 'One-string-width of sky', the name given to the narrow
space between two precipitous rocks on the Island of Puto in
Chekiang Province. There is a superstition that anyone
especially fortunate or possessing divine attributes may see,
near the right end of these rocks, the image of Kuan-Yin,
Goddess of Mercy, sitting on a lotus flower or in a little golden
shrine. Personally I had never caught a glimpse of the Goddess
when visiting Puto, but any regrets I might have felt were
now effaced, for the little Trinity Church I could see at the

far end of Wall Street became my shrine of Kuan-Yin. I felt that I must after all be a lucky person.

In front of the Bank of Manhattan building I tilted my head back to see the top but found this a strain. I recalled that once in London I asked a rather short compatriot what was on top of a nearby policeman's helmet. My friend's own hat fell off and he complained that the job made his eyes ache. I could sympathise with him now. After finishing my business in the Bank of Manhattan, I was told to take a lift up many floors to the Bank of China. The lift seemed to be a non-stop affair. Just as I was about to enter it for the downward journey, some young ladies darted out from a nearby door as if by magic and were borne off. Whether I would or not I was left standing. Young men and elderly men next appeared and disappeared with the same speed. The lift went without me again. However, I was swept into it with the next rush and reached the ground-floor with a sigh of relief. It was the first time in my life that I had entered two banks within half an hour. At this rate I might very soon land myself within four bare walls!

I passed the statue of George Washington in front of the Sub-Treasury and then approached Trinity Church. Its smallness puzzled me. I have been living in England for many years and have also visited a number of places on the continent of Europe, over all of which soar church towers, spires and domes, such as that of St. Paul's Cathedral which rises above the buildings surrounding it in the City of London. I have realised as an outsider how strong a hold religion must have on the hearts of the people of those countries. It should also be deep-rooted in the hearts of New Yorkers, as most of them are of European stock. Why, therefore is Trinity Church not higher than the neighbouring buildings in Wall Street? It seems to me that in New York science has become a menace to religion, as far as architecture is concerned. Money must be the principal consideration of those people who build the skyscrapers, and religious bodies cannot compete with them. I conceived the fantastic idea that it might be possible to raise the original church above the level of the skyscrapers, using the storeys underneath as offices. I would like to see religious thought or moral teaching help to keep our minds balanced in these days of rapid scientific developments.

The neighbourhood of Wall Street invited me to stroll.

Perhaps *strolling* is hardly a suitable activity in this part of New York, but I had no reason to hurry. I read the street names—William Street, Pine Street, Exchange Place, Beaver Street, Nassau Street, Liberty Street and so on. They conveyed little to me as a newcomer. It was now about lunch time. People were streaming through the revolving doors like puff-corn out of a machine. On reaching the pavement, they were brought more or less to a standstill, for there were so many others already there. Countless cars, seemingly chained together, blocked the middle of the narrow street. Before I came to New York many people told me that New Yorkers were noted

Paper-stand in Wall Street

for efficiency and speed, but now I realised that they could also be very slow and patient! Not so very different from other people, after all.

Cars cannot pass through Needle Lane in London, so during the lunch hour many people, almost all men connected with financial business in the City, come out and stand in the middle of the street, talking and joking at their leisure. Before the war most of them wore top-hats and smoked big cigars. It was an impressive sight. During the war the top-hats and cigars disappeared, but the men still stood and talked there even during the blitz and flying-bomb days. I often wondered where they had their lunch as there are very few restaurants about, apart from some pubs. I think they had probably had some drinks beforehand! In Wall Street there is no similar sight. I cannot recall any such scene in my own country either.

I wrote in my *Silent Traveller in London* that the streets around the Royal Exchange and Gracechurch Street must be the last destination of spring, as they are the haunts of men instead of fashionable ladies. The City of London seems to be an all-men affair, and their clothes mark no change of season. But in Wall Street there are women as well as men. Perhaps there seemed more women than in fact there were because their

Shoe-shine

dresses were so colourful; though even the men's clothes here are not so uniformly navy blue or black as in London.

I wandered towards Fulton Street. I had already been amazed at the number of newspaper kiosks with masses of brightly-covered magazines and thick papers which were situated at most street corners. Now I noticed a new type of stand. It was a tall, narrow wooden box, painted green, with glass doors, bearing the trade sign 'SHINE' in red. I went up to it and found that it was a place to get one's shoes polished, so I stepped in boldly to have mine done. There was a row of two raised seats for clients and one elderly man doing the polishing. It was a comfortable and practical arrangement. In London one has to stand to have one's shoes polished, while the polisher in his scarlet coat kneels on the ground; this is not comfortable for either party. Here I had to put my feet on two little stands, while my arms rested on the arms of the chair. In that position I felt like the statue of some Egyptian deity. Many figures in early sculptures, including Chinese, are seated like that. I might have been the Chinese God of Earth, who is to be seen far and wide in our countryside, sitting in that position in a little narrow shrine (though I have not acquired the long, white beard yet) and the shoe-polisher a priest or peasant bending to burn incense or pay respect to the god. In my *Silent Traveller in Oxford* I described how I once became a ghost. Here in New York I had become a god.

Though temporarily I may become a ghost or a god, I remain fundamentally a man and must eat. Looking around I noticed a large number of people streaming in and out of a shop. I stepped in. The place was packed with people eating. Many sat at the counter; others leant against the walls. There were no tables, but the lights were very bright and everything looked well-appointed and clean. Shapely dark-skinned girls all dressed in green were busy serving ice-cream, sandwiches, orangeade, grapefruit juice, and other items. They must have been well-trained for the work for they moved as if by clockwork without uttering a word. I got a seat and echoed my neighbour's order for two hot-dogs. This was the first time I had tasted them though I had heard of them for years. I ate the two with enjoyment. I wondered how the name 'Hot-dog' originated. Some years ago I read a travel-book on China in which the Chinese in some part of the country were described as eating dogs. The writer condemned this practice. I read of

Hot-dog and Coca-cola Push-cart

it with an uncomfortable feeling, for I had heard of dog-eaters in my youth but had never seen one. Now I was actually one myself, and the thought made me shudder.

I left the restaurant and made my way to Trinity Church. Although the surrounding buildings are high, this comparatively small structure seemed to me more dignified and impressive. I found three reasons for this. First, a good-sized churchyard separated it from the neighbouring buildings and offered a welcome breath of fresh air to passers-by. Without the church-yard the tops of the skyscrapers gave the impression of falling on to the church and squashing it out of existence. Secondly, it has a style of architecture which can be easily grasped at a glance. I am no expert on this subject, but after the monotony of the lower storeys of the skyscrapers with ranks of identical rectangular windows, the classical style of Trinity Church was pleasing to my eyes. Thirdly, the dark, almost black colour of the building contrasts strongly with the surroundings.

I learned that the church was built by the English. It was no wonder, therefore, that it had a London look. I read that the spot on which it stands has been consecrated to religion since 1697, when King William III, of England granted a charter to the 'Wardens and Vestrymen of the Parish of Trinity Church in the City of New York'. The first church was opened on March 13, 1698, 80 years before the signing of the Declaration of Independence and 70 years after Peter Minuit purchased the whole of Manhattan Island from the Indians for twenty-four dollars! It was destroyed in the great fire of 1776. The second was pulled down, as unsafe, in 1839. The present edifice, the third to be erected, was completed in 1846. I was interested to learn that the church was opened on March 13th, a date of significance to Western superstition, and that New York as well as London had had a great fire.

A few people sat about the Church in meditation or prayer. It was remarkably quiet. A priest in a black gown was tidying up the Bibles and Prayer Books on the long tables and adjusting the ropes which divide one section of the church from another. He handed me a printed sheet and I gave him a deep bow to show my respect to him. I think of the long black gown as a kind of priestly uniform, differing from that of a soldier in that it implies authority for the construction of the mind rather than for its destruction. Anyone who wears it, I feel, is worthy of my deep respect.

Coming out of Trinity Church, I strolled round the church-yard for a while. I noticed a marble cross, erected in memory of Mrs. William Astor, with carved panels all round illus-trating the life of Christ according to St. Luke. My attention was also attracted by a most conspicuous monument to 'The Martyrs', situated in the northeast corner, near the street. This was erected by the Trinity Corporation in memory of the American patriots who died in British prisons in New York during the War of Independence.

It was time for me to stop wandering, and I entered a subway near the church to return to my hotel, relying for the purpose on my experience of London, where, once in the Underground, one can reach any destination. After a long time I still had not reached the station at which I should have got out and I began to ask myself whether I was riding in the right direction. Nobody seemed able to tell me, or else they did not know the station which I named. Finally I got out and tried to find a porter, but there was not one about, nor was there a clear map to be found. Someone on the platform told me to change to an Uptown train, and others declared that I should go Downtown and then Uptown. I asked what the difference was between Uptown and Downtown. No one could tell me; or anyway they were all very busy and quite indifferent to my difficulty. At last someone who looked like a porter told me that I was in the wrong subway, but that I should carry on as far as a certain station and from there take a street car to the other side of the bridge. Then I should go back into the subway and find an Uptown train to my destination. He was extremely busy and did not have time to linger with me. The London Underground would be equally confusing to a stranger were it not for the clearly-mapped directions at the stations and the many helpful porters. And there are interchange stations by which one can get from one line to another. Here I was entirely at a loss and did not know how far I had come from my hotel. The easiest way for me to get back would have been to take a taxi. But I wanted to find my way about, so I pro-ceeded to try to carry out the complicated instructions given me. At the appointed station I asked for the street-car. Fortunately an elderly man told me to follow him, as he was

Wall Street at Twilight

also going to the other side of the bridge. In the street-car we sat together and he told me that he came from Italy and had lived in New York for the last twenty-five years. "New Yorkers do not know anything about places," said he, "but only how to make their way home to bed late at night." There was certainly something in what he said. It took me two hours to get back to my hotel, and I paid one nickel for the subway, one nickel for the street-car, one dime for a bus and another nickel for another subway. The hotel-boy had told me that one nickel would take me right round New York. I now realised that he had been pulling my leg!

Line-up at the Letter-box

V

NON-OBJECTIVE SKETCHINGS

By a happy chance, during my first few days' wanderings in New York, my eye fell on a signboard of the 'Museum of Non-Objective Paintings'. I did not visit it at once, but it gave me the idea of doing some non-objective sketches myself. Lest there be any misunderstanding, let me explain that my sketches are written ones, composed entirely without objective.

I should have bought a guidebook and map of New York the day after my arrival. But I did not. A guidebook may help one to see things in an orderly and easy way, but I dislike its imperative tone: 'This the visitor should not miss'. I like to see things of my own freewill. I do not attempt to see everything, nor do I mind missing something important or outstanding. Life is too short. It can, however, be lengthened . . . Just before the war ended, a doctor in the American army, stationed in Oxford, was brought to see me by a mutual friend and we spent a pleasant hour together. The doctor asked if I would like my life prolonged. I thought he had come to see some of my paintings and to talk about Chinese art, and his question took me by surprise. "Certainly," I replied, "I think every human being would like to have his life prolonged, provided he can retain his vitality. Personally, I feel that my life has already been lengthened since I came to live in England. For example in China, if I wanted to see a friend who lived in the country, I had to devote a whole day or more to the job! In England I can spend a few hours with a friend in the country as just one item in a day's programme. I think I accomplish twice as much each day in England as I would have done in my own country. This means that my life has already been doubled. Now I am hoping to visit the U.S.A., and I shall expect the length of my life to be trebled." We all laughed.

Before leaving England, I had of course heard of many interesting places and things to see in New York, but I decided to try first to become acquainted to some extent with the American way of living. One is bound to find some things different in a new country and I could not immediately accustom myself to life in New York. The best beginning, I thought, was to become familiar with the hustle and bustle of the crowds. At the same time I did not want to be *in* the crowd incessantly, so I compromised by riding round and round in the subways, street-cars, and buses. My first week in New York was mostly spent in this manner. Each time I went in a subway, I felt as though I were having a joyride on a particularly lively merry-go-round. I used to get out at one subway stop, look round the neighbourhood, then go down the subway again. Or I might ride on a bus between one subway journey and another. I felt rather like the London schoolboy who evaded school by spending whole days in the Underground. He left home in the morning as usual and came back in the evening. His mother thought he was at school and his teacher thought he was at home. In the end the educational inspector found out that he spent his days on the Underground, going to the terminus of each line in turn. I had the advantage over him that no educational inspector came to bother me! Our great philosopher, Lao-Tzŭ, once lamented that there would be no peace in the world until mankind returned to a childlike state of mind. Confucius' best disciple, Mencius, also said that a sage should retain his child-like mind. My behaviour has sometimes unconsciously resulted in childishness, perhaps because I have been brought up in these philosophies! It is strange that people do not like to be called childish. An elder, scolding a boy or girl, says "You must behave in a manly way" or "That's not ladylike". A boy always wants to be looked upon as a great hero. A girl is offended if told she is too young to join in social functions. Women both in the West and East enjoy the compliment: "You look younger every day". But when told that they know very little about life because of their youth, they are displeased.

A few days' joy-riding in the three subways afforded me many aspects of American life and a general idea of the geography of Greater New York with its five boroughs: Manhattan, Bronx, Brooklyn, Queens and Richmond. All three subways run the main part of their lines on Manhattan, and connect the island by way of tunnel or bridge with the boroughs of Bronx, Brooklyn and Queens, but not with Richmond, which is too far distant. I thought that as the whole area of Manhattan could not be bigger than that of London, one subway system ought to be sufficient. But I noticed that all three maintained exactly the same standards of cleanliness, brightness and noise. I can now well understand why New Yorkers move faster than the inhabitants of other cities. It is because they spend so many of their valuable minutes, even seconds, catching connections between subways and buses and street-cars.

I speedily grasped how to tell whether one is moving Uptown or Downtown, terms which had puzzled me on my first day. It could not be simpler. If the street numbers are

Bubble-gum

ascending one is going Uptown, if descending, Downtown. I also learned that the Underground is called the Subway in New York, because it is not very deep under the ground. In places there are lines elevated above the streets. Watching people moving about in the streets and houses from the windows of a train on the elevated gave me a new slant on them. I also saw many interesting things inside the subway trains. In certain parts of the City, most people got into the train chewing gum. They reminded me of the inhabitants of Singapore, Penang, Malaya, and some southern parts of China who chew pingnan, areca nut or betel nut, which gives a reddish stain to the mouth and lips which is considered attractive. I remember that a Chinese writer of the eighteenth century wrote that he often shut his eyes so as to try to imagine the taste of the fruit inside the eater's mouth rather than to watch the facial movement, though he could not help hearing the little sucking noise produced from time to time.

I very seldom tried to sit down in a train in case I had then to practise the courtesy of letting-the-lady-have-the-seat which I learned in England. Actually there was hardly a vacant seat in a subway. In every coach there is a detailed map of the line about three feet square but the words on it are in very small print because the name of nearly every station is given. I seldom dared to look closely at it lest I should fall. I would not have minded falling on a man, who could at most have given me a punch on the nose. But suppose I fell on a lady? 'One can't be too careful' was my motto in New York. And anyway the subway map is generally in a corner or near the door and I could not often get near it. I was much struck by one notice on the windows warning the passengers in big letters not to do 'unlawful things' in the train, otherwise they would be heavily fined or sent to prison. I could not guess what the 'unlawful things' might be. The notice reminded me of a similar warning appearing beside the communication cord in the London Underground, saying, but in very small letters, 'Penalty for improper use £5'. Five pounds seems to be practically a standard sum for a fine in London.

In the Underground, there are different compartments for smokers and non-smokers. In New York Subways smoking is absolutely forbidden. I often wondered how heavy smokers could endure this prohibition, for they have to stop smoking as soon as they enter a Subway station. Surely not all can afford to travel by taxi all the time!

Most passengers on the Underground smoke either a pipe or a cigarette or do one of the crossword puzzles in the daily papers. They generally look very calm and sit at ease. I found that Subway passengers, being forbidden to smoke, did not so entertain themselves. In the morning some of them were still rubbing their eyes and yawning. At midday they were busy wiping the sweat from their foreheads or exclaiming: "Hot". In the evening and late at night I enjoyed studying the different positions of drooping heads and relaxed bodies. But no matter how late it might be, all came to life again as soon as the train stopped at 42nd Street, preferably at the side of Times Square. Times Square has a magic power of revitalisation.

Sometimes the passengers inside a Subway train were entertained by one of their number. Once, in a train not as full as usual, a big man with a bushy beard like Robinson Crusoe got in. He stared dead ahead and was obviously blind. He walked slowly and steadily and his wide-apart feet were wrapped in some sort of red bindings. He did not utter a word. Some of the passengers dropped a nickel or a dime into the

Beyond Times Square   Approaching Times Square

hat he held out. I thought he must be collecting for a religious charity, so one of my nickels went into his hat too. But then I was informed by my neighbour that he was a beggar. Another time someone in the middle of the train suddenly shouted details of the goods he had for sale. He even displayed a few of them and asked the passengers to pass them round. So one way or another the travellers are prevented from becoming lethargic.

I am well acquainted with the rush hours in London. I had anticipated that every hour would be a rush hour in New York, but I found that there are specially busy periods there too. The first seems to begin about three o'clock in the afternoon and to reach its climax at half-past five. Then between seven and eight in the evening there is another big rush for Times Square. I may be wrong, of course, but that was my impression. I wanted to sample a New York rush hour, so one day I purposely went down a subway in Times Square just after five o'clock. Once en route I dared not hesitate or I should have hindered the people behind me, who were either squeezing me aside or pushing me on. At one point I tried to stop but in vain. Fortunately I could not understand what one or two people said to me! I suppose I should have been as annoyed as they if I had had to count the time minute by minute. I moved on non-stop in a single file until I reached a gap, presumably opposite the train's doors. Except for a small space round this gap the whole platform was full of people. The other platforms were equally crowded. I was shoved aside by a dark-faced porter and made to line up, unlike London queues. Soon there were crowds of people behind me. There were iron chains on either side of the gap to keep back the waiting crowds. As soon as the train doors opened, a flock of people poured out like the huge volume of water down Niagara Falls. At the same time, I was involuntarily moved forward. If the railings and chains had not been made of steel we should have broken through them. I say 'we' because I could not have avoided taking part. While the train was emptying, the porter had to hold on to the railings, with his back strained against the crowd, from which he was protected by the chain. He looked like Joe Louis posing before a fight for the world title. When he eventually undid the chain, he at once vanished from sight, and I did not see him again until he relocked the chain. For the train moved off without me. But I was now near the chain and stood a good chance of getting on the next train. It soon arrived, but I was pushed aside by the crowd who streamed into the train as if they were being chased. Once again, I was left standing in the same gap as before close to the chain. The third time I was carried into the train, with my feet suspended a few inches above the ground, which made me feel like an ancient Prince or a modern hero returning in triumph from the war! It was better than any Circus show. I held my breath at first and when I did venture to breathe out and then try to breathe in again, there was no room for my lungs to expand. My arms had to be kept folded in front of my chest and my shoulders were bent. Despite the great noise produced by the friction between the wheels of the train and the track, I could hear the faint music of chewing gum quite close to one of my ears!

At last I reached my destination and had a meal to calm my excitement. I have had three similar experiences in London, once on the Jubilee night of the late King of England, George V, again on the Coronation night of George VI, and the last on VE day at Piccadilly Circus Station. I think I could have had one in New York every day if I had wished.

Rush Hour in the Subway

Apart from the sights inside and around the trains, there were many interesting things to see along the platforms and at the entrances to the subways. Sometimes it would be a stout figure in a beautiful white fur coat and hat of whom no one else took any notice; sometimes a group of carefree girls in bright-coloured dresses humming a Frank Sinatra or a Bing Crosby melody, looking 'adorable' and as if they would not mind in the least if Heaven fell or Earth turned over. Sometimes I would see, shouting and scampering under the arms of the crowds, squeezing from pillar to pillar inside the subways, a number of dark-faced youngsters with startlingly white eyes. I only wished I could have made some paintings from life of these figures. The French artist, Honoré Daumier, would have enjoyed sketching here much better than in the third class carriages of French trains. And I wondered what Henry Moore, the modern English sculptor, would make of New York's Subways to compare with his impressions of the Underground during the war!

There are very few women flower-sellers in the New York streets. I noticed men selling flowers inside the subways, but I very seldom saw a passenger stop and buy any. Yet presumably they must do a good business; certainly their stocks of flowers were always attractive. On one occasion I saw near a subway entrance two smartly dressed young men with beautifully pomaded hair and shining shoes, one of whom was looking after a big box of flowers while the other, wearing white gloves, barred the exit by holding out a button-hole. He did not utter a word but tried to pin the flower on the coat of each lady who approached. I watched him pestering several ladies, who had to be protected by their male companions. Some of them looked embarrassed, and some of the men pushed him roughly aside; but he was not discouraged. He went on with his job very patiently and persistently. He and his partner must have found this a good way of doing business, and I expect they did not leave until they had sold all the flowers in the box.

One acquaintance I made at a luncheon party given for me by Paul Standard told me that in New York one had to be rough and tough. If I may say so, I found some New York women tougher than the men, if not rougher; I watched them getting into trains and securing seats . . . New York men do not always let the 'weaker' sex have the seats. Kindness comes after necessity and they do not feel like giving up their seats when they are exhausted after a hard day's work. I must admit that several times when I was dead tired I did not give up my seat on the Subway. Who expects kindness from a hungry tiger? Nevertheless, though there was constant movement and roughness inside the subway, I was pleased to notice gentleness and calmness there as well. In one subway I saw a nun sitting by a pillar, quietly reading a book, and apparently unaware of all the bustle around her. Some passengers left money with her in gratitude. I mentally gave her a deep bow of respect for what she represented. A Chinese saying 'Hsin chin tzu jan liang' means 'The heart at peace naturally finds coolness', and this is

A Nun in the Subway

a phrase we often use to anyone who seems restless or who cannot refrain from complaining about the heat on a summer day. In New York, as elsewhere, one can enjoy oneself in one's own way if one's heart is at peace.

Two kinds of buses used to run in New York. One was a double-decker, similar to London's red buses, painted light yellow with green strips and called Fifth Avenue buses because they passed through Fifth Avenue at some stage of their route and terminated at Washington Square where Fifth Avenue begins. I did not find these buses going along any other avenues. They differed from London buses in their interior construction. All the seats were very comfortable, but passengers on the lower deck really needed steel helmets, for sometimes the roof over their heads seemed to droop! The designer of these buses made good use of every inch of space. There was one small seat placed high above the front wheel on the off side. I thought at first that it was intended for children. But then I noticed grown-ups, even quite elderly ones, sitting on it. In a spirit of childishness I wanted to try it myself, but it was not easy to find it unoccupied. The driver urged everyone to get off the bus quickly and the conductor— there was a conductor on this kind of bus to collect fares upstairs—pushed all the new passengers inside as far as possible. The space between the stairs and the driver's seat was very small and as it was partly occupied by the conductor while the two streams of people went up and down, the congestion was extreme. The driver and the conductor were not too patient —nor would I be in their circumstances—so the bus often moved on far too quickly for some of the passengers. Therefore anybody who was lucky enough to get aboard secured the nearest seat, and that small seat above the off front wheel was handy and always occupied at once. However, one morning I did manage to become the honoured occupant of it. It must be understood that whenever I got a seat in a bus during my first few days in New York, I did not part with it until the bus reached its terminus. This occasion was no exception. Naturally I felt proud on this seat, because it raised me above the rest of the passengers as if I were their leader. Presently I felt that all my blood had concentrated in my toes, so I had to curl my dangling legs up for a while. Unfortunately it proved impossible to stretch them again when I wanted to because of the crowd. Sitting with my hands grasping my curled-up legs I imagined myself becoming more and more like a monkey sitting on a bar in his cage in the Zoo. I have always wanted to become some other of Nature's creatures for a time, but to be a monkey sitting motionless all along this bus route proved a little too much for me!

I liked best to have a seat on the upper deck of these Fifth Avenue buses, for through the windows there was always a good and interesting view. The only drawback was that I had to make a flying leap to get off in time when the bus stopped at my destination. Some of these buses had open upper decks. This was a great attraction to me and I went on top of these whenever I could. I remembered my few rides on the open decks of London buses in the first year of my arrival in England. They all seem to have disappeared now, probably on account of the London weather. Who could enjoy the view in the constant London drizzle unless his mind were as 'inscrutable' as mine? New York days were dry and sunny even in wintry February, so I usually found many other people sitting on the open upper deck. Even these New York residents must have found the views as endlessly interesting as I did. Most of my fellow passengers looked down on the streets, but I kept my gaze at eye-level and sometimes above it. When I rode on a London open bus, I felt very grand, because I was so high up that I could almost touch the roofs and chimney-pots of the houses. But in New York I did not get the same feeling, for when I looked at the tall Fifth Avenue buildings, I seemed still to be very close to the ground and as small as ever.

Once or twice I had occasion to wish that I had not ridden on top of an open bus.* There was no drizzle in New York during my first few days' stay, but once there was a real downpour of rain! My fellow passengers cut their journey short and hurried down at the first possible stop. I did not wish to give in so I sat on, feeling as if I had been ship-wrecked. I must admit

* Open-top buses were discontinued in New York late in 1948.

that it was not easy to do so, but it made me feel an even keener admiration than previously for those ship's crews who braved indescribable storms to carry food and other goods across the seas to England during the war. Another time I was on this kind of bus on Riverside Drive on a very windy day. Suddenly my hat blew off, right through the window of a big apartment building. I could not go back five blocks to fetch it. I had on my overcoat, but had to grip the edges of the collar firmly to keep the wind from my chest. At the same time, the fluttering silk scarf of the young woman sitting in front of me continuously flapped in my face. She did not notice this, probably because she was having a similar struggle to hold her coat together. I did not mind this, but I did mind having to spend some of my limited allowance of dollars on another hat!

Single-decker buses, similar in appearance to a London coach, are to be seen almost everywhere in New York, mainly plying from East to West and vice versa. They are painted in a variety of colours—red, yellow, blue, green. I was never quite sure where they would appear or stop. I don't expect that I would have known all the buses well, even if I had stayed in the city for a long time, because I cannot claim to know all the London bus routes after many years' residence. I tried many of these coloured coaches in New York and often landed at a place from which I could not find my way back. There are no conductors and the driver has to do a variety of jobs. He collects fares and gives the passengers transfers. He opens the doors mechanically to let passengers out and in. He has to watch the traffic lights in order to drive on as soon as the green light appears, and so he cannot always pay attention to the passengers who are getting on or off. On one occasion I missed my grip on the bar inside the bus and fell on top of someone when it moved forward unexpectedly. Fortunately I was not the only one to fall, otherwise I would have felt much more embarrassed than I did. To my surprise all New York bus passengers are very tolerant. No one complains, even if all the passengers lurch at the same time. I think that some London passengers would speak their mind or display their renowned sense of humour in similar circumstances. Someone did complain once, but the driver had a store of answers ready. How can anyone be expected to do several things very well at the same time?

Another means of transport in New York is the street-car, or tramcar as it is known in London. Tramcars are gradually disappearing from London streets as they are considered uneconomical, inconvenient and noisy. So I was surprised to see them still running in New York, particularly on Broadway. If New York does decide to replace them, it may be done over night, whereas it would take a considerable time in London and at least a hundred years in China! To my mind street cars are perhaps the best vantage ground for the sight-seer in New York. They move steadily and slowly and stop about every two blocks. For fun I worked out that it would take more than half-an-hour in a street car from 103rd Street, where I stayed, to Times Square, as compared with about ten minutes in an express subway. The street cars run down the middle of part of Broadway, and I found it alarming to stand in the middle of the street waiting for them, while motor vehicles and taxis dashed past. The taxi drivers in New York avoid collisions by a hair's breadth. Imagine my feelings when I was only missed by that amount of space!

The bright yellows and reds of New York taxis look very smart by comparison with the dark colours of those in London. I understand that London taxis have to be constructed like high boxes so that wearers of top-hats and stiff shirts can sit in them in comfort. Now I learnt that the inside of a New York taxi is designed on spacious lines for relaxing in comfort, with a girl-friend humming Frank Sinatra's tunes alongside. The designers of both vehicles were motivated by humane intentions.

I saw none of the old, heavily moustached drivers so familiar in London. Instead the driver might have a moustache à la Fairbanks or resemble Edward G. Robinson's partners in his early films. There are many hack-stands (taxi-stands) in New York, but I never found a taxi there. Catching one was a breathless business and I certainly had no time to observe the driver's looks as I got in, but facing me as I sat would be a photograph of him together with his name, address, age and the number of the taxi. Once or twice I wanted to get out as soon as I saw the photograph, but as I was by that time speeding along, I could only shut my eyes until my destination was reached. The driver usually turned the wireless on to give me quiet music; I appreciated his thoughtfulness. I am no musician and understand very little about Western music, but I can usually guess when a piece is nearing its close. To my surprise, the music would soon be cut short in favour of a loud voice, urging me, with many valid reasons, to sell such-and-such a company my old car. A good price was assured. I wished I had a car! Immediately afterwards a doctor might urge me to find out if my eyesight was perfect and if not to go to such-and-such a company where I could obtain a pair of excellent lenses. This helpful attitude touched me, though I had had my eyes seen to before I left England. Other voices followed, urging me in friendly tones to do this or to buy that. I found this a little overwhelming and would have liked the driver to switch

New York taxi

the radio off. But he couldn't or wouldn't hear me. I was usually very relieved to reach my destination.

I complained about this to the friend who had assured me that I could be silent in New York. He retorted that he had not meant in a taxi. Where had he meant? Wireless boomed all day and night in the hotel where I stayed. I can be silent amid a big roaring noise, but how can I keep quiet when someone shouts friendly advice in my ear or tries to persuade me to buy something, which I had no American dollars to do? Sometimes the drivers themselves were talkative. One of them wanted to demonstrate how fast and safely he could drive his taxi and said that he could pass at least ten blocks in Park Avenue between the change of lights. At the back of the Grand Central Building, he began to try to do this, but was stopped behind many other cars every three or four blocks. Each time he shouted "Fool, damn fool" to the people in front of him. In the end the fare was double what I usually paid for the same distance. It seemed to me that I was the fool.

A Chinese phrase 'Chi hsin kao chao' or 'Lucky Star is shining high above' is always used to compliment someone who is lucky. The Lucky Star was shining high above me while I was in New York. I soon made a number of friends, many of whom had cars of their own, in which they were so kind and thoughtful as to take me sight-seeing when they could spare the time. I enjoyed many such outings, but I always felt very sorry for them when it came to searching for a parking place. Once I went with a friend to an art exhibition. The car could not be parked near the exhibition building and eventually he had to park it ten minutes' drive away. We then had to take a bus and finally walk for five minutes to reach the exhibition again. My friend told me that it was a curse to own a car in New York; one was continually worrying where to put it for the night and where to park it for the day. Sometimes it was quicker to go to one's destination on foot or by bus.

A day or two after my arrival in New York, I wrote to my good friend and publisher, Alan White, that so far I found the city very brusque. He wrote back in his usual friendly and persuasive manner that I would soon find it agreeable. He was right. By the end of a week of joy-riding on every possible means of transport my feeling towards it had entirely changed.

Glass-cutter Seller seen near Washington Street

VI

ROUND TIMES SQUARE

THE number of times I was in or around Times Square in the course of my comparatively short stay must have approached three figures. This is not because I have a passion for crowds and noise; nor that I am a spendthrift, and in any case I had not many American dollars to spend ; but simply that I found it impossible to avoid Times Square whenever I was sight-

Times Square

seeing or meeting friends. Every means of transport seemed to bring me to this hub of the city.

Times Square occupies a small section of Broadway, which is supposed to be the most 'provincial' district of America. Broadway, I was told, used to be called by all New Yorkers *the Great White Way*, on account of the coloured lights and neon signs which illuminate it at night. I have seen Times Square at all times and in all weathers. Before I visited America a Swedish friend informed me that there was no nature in New York and that one never saw the sky. Everyone ate, worked, played, talked, and slept entirely by electric light. This made me picture New Yorkers as extremely busy creatures, working like moles inside solid, square, concrete buildings, and making use of every minute to produce something for sale. I

48

soon discovered that my picture was wrong. Though there are so many means of transport, it seemed to me that people *walk* in New York much more than in any other city, and particularly so in Times Square, where they stroll in large or small groups at any time of the day or night. On a sunny day—and New York has plenty—indeed on practically any day, people can be seen sitting on the public seats, oblivious of the roar of the traffic on both sides. New Yorkers seem in fact to have a great passion for the open air, and generally to prefer being out-of-doors to being inside their electrically-lit homes. They did

Peace in Times Square

not seem as busy as I expected, yet it was impossible to believe that most of them were people, like myself, only on short visits to the City. I wondered what was responsible for such a false conception of the New Yorker, for, if the Times Square crowds are any criterion, they have more leisure than any other people in the world.

The roads in the Square looked to me like the capital letter X with the Times Building at one end and a huge Coca-Cola advertisement at the other. In front of the advertisement is a fine marble dais on which stands the statue of Father Duffy. The steps of the dais seemed to be full of people from early morning till evening, standing or sitting round the statue, feeding the pigeons—and themselves—with *Jumbo* peanuts. In addition to peanuts, popcorn, sweets, oranges, ice-cream and

E

even hot-dogs are consumed. Innumerable eating places round the Square make it easy to replenish supplies. Money never seems to be lacking. I was amazed at the New Yorkers' capacity for food. The many restaurants and eating stores appear always to be full, and there seem to be no definite times for meals; one eats when one feels like it. I found this had its advantages but disturbed my sense of the time of day. Presumably the crowds do not go to Times Square specially to eat. What then, do they come for?

A friend of mine happened to be staying at the Hotel Astor, so I had the good fortune to enjoy the view from its roof. This hotel is an old landmark of New York, and though it cannot now be ranked as a skyscraper it must originally have been considered a tall building. There are many potted plants along the parapet of the roof and I could imagine how they looked when the flowers were all in bloom. Looking down, my eyes were just able to separate people and cars. The people were like ants, the cars looked like black and coloured beetles! Our ancient philosophers ranked Man in the same category of Nature as all other creatures, even insects. They were right. The human mind, no matter how hard we try to distinguish ourselves from other types of creatures, always unconsciously evolves forms borrowed from Nature, as witness these New York cars!

Three weeks or so after my arrival there was a very heavy snowfall, which for me gave the whole New York landscape a changed and exciting aspect. I wanted to see Times Square with a snow covering and thought I could be the earliest sight-seer if I went there first thing in the morning. But no; I was lost in the midst of a strolling throng, as on many another occasion. There were drifts of snow several feet high piled up along the pavements of the Square, despite the teams of road-clearers. As I passed the Hotel Astor, a big lump of snow fell on me. Unintentionally or intentionally? I looked up quickly and saw that it was caused by two workmen; but some ladies walking behind me received similar treatment and took no notice of it so I gave the men the benefit of the doubt. Their composure was admirable. Perhaps they had cultivated the habit of indifference to the weather. Indeed inside my hotel, or any other building in New York, it was impossible to tell whether it was sunny or windy, raining or even snowing.

One early afternoon, as I was turning out of 44th Street under the signboard of the Hotel Claridge, I noticed that the sky had suddenly become so dark that it was almost impossible to see the tops of the buildings. I was greatly struck by such a rapid change, for it had been bright and sunny a few minutes before. I was glad to see Times Square in darkness such as I had never yet seen there at night. Then a peal of thunder rang out and torrents of rain poured down. Everyone rushed for shelter. So many people surged in one direction that some had to retrace their steps. Others dashed into the Subway, blocking the entrance. The elder and weaker members of the crowd naturally got left at the back. I heard someone say that old and frail people should not try to travel at such times, but who could have guessed that there would suddenly be such a downpour in Times Square in the middle of the day? I took refuge myself under the canopy in front of a cinema facing the Times Building. Apart from long lines of cars the streets were empty. There was not a pedestrian in sight. The noise of the traffic was subdued by the thunderclaps. I decided to record the unusual scene in a painting entitled 'An Afternoon Storm over Times Square.'

In my *Oxford* book I refer to rain as the 'wine of Heaven' and I have often expressed my fondness for it in other writings. I like rain because it washes away the dust, refreshes the air, makes the grass greener, flowers more colourful, and buildings cleaner. I often deliberately walk in the rain out of pure joy in it. However, this torrent in Times Square had little appeal for me. It recalled those rainy seasons, called 'Mei-yü' or Monsoon Rain, which I had experienced in my boyhood in China. Those torrents went on for days, sometimes weeks, on end. Rain, like the human mind, can be constructive or destructive. One has to take it as it comes.

Or that is what I should have thought, but a wartime anecdote about General Patton makes me wonder . . . Just before Christmas 1944, many wet days helped Rundstedt in the Battle of the Bulge. No reconnaissance planes could fly, and American tanks could not find the enemy in the downpour, so Patton decided that the rain must stop, and he went about it in characteristic fashion. He summoned the Chaplain. "I want," he said, "a prayer to stop this rain. If we got a couple of clear days we could kill a couple of hundred thousand of those

Krauts." "Well, Sir," replied the Chaplain, "It's not exactly in the realm of theology to pray for something that would help kill one's fellow men." "What the hell are you, a theologian or an officer of the U.S. Third Army? I want that prayer." The prayer was printed on thousands of cards with Patton's Christmas greetings on the back. It reached the troops on the fifth day of rain. On the sixth day the *sun shone*. I was most interested in this story, not because I am superstitious, but because it made me wonder whether the many legends and miracles which we read of in connection with great men of the past may or may not be true. Our peasants often pray to their local gods for rain during a drought, but I do not think it ever occurred to them to pray for the rain to stop during the Mei-yü season.

The torrents of rain in Times Square did not last long. As soon as they stopped the life of the streets was resumed.

As I moved on I wondered what Times Square would be like really early on a Sunday morning. I decided to see. I got up at 5 a.m. and reached 42nd Street half-an-hour later. There were two or three persons snoring on the wooden seats in the subway. They must have been too tired to go home. In the Square a young fellow in a bi-coloured coat was riding a bicycle. This was the first time I had seen a bicycle in the heart of New York. The sun was not up and there was a thick morning mist, making the scene at once strange and familiar: it was more like Piccadilly than Times Square. (I was by now used to tall buildings and regarded them as quite normal). The Times Building, high and narrow,

its many windows made vague by mist, resembled the long column of the Duke of York's Monument off Pall Mall, seen from the top of Lower Regent Street early in the morning. The shape of the Times Building is unforgettable. It must have been specially constructed to fill exactly the space available and be visible from many angles, and of course to give the Square its world-famous name. One might confuse the Nelson Column with the Duke of York's Column in London but no one could mistake the Times Building for any other.

Though New York weather is very different from London weather, New York does have drizzling rain as well as bright sunny days. When it did drizzle, I was inevitably reminded of London, where it can be expected at intervals all the year round. Many Londoners *never* go out without an umbrella. I have oftened featured a large group of umbrellas in the centre of my scenes of London in rain. But New York in rain cannot be represented in that way. These people seldom carry umbrellas; when it rains unexpectedly, they run for cover or manage as best they can. Once or twice I noticed a man sheltering beneath an obviously feminine silk parasol without apparent embarrassment!

Watching rain in Times Square after dark is a novel experience. Certainly by night it is the brightest square in the world, but I would not describe it as 'lighter than day'. The artificial light only reaches a limited height: above is darkness which the dazzling brightness below makes the more profound. The criss-cross lines of rain reflecting the light look like skeins of silk threads suspended in space, the thronging crowd seeming like puppets attached to the strands.

Visiting Times Square made me feel like a 'country cousin' who had never been to town before. I looked up and down and round about, and peeped through windows and round corners. My eyes were never still. I don't as a rule behave like this, but here I found it impossible to do otherwise. One day I found an enormous ball in the middle of the Square. It looked like a geographical globe except that there was no map on it. Instead it was painted in bright blue, red and white. Occasionally the face of a 'lovely' framed in golden hair would appear at an opening, and I realized at length that the purpose of the ball was propaganda for the American Navy. A few days later the structure was replaced by another in aid of European Refugees; then by one for Child Welfare; and so on.

Once I was resting for a while on the steps of the statue of Father Duffy, watching the pigeons being fed, when a loud-speaker blared and made me jump. Some celebrity, standing on a huge new structure, was appealing for help in 'the War against Cancer'. It made me feel less provincial to notice that even some of the pigeons were startled too. An old fellow by my side, wearing an open-necked shirt, murmured; "Don't talk such nonsense. Give me peace to feed my pigeons."

Another time, trying to trace the source of some stentorian music, I stopped in front of a shop bearing the sign 'National Beauty Parlour', and I was speculating whether this provided free beauty treatment when I discovered that the sound came from a big pale yellow coach. One of a group of soldiers standing by jumped in and out as the record needed changing. About me people were tapping their feet and moving their lips in time with the music. A dark-faced young man and a Chinese-soya-sauce-skinned girl, unable to resist the rhythm, began to dance on the pavement. Painted on the coach were some such words as 'Recruiting Unit for the American Army', but I could not imagine what the music had to do with the Army. It was, I suppose, a way of attracting notice, but I did not see anyone approach the coach to ask for information. To Americans there, street phenomena are commonplace. To me they were like things out of Baron Münchausen.

Sometimes, after dusk, Times Square reminded me of some big exhibition such as I had seen at Olympia in London before the war, the stands of the exhibition vying with each other in the brilliance of their illumination. The shops were outshone by the dazzling Neon lights around the canopy of the New Yorker Cinema and its rectangular signboard, while Loew's, not to be outdone, had great revolving pictures of the stars in the current show. The huge Coca-Cola advertisement, occupying the best position in the Square, almost beat the cinemas. The makers of Camel cigarettes, not to be overlooked, displayed the colossal face of a man in an army cap, puffing smoke as he enjoyed a Camel cigarette. Yet none of these advertisements is more effective than the moving-shadow-show of Schaefer's Beer. I watched it more than once. Sometimes it showed a pair of monkeys fighting, then a pretty girl dancing, or a fisherman who eventually landed a bottle of Schaefer Beer. There were always people watching these signs attentively and laughing. I became quite blind after watching them for a while and would find myself bumping into people. I saw this happening to others too, but the crowds were good-natured and no one seemed to mind.

Continuing to act like a country-cousin I sampled the hot-dogs, the milk-shakes, the coca-cola, the popcorn, the root beer and many other things I had never tasted before. Once I stood with a crowd inside a shop near Times Square, and watched a woman shouting as she auctioned something, but I could not understand what she said. Another time I noticed a shop selling small green turtles with their shells painted

Interested Customers

with brightly coloured designs such as the American flag, a house and garden, a bunch of roses, a horse, a base-ball player. They were kept in a square water tank. At first I did not recognise what they were, because the coloured designs were so vivid that I did not suspect there were living creatures underneath. Then I noticed that they were moving about in the water and I grasped what they were. They were all of about the same size, a little more than an inch in diameter, not perfectly round. They made a direct appeal to me because I had a passion for keeping turtles in my childhood. I enquired what kind of turtle this was which had head, legs and shell of dark green, but the man in charge of them was too busy to be bothered with biological questions. There was a notice on the tank saying 'We mail them anywhere in the world', so I asked if he would mail some to me at Oxford. The man shook his head and remarked: "China is a long way away and they would have to go by aeroplane. We can't do that yet." So I said "England". He shook his head again. That couldn't be done either. When I pointed to the word 'World' on the tank, he laughed and said "The world of America". Well, to those who live in America I suppose America *is* the world. It feels like that.

"Historic dates," says an editorial in the *New York Times*, "continue to multiply. If some, once considered important, were not forgotten, the school children of generations to come would be in a pretty situation. But perhaps the dates that matter to most of us are not the ones likely to be celebrated in the histories. V-E Day and V-J Day caused general rejoicing, but a particular family may think of the war's end as the day when word came that a missing Bill, Ed, or George was safe and on the way home. . . . Normal people love their country. Normal people are pleased when something happens, like a new cure for an old disease which benefits the entire human race. But we all have a healthy interest in our own private lives. We are not entirely the creatures of governments and institutions. If we pound our thumbs, we momentarily disregard the menace of the atom bomb. If a friend or relative is seriously ill, we cease to speculate about Congressional elections. If you are X's, down the street, who have so long wanted a baby, and are blessed with an eight-pound girl or boy with blue eyes, we are as glad as we would be if Congress passed a law absolutely, positively and democratically curing all our economic ills. The day is a holiday on our street. And this fact, no doubt, is the reason why the human race keeps as contented as it does in spite of the drums and trumpets of big-scale history."

I endorse every word of this. It applies not only to Americans but to us Chinese, indeed to all mankind. I used to share the sentiments of compatriots who were pleased when someone showed great interest in China or praised her, but turned sad or scornful when no one referred to China in their presence. All human beings are likely to be so interested in their own private lives as to forget that others are equally interested in their own lives. Thus do many misunderstandings arise. However, I was happy to have met the turtle seller, who continues, I suppose, to sell and mail his turtles to any part of his world!

One evening, strolling through Times Square, I heard a sudden bang. A giant toy balloon—one of many being offered for sale by a couple of men at a street corner—had burst. The men were shouting: "Biggest balloons in the world, thirty-five cents each". Americans are supposed to be fond of claiming that they have the *biggest* of everything in the world. Similarly, British people love to say that they have the *best* in the world. In China we have a saying: 'Tien hsia mai yu tsai hao ti' or 'Nothing better under heaven'. Evidently we are none of us unique.

In search of further amusing wonders I came upon a photographer's shop where one could be photographed as an Indian Chief or a jockey, by simply putting one's head through a hole in a painted board. Another photograph shop advertised '5 in 1' photos—five different positions in one shot. I was standing behind a glass-pillar looking at some of these when a middle-aged woman—at least she looked middle-aged to me—approached me and asked if I could help her buy a lipstick. I concluded that though I felt like a 'country-cousin', outwardly I must look like a country-aunt.

A crowd outside an eating place aroused my curiosity. They say that bees in a swarm, though they look like a stationary mass, in fact keep moving all the time towards the centre or the perimeter of the swarm. The same applies to a crowd of people. I placed myself on the fringe of this crowd and in a few minutes reached the centre of attraction. A tall man, whose face I could not see, was wrapped in an old yellow overcoat with a hood and his whole body bound with cords. He wore no shoes; his feet were wrapped in some sort of cloth or canvas. He stood so still as to be almost inhuman and at first I thought him a robot. When I could get round to the front of him I found he had a very pale, sad face, and a rather thin, black-brown moustache. He was not more than thirty-five. His eyes were downcast and he seemed to have lost the sight of one of them. He was perfectly silent. The crowd pushed and shoved to see him, and some laughed, but his extraordinary motionlessness made me feel uneasy. On his chest hung a square of thick cardboard with the words 'Establish New World Sovereignty.' Everyone, myself included, expected him to say something. One or two tried to stimulate him to speak. A soldier remarked loudly : "What does he mean by World Sovereignty?" Another asked, "Why world sovereignty?" Several girls shouted: "Goodness knows." One spectator said to his friends : "Well, this is New York. You can find anything in Times Square. Nobody knows what may be going on here tomorrow night." The question I should have liked to ask was : "When and where does he go from here?"

The population of Times Square is in direct ratio to the time of day. The later it is, the bigger the crowds. After eleven p.m. there seems no room for another soul, let alone body, yet more people keep pouring in from the fountain-like entrances of the subways. When the theatres finish, the audiences stream out and still everyone appears at least to have his feet on the ground. I went a few times to the theatres and on each occasion it took me about half-an-hour to get to the Square and some time longer to reach the subway. No one seemed in a hurry. There was always gaiety and insouciance in the air. My eyes were dazzled by the sparkling jewels and glittering dresses, my ears filled with the pleasant noise of kissing, good nights, gossip and laughter amidst the hooting of car-horns. If only life might always be so joyful and prosperous for everyone on earth all the year round!

No one seemed to pay any attention to the traffic lights. I do not see how they could have done so even if they had wanted to. Once or twice I stepped aside onto the door-step of a house or other building to see the crowd as a whole. The bodies formed a solid mass. Very few faces could be distinguished, but heads bobbed up and down as if the necks were on springs. It

Paper-selling after midnight

reminded me of the hot wood-pulp in a paper factory. You could not see what anyone was wearing—any more than you can at a cocktail party. But that consideration does not lessen the time people spend on designing, making and donning expensive dresses and jewels!

Crowds still throng Times Square long after the theatres

have ended. The buses stop running at a certain hour but the subways and street cars give a twenty-four hours' service. So do some cinemas and all kinds of eating places. The sight of people entering cinemas after midnight always astonished me. When an acquaintance on the *Queen Mary* informed me that "There is life in New York after 4 a.m. but in London none after 9 p.m." I had been sceptical. I could not contradict him now. It was not only the eating capacity of New Yorkers that amazed me but their ability to keep awake. No one seems to want to go home to bed. I got the impression that they would be glad if they could do without sleep altogether; and I thought that there was a million dollar fortune to be made out of the invention of a pill to prevent sleep.

The word 'million' crops up often in New York. I became affected by it. The Chinese phrase 'Hsi su yi jen' meaning 'conventional habits alter man' is very true. The late Professor Mackail, Professor of Poetry at Oxford from 1906 to 1911, and one of the world's great classical scholars, predicted that family life would eventually cease to exist, the house as a home cease to function, all existing domestic architecture become derelict, life resemble that of ants or bees, and housing a beehive or anthill. I wonder if he was ever in Times Square? I admit there are things in modern life tending to fulfil his prediction, but I think he overlooked the fact that, first, human reproduction would need to be speeded up to the pace of bees and ants. Oysters are said to multiply more quickly than any other creatures, but even they do not yet occupy one whole sea. There will always be people living leisurely in the country as well as rapidly in the town. For many ages yet there will only be one Times Square.

A Statue in Herald Square

VII

ALONG PARK AVENUE

I went to Park Avenue for dinner the evening after my arrival, at the invitation of an old friend who occupies an apartment in Mayfair House.

The China Institute of America is not very far from Mayfair House. Its director, Dr. Meng Chih, seems to have taken a great fancy to the cooking there, for he is a frequenter of the dining hall, though not a resident. In the entrance hall of Mayfair House some Chinese *objects d'art*, such as mahogany chairs inlaid with mother-of-pearl, huge porcelain vases, and carpets, are noticeable. Once Dr. Meng took a big party there. After the dinner, when I went to fetch my hat and coat, I was mistaken by the girl attendant for either a diplomat or a Chinese delegate to U.N.O. I tried to explain that I was neither, but she had a lot to tell me. Many grand people had come her way. Once a Russian prince and princess, another time an Austrian Duke's family, then the Peruvian Ambassador and his wife, an English Marquis and Marchioness, and so forth. According to her, the visitors to Mayfair House were very international. What really surprised me was that she should remember so well the details of the ladies' dresses and jewels.

Once I walked from 70th Street towards New York Central Building during a snow-fall, the flakes growing gradually bigger and falling more thickly as I went. The air was quite still except at the street crossings and the snowflakes did not fall straight but floated or danced in the air. They reminded me of the fluffy white willow flowers drifting about on spring days in my part of China. There was no sunshine at this moment and the masses of snowflakes formed a close-meshed veil, behind which interesting buildings appeared far away and unreal. Several lights shone through the windows, particularly through those of New York Central Building, and, together with the gilded roof, reminded me of fairy stories. The more I looked, the more I wanted to go nearer, like a child longing to visit an imaginary castle in a fairy tale. The more eager my longing became, the more densely fell the snow, and the further away the buildings seemed. Their true aspect became more elusive every moment. I was brought back to reality by the lack of trees and rocks, while the roar of cars drove away the last of my fantasies.

Park Avenue

Gradually the fall of the snowflakes became thinner. When I half-closed my eyes the upper part of the New York Central Building looked to me like the towers above the main gates of the city walls in Peking. The symmetrically arranged windows were not very different from those in the towers of Hatteh Meng and Chien Meng. The buildings on either side of the Avenue were temporarily transformed into shops beside the gates, the cars into the traffic of mule carts, donkey riders, and camel caravans, only modernised and faster moving. However, the roofs of Hatteh Meng and Chien Meng were not gilded. It may be that Chinese taste prefers natural colours rather than showy ones, while Chinese architecture aims to achieve harmony with nature rather than distinction from it.

In Park Avenue I found a number of people who apparently spend their life, day after day and night after night, entirely indifferent to the hurly-burly of the cars around them. These are the uniformed porters of the big apartment houses between 70th and 86th streets. With their neat, coloured uniforms they make very impressive figures. Sometimes they stand near the edge of the pavement gazing round at ease; sometimes by the entrance of the houses to which they belong. Sometimes they walk up and down, or to and fro between the entrance of the house and the edge of the pavement, with dignified mien and measured tread. Once or twice I happened to bump into one of them when we were both looking at the tops of the nearby buildings, so I had to apologise, but received only a sharp look in reply. I have seldom seen such motionless faces as theirs. Their Union must train them to be like that.

There are plenty of fashionable shops with good window-displays on both sides of this Avenue, so presumably people must come and gaze at them. But I very seldom saw any, and I was told that people living in this neighbourhood order by telephone and that well-trained shop assistants, knowing their customers' characters and tastes, can supply the right things. Why then should the managers bother to make window displays? It seems to me that they are not as practical as I am, though we Chinese are supposed to be most unpractical. The windows certainly kept me amused and interested. The two large ones on either side of Prince de Condé, for example, had a fresh show each time I passed by. Involuntarily I would stop to admire the well-displayed goods, the ingenious lighting effects and the colourful backgrounds. I still remember vividly the display of Mother's-Day chocolates. Through the windows I could see all along the gilt walls which were decorated with long strips of purplish red satin. If I remember rightly, the counter, lamp-stands, chairs and small tables in the classical French style, were all gilded. On the floor was a vermillion-coloured carpet. I have a passion for this colour which seems to me unsurpassed in richness and dignity. Consequently for me the Hall of Prince de Condé had an air which seemed particularly suited to Mother's Day. I expect I was being influenced by my Confucian upbringing, for I was taught to revere my parents as being full of experience and dignity who could guide me in the right conduct of life.

Few things I saw in New York induced in me more mixed feelings than the poodle puppies in the window of Irene Hayes. There were three of them and their movements made me laugh aloud. The hair of the two older puppies was shaved in the comical manner employed, for some reason, for poodles. A tuft of long hair was left at the tip of the tail and other tufts here and there over the body and legs. Each dog was treated differently. I had seen shaved poodles in England, but none that

looked so ridiculous and amusing as these. One had green and the other had red satin ribbons tied in bows on its tail and legs; and the remaining hair had been brushed with the utmost care. The light inside the window, reflected on the shaved parts of the bodies, revealing the pinkish flesh, which looked so soft and delicate as almost to make one weep. Though outside it was snowing heavily and it made me feel bitterly cold to look at these dogs, inside the window the shop was air-conditioned and the poodles were in fact perfectly warm. They could not have been better cared for. But I wondered who it was who first thought of shaving poodles—rather than any other species of dog. Nature has given the poodle a coat to protect him from cold and sudden attack: man denies him its use. Men strive to produce mechanical objects which resemble living beings, and turn the poodle, which is a living being, into something artificial. It is very peculiar.

The cult of the poodle in the west must be as absorbing as is that of the Pekingese in my country. The Chinese consider that the head of the Pekingese should be large, the chest wide, the ears big, the neck short, the eyes prominent, the legs short, with the two front ones bent to form a circle, the tail curled upwards and not inclining to one side, the nose flattened. Well, they are *not* all born like that! There is a story that in the imperial days of Peking, each palace dog had a court-girl assigned to wait upon it and massage its nose into the requisite flatness. In addition a piece of dry meat was hung up against the wall just out of reach of a dog, which would try and try in

vain to snatch a bite, succeeding only in flattening its nose in the process, while its eyes almost popped out of its head with eagerness and desire. This sounded cruel to me when I was a boy. But who thought of a little cruelty when he had spent a large sum of money on the purchase of his pet? Similarly in bygone days a Chinese mother was willing to bind her daughter's feet in the cause of 'beauty,' while ladies in Europe tight-laced themselves to achieve a wasp waist. It is a sad fact that human nature always seems ready to turn the natural into the unnatural.

Near New York Central Building, I noticed two big blocks of apartments, one on either side of the Avenue, with a large courtyard in the centre of each. This was an unusual sight here and I went into the block on the east side and walked round, looking at the trees, the flower beds and fountains. They must look very nice in spring and be a delight to the tenants. It was a generous thought of the owner to provide these courtyards.

To my delight, two weeks before I left New York, I was asked to take tea with Mr. Richard Walsh and his wife Pearl Buck, the Nobel Prize Winner for Literature of 1938, who lived in one of these blocks. It was the first time I had met Mr. and Mrs. Walsh, but I felt that I knew them well. I need hardly say that I had read many of Pearl Buck's books. She knew my native city Kiukiang, and also Nanking, where I spent my college days. As Mr. Walsh had also visited my country, we had a great deal to talk about. But they were both very busy and I was on the move, so I couldn't stay long. After leaving, I chuckled to myself at Mrs. Walsh having asked me to take tea instead of coffee, as if suggesting that as I had been living in England so long, I must be entertained in the English fashion. However, she did not give me a Sergeant Major's cup of tea made from those strange leaves grown in Ceylon!

In *A Corner in Women*, the American humourist Tom Masson wrote about geography :

"Well, pa, where is New York?"

"It's situated on the first floor of the Waldorf-Astoria."

"What's that? A Country?"

"No, it's a caravanserai."

"Oh, my, what a word! What is a caravanserai?"

"You wouldn't understand if I told you. It's a sort of a place of public irreverence where people go who are too rich to live in homes. Ask me something easier."

The son did not pursue the enquiry. The explanation did not help me to understand the word either. But certainly New York *is* situated on the first floor of the Waldorf-Astoria. In a short visit to London, one might not even know of Claridge's or the Dorchester, for they do not stand out above other buildings; but even a visitor of a few hours could not escape the Waldorf-Astoria in New York. Its name is printed in all papers and its twin towers overlook one almost everywhere one goes. It occupies a good stretch of pavement along the east side of Park Avenue. Of course I took myself there to see 'New York,' for that, after all, had been my sole aim in crossing the Atlantic. I was given a chance by a friend who happened to be staying there. He took me up on the roof for a short while, but I enjoyed myself more moving about on the first floor in the grand manner. One *must* move about there in the grand manner. On entering I did not find the lordly calm of Claridge's, nor the spacious pleasantness of the Dorchester. Instead, I was surrounded by a gay and fragrant atmosphere, with perfumed women on comfortable sofas and smartly dressed men standing round or moving about. Lights outlined every decoration and ornament on the walls, on the ceiling cornices, under the lamp-shades, and round the pillars. I could not quite follow the scheme of decoration, but that may have been because there were always a large number of people about and I could not see everything in one glance. It seemed a kind of profusion of colour and flesh. Many telephones for the visitors' use kept ringing, interrupting the murmur of the crowds. All kinds of flowers in pots were arranged here and there. Particularly beautiful were the lilies which lined the steps inside the main entrance when I went there the day after Easter Sunday. The masses of pure white jade-like flowers, supported on their single straight stems with dark green leaves all round, was an unforgettable sight.

When I was invited to go to the Waldorf-Astoria for the first time, I was told to put on my best clothes and to walk in a grand manner in case I should unconsciously create trouble for the management. Fortunately I had used my whole year's clothing coupons on having an overcoat specially made for me by a London West End tailor. As winter in New York is much colder than in London it was of particularly thick material. I was very proud of it and glad to put it on for this visit. The London West End tailor had obviously foreseen the necessity of my walking in a grand manner and had given the coat well-padded shoulders to cover my own sloping ones. I thought that if I walked in a grand manner into Claridge's or the Dorchester I should be asked by the porters if they could help me, but no one approached me in the Waldorf-Astoria. I walked into the enquiry office and was told to ring my friend myself through the visitors' telephone, which I did. The overcoat had at least helped me to walk in without trouble, but while walking inside it troubled me directly, for there the temperature was totally different from outside. But I could not very well take it off on the first floor of the Waldorf-

Astoria. It was fortunate that I was a Chinese who could be tolerant, even if the sweat was running down inside my shirt. The New York central-heating system is certainly efficient. Nobody noticed how hard I pressed my lips together to live up to my name of *Silent Traveller!*

Another time I went there with Eric Underwood to a cocktail party given by Mr. and Mrs. Douglas Chandor for the private view of the portrait of Mr. Winston Churchill which Chandor had just finished. I first met Eric Underwood some twelve years or so ago at Parcevall Hall, the house in Yorkshire of our mutual friend Sir William Milner. I heard that he was in England again just after the end of the war, but I could not get into touch with him before I left London. One morning I received a note telling me that he would be on the high seas for New York in a few days and that we must meet. He had got my New York address from Sir William. He is an Old New York Hand (I use this term by analogy with the American term, Old China Hand, used to designate those who have lived in China for some time). He has lectured very successfully all over the U.S.A. during the last few years, so he has made a large number of friends. When I went to see him, just after his arrival, in a new apartment at 630 Park Avenue, which he had apparently had no difficulty in finding, an amusing little incident occurred, which I have never mentioned to him until now. I arrived at No. 630 punctually, to be told by the two porters that they did not know the person for whom I was asking. However, after a moment's hesitation one of them told me to wait while he made inquiries. He rushed around with no result. Then he asked the telephonist in the corner by the entrance but she couldn't help either. Suddenly the other porter laughed and said "Oh, yes, I know. That English fellow who came this morning." I was relieved. Then he directed me to the lift and took me up. On the way I asked him how he knew the new arrival was English. "Ah," he said, "he had such well-tailored clothes on!" I glanced down at my West End tailored overcoat and reflected that it could not turn me into anything but a Chinese.

Eric Underwood had a little difficulty in discovering on which floor the Chandors were. In the end we followed a number of other people, and I was introduced to the host and hostess and to many guests. The Chandors occupy a spacious suite with big windows. Mrs. Chandor was busy pouring out all kinds of drinks and handing them round. I received a Martini Cocktail. Douglas Chandor took several of us into another room where there stood on the easel the portrait of Mr. Winston Churchill which he painted on the occasion of one of the meetings between Mr. Churchill, Generalissimo Stalin, and the late President Roosevelt. The artist's style and talented brushwork is well-known and I need say nothing about it. Chandor explained why there was no cigar in Mr. Churchill's right hand. The portrait was only a part of the whole, which depicted the scene of the meeting. Mr. Churchill had laid his cigar down and was talking to President Roosevelt.

Presently some more guests came in, among them many ladies wearing smart dresses and interesting hats. The artist had to begin explaining again. He also showed us a portrait of Mrs. Churchill painted at the same time during the Churchills' visit to New York.

At last the guests gradually thinned out and Douglas Chandor drew a deep breath and said "I can't say the things which they like to hear about what the sitter does. Now let's talk our own artist's language. I envy you calling yourself *The Silent Traveller*," he continued, "so that you shan't be bothered by people asking questions." I laughed and said: "You bet. Many people want to put more questions to me just because my name sounds so mysterious." Both Eric Underwood and I had another engagement, so we bade good-bye to our host and hostess. I could hear the Chandors still laughing after they had closed their doors. What a happy occasion!

Nothing could be more startling to me in all the years of my residence outside China than when I was asked to have breakfast at the Waldorf-Astoria by a friend of mine, Dr. K. C. Wang. I have had invitations for lunch, dinner and supper but never before for breakfast. At first I took it as a joke and then went with our mutual friend, Mr. F. C. Tien. We did not arrive until a quarter past ten but Dr. Wang came down quite calmly to take us to the hall for breakfast. In England one does not usually have breakfast after half-past-nine, but here many people were about to begin eating and many more were just coming in. The menu was handed to me. I looked through a number of interesting items and found one with the wording 'Breakfast in the English fashion,' under which was 'bacon and

Skyscrapers above evening cloud and mist

two eggs.' I ordered it and my friends endorsed my choice immediately. Dr. Wang had come from Washington to New York for a short visit. This was the only time he could be free to see Mr. Tien and me. Fortunately there is no difficulty in obtaining meals at any time of the day in New York. There is a term 'brunch' used to describe a telescoping of breakfast and luncheon, just like the English 'high-tea' which is a combination of tea and supper.

The day was Sunday, but after breakfast both Dr. Wang and Mr. Tien had business to see to, so I was free again to wander round Park Avenue. Noticing a number of people getting out of a taxi and going into St. Bartholomew's Church, I followed them. The stone carvings on the tops of the doors of this church were very interesting to me as I had seen the original sketches in Dublin. This Church differs from the other buildings in the neighbourhood in being built of brownish brick, and I was interested to notice that the General Electric Building, one of the tallest skyscrapers in New York, was of the same material. I wondered which was built first or if perhaps they were both built at the same time. When I got inside the Church, I found it full and a service in progress. Two gentlemen in black suits with dark red roses in their buttonholes invited me to sit down. I followed one of them, who was extremely kind and polite. Though the church was full to capacity, I could hear the sermon very clearly. I have often been inside churches in Europe while a service was being held. On those occasions I have sensed a feeling of antiquity, but here I breathed an air of richness and modernity. Instead of feeling transported to a bygone age I was in the world I knew. The church was very well lit and the lights were reflected on the myriad gilded dots on the walls. After the service, as I had been sitting near the doors, I walked down the steps in front of most of the stream of congregation. Everyone was smartly dressed, especially the young ladies, all of whom wore fresh flowers and, apparently, new hats. I have never seen a church service so well attended by so many well dressed people. It impressed me very much.

When I had explored the southern part of Park Avenue I wanted to see how far it extended to the north, and so I decided to spend a day walking along the pavement from 65th Street upwards. The plain box-like appearance of Hunter College at 68th Street did not seem to me very suitable for this part of the Avenue. I learned that this is a free college for women which was established in 1870 as part of the public education system of New York, and is governed by the Board of Higher Education for Women. There is a strong tendency for modern buildings to be severely plain in appearance and economical and practical in the use of material and space. I entirely agree with this for commercial premises; but as I have said in other books, I hold the opinion that one is entitled to be a little extravagant over the things one likes. I see no reason why a lady should not indulge herself in spending time and money on a hat she likes. Nor did I restrain myself from taking one more hot-dog when I began to like them, despite their disagreeable name! So why should not a women's college be attractively planned?

I began to feel tired after walking about forty blocks. But I revived when I saw a number of people going in and out of the 'Public Market,' between 111th and 116th Streets. This is said to house about 480 small retail merchants who were originally barrow pedlars. I walked right down one side of this market and then back the other side to my starting point. My head kept turning from left to right all the time. It is impossible for me adequately to describe the variety of food

and other things displayed. One section was devoted to fish, with many unfamiliar varieties, and the strong smell of it almost overwhelmed me. Another section was full of salad greens and vegetables, many of them from South America, with names quite unknown to me. There was a big section selling cloth and clothes of all descriptions. I was reminded of London's Caledonian Market, but here everything was much neater.

Hotel in Upper Park Avenue

I need not mention the varieties of the sweets, candies, nuts,
poultry and other forms of food.

Walking back a few yards I found a building called Park
Hotel, which had escaped my notice before. I thought of
going in to book a room, as I was likely to be turned out of the
hotel where I was staying, but then I saw a notice saying 'Full'.
Outside this hotel were a number of big wooden boxes full of
coloured linens which were apparently for sale.

Not long after my arrival in New York, I was entertained
to dinner by some friends. In the course of conversation Park
Avenue was mentioned and one of the guests remarked that
he wanted to find an apartment there, round about 114th
Street, and that he would then have the address Park Avenue
printed on his notepaper to impress his friends who did not
live in New York. Everybody had laughed except me. Now I
saw the joke.

Near Pennsylvania Station

VIII

IN CENTRAL PARK

LIFE is a continuous procession of experiments. There are people who aim at definite results from scientific experiments, but it is not easy for anyone to know exactly what to aim at in the experiment of life, which cannot be carried out in any scientific laboratory, no matter how well-equipped it may be. There is an intangible quality in life which science cannot measure, and which changes as life goes on. The appearance and shape of a flower had a different meaning for me when I was a child from when I was a schoolboy, and a different one again when I reached maturity. Now that half of my life is spent I often find myself recalling how I felt about certain things at earlier periods of my life.

Differences of climate affect people's feelings. The Eskimos, for instance, can hardly see the same beauty in snow scenery as I do. People in England joke at my fondness for rain and fog. The difference between looking at a flower with one's heart filled with the bitter-sweet ache of love and when one has suffered some calamity is often overlooked. A fresh, bright-coloured flower seen in Antarctica or in the Sahara desert would certainly affect one differently from one seen in New York.

When I was a boy, knowing only the part of China where I was born, I regarded the year as equally divided into four seasons of three months each. Then I spent some time on Hainan Island, the southermost part of China, where I found practically endless summer. Two lines of a poem by Su Tung-p'o, a poet who was also governor of this island during the Sung dynasty (A.D.960-1276), describe it well:

"The four seasons are all summer,
But one fall of rain changes them into autumn."

During my years in England, I have hardly experienced a single real summer in our sense, and autumn is only a short prelude to a long winter. In New York I had the new experience of finding spring much too short. This does not mean that there is very *little* spring in New York. There is far too much of it. There are always brightly coloured flowers inside the houses, and as the houses are centrally heated most people, particularly women, wear clothes of silk or thin linen even in winter. Then one is always hearing love-songs about 'spring in the air' and romance. Everyone in New York seems to wear an expression of eternal spring, or at least they try to look youthful, lively and restless. Perhaps this is because they see so little real spring, or else because they have such a deep love of spring that they cannot live without it. Since the beginning of history every creature of Nature has welcomed the advent of spring. I don't think I could ever enjoy myself in an artificial atmosphere of spring as much as in Nature's springtime. Even a pet animal does not enjoy an indoor spring for long. As soon as I learned that spring would not stay long in New York, I hurried off to Central Park to enjoy the real thing while I might.

I read the following passages in the New York Times :

"But if you would have the loveliest color of spring knock your eye out—and make your heart leap—look down on Central Park from one of the high windows south of it. A tapestry woven in a feathery pattern of all the tender greens of the new leaves in the treetops is spread over the whole expanse of it. The towers of the City, east, west and north, are a baroque frame about it. Spring is caught in the embrace of the monster of steel and stone and brick that is New York—and is not ruffled or put out of countenance.

Capture the magic of it while you can. The spring greens will not keep. Summer is on the way to paint the landscape in deeper tones of leafage. And, for choice, take it when the last lingering rays of the setting sun are upon it. Then watch while the day fades, the Park becomes a panel of darkness, and the frame is transmuted into a jewelled band of lights against the sky."

I was glad to know that I was not the only person finding spring too short in New York, but I think one should not just look at Central Park from a high window but go right into it. I was fortunate to stay in a hotel only two blocks from the Park, so I walked there nearly every morning. In China, spring was heralded by the appearance of mei-hua, an early leafless plum blossom, and we acknowledged its arrival by gradually shedding our thicker clothes. In England I hailed the crocuses as the harbingers of spring; though I was never sure whether spring had really come, for it might still be very cold. In New York as soon as I noticed a few tiny leaf-buds along a slender twig, I felt a kind of pressure all round me, particularly under my feet, and knew that spring was coming with a rush. Although in England some young leaves may be reluctant to emerge from their sheath for fear of cold winds and frost, and in China from a wish to retain their appearance of immaturity as long as possible, in Central Park, they are all forced out at the same time, like passengers from a crowded subway train into Times Square Station. In a few days all

Spring comes to Harlem Meer

these young leaves grew to full maturity, lost their youthful yellowish tinge and turned dark green. They experience life at high speed. I have not ceased to wonder why spring behaves in this peculiar manner in New York and pays it so brief a visit.

Spring in Central Park is certainly something to remember. Famous poets of my country in the old days often asked in their verses whence spring came and whither it went. I had never before attempted to answer these questions, but now I felt I could say that it had come direct from the bottom of Manhattan Island up to Central Park. Of the four seasons only spring comes up from below the earth; summer, autumn and winter all come from somewhere in the sky!

At first I learned with amazement that Central Park stretches for fifty-one blocks and is two and a half miles long and half a mile wide, with ponds, lakes, reservoir, lawns, playgrounds, ball-fields, etc. By and by I managed to go round almost all of them—and not only in spring. I was there in snow, in wind, in rain, in mist, in bright sunshine, at sunrise, at sunset and almost at all times from February to June. Each time I gained fresh inspiration or a new colour scheme for a picture. To any landscape artist Central Park offers an endless variety of subjects.

Among the many different types of trees, sycamores, field maples and planes are most conspicuous. Here and there a few silver birches stand elegantly among the others, and once I found a good-sized beech—at least I thought it was a beech. There were no chestnut trees about, and I was told that they were all killed by a blight some twenty years ago. Nor did any of the mast-like Lombardy poplars, so common in England, strike my eye. Near the American Museum of Natural History is a group of lofty pines.

The trees which held my attention most and touched my deepest feelings were the weeping willows. I have met weeping willows in England, but not in such numbers as here. There are about twenty different species of willow, but the weeping one is a native of China. How could I refrain from being emotional about it for this obvious reason? We call this tree 'Trui-liu' or 'Hang-down willow'. I do not know why nor how it came to be named 'Weeping willow' in English. Some used to attribute the name to the words of the Psalmist (cxxxvii 1,2):

"By the rivers of Babylon, there we sat down, yea, we wept, when we remembered Zion. We hanged our harps upon the willows in the midst thereof."

But later scholars found that the tree mentioned in this passage was not in fact *salix babylonica*, but a poplar. In my book *The Silent Traveller in Oxford* I have written at length of the big part played in our daily life by this willow, particularly in our literature and pictorial art. Very few Chinese landscape paintings lack a willow. Many of our most famous poems contain some reference to it, to suggest a feeling of attachment:

for its long slender branches blown by the wind seem to cling to the departing person. In this sense the English name 'weeping willow' is appropriate. But, on the other hand, we imagine the rhythmical swaying of its branches to be a lighthearted young girl dancing gracefully in the spring wind. Indeed, the willows in Central Park are full of gaiety. Three groups of them persuaded me to linger.

After crossing the road which faces the Avenue of the Americas, I used to follow a narrow foot-path leading to the Pond. On the right there is a rocky mound, left in its natural state, on top of which two large willows grow amidst many other trees. It was an early morning of late February. Most of the trees were bare, with dark trunks and blackish branches, but the long, hanging branches of these willows became bright fresh yellow in the sun, tossing in gentle masses like golden silk tassels. I murmured to myself at once that spring had already come and was disporting itself in the willows. With the tall buildings along Central Park South as a background far behind the footpath, these two large willows looked most picturesque.

Inside the children's playground stands a group of fine willows. They rewarded my attention one bright sunny day in May. Though I could not feel it, there must have been quite a strong wind, because their long dark green tassels were being shaken from side to side. They looked like a chorus of ballet dancers. Or would they be better described as the hands of Mother-Nature caressing the lovable heads of a number of young children playing and laughing below? The children's tinkling laughter added to their charm.

On another occasion I was near the Grand Stairway. Many people, mostly young, were either rowing on the lake or idling by the lakeside. The wind brought me the noise of their chatter from time to time. I stepped up the slope of a mound, with the lake on my left and the Grand Stairway to the right facing the fountain, the water of which was being blown aside in a fine spray. In the distance behind the fountain was the big willow. Its slender branches were tossing in the wind almost identically like the spray from the fountain: at one moment I mistook the long spray of the water for willow branches, at the next vice versa. When sunbeams fell on one of them, the willow branches became golden and the water silvery. This

Spring comes to Central Park

intermingling of gold and silver movement impressed me with its artless beauty. My personal attachment to the willows in Central Park is expressed in the following little poem which I composed there on one occasion:

異地初為客
相見也依依
春來戒若歸
絲絲園裡柳

一湖渺渺停春水
愛夕陽天欲晚
雲樓排立靜群喧園最
怪石巖畝挿滿園

湖遠邊槭一著怪新石裝
小坐領春光
小艇飄然去
層樓鶯任竟天際翔

薰風欲醉我
吹面思茫茫
輕鷗任意竟天際翔

松鼠公然不避人
間嘗慾多如此
寄語園丁莫浪嗅身去
立當高槭覓怎身

右元貢性之松鼠絕句

一路好風吹
落花亂馬足
兩傍春槭綠
纖手拂鬢絲

I come to this strange place as a guest;
At the arrival of spring I feel like returning home.
The tassel-like branches of the willows in the Park
Cling round me during our meeting.

Of flowers there is a great variety in Central Park. In the Conservatory Garden, which is a small part of the Park, I saw the wonderful shows of tulips and roses and wistaria. When I found myself in the Shakespeare Garden my mind went to pieces in the effort to remember this or that line from Shakespeare's work and so identify a flower. At length I acknowledged that I was not an Englishman, and gave it up. I wondered how many English men had stood the test here before me, with any success. But two flowers, the cherry blossom and the magnolia, did delight me immensely. Both have their origin in the East, and neither shows its face for very long in the year.

Cherry trees in bloom cannot feel much affection for the wind, especially the strong wind of New York. On the other hand, they would smile at a gentle breeze as I saw them do in this Park on several occasions. I noticed two little cherry trees when I walked by the west side of the reservoir towards the American Museum of Natural History. They were of an unusual species, having a number of flowers with double or multiple petals blooming together like a small ball on the tip of each twig, instead of blossoms all along the branches. Very few leaves had come out yet. The slender branches bearing only the clusters of blossom were very beautiful.

Cherry Blossom

One evening after strolling round the Park for some time, I came upon an antique-looking building high up on a rocky hill. Going up to it, I read the words:

"Belvedere Tower, erected in 1869 as a look-out. It now houses the New York Meteorological Observatory, which was founded in 1868".

It was built of dark grayish stone which gave it a weather-beaten appearance. A few boys and girls were playing round it. Their happy laughter seemed to receive approval from the soundless smile of masses of cherry blossoms by the side of a small pond below. Moving towards the trees, I quickly realised that I was on the wrong side of the pond, facing the cherry

blossoms instead of mingling with them. The inverted image
of the Belvedere Tower in the water was somewhat obscure
and decorated with the pink and red dots of the petals which
the east wind had blown down. The same wind was making
thousands of tiny ripples on the surface of the pond. Stronger
gusts made the cherry trees bend their heads to let the wind
pass over them. The air became alive with fluttering petals. The
sun was setting and a big bunch of white clouds floated high
above, motionless despite the ground wind.

Cleopatra's Needle

Moving among the trees I let the rain of petals fall on me.
Near the pond there were a number of magnolias in bloom.
I was particularly attracted by the few growing on a little
mound where the Egyptian Cleopatra's Needle was erected
not far from the back of the Metropolitan Museum of
Art. The Needle commands a wonderful and imposing view
over a wide area directly facing the Belvedere Tower. Though
it is a very old monument with a weather-battered face, it
retains an unbelievably youthful look, perhaps enhanced by
the presence of the many cheerful faces of magnolias, swiftly
urged to full bloom by the hurrying New York spring.

The back of the Metropolitan Museum was painted a brownish colour at the time of my visit and this reminded me of the outside wall of an ancient Chinese monastery in the countryside or high up a mountain. Seeing the magnolias in full bloom in front of this brownish wall I felt nostalgic; even the Egyptian Needle did not seem out of place.

I have one regret concerning the birds in Central Park : that I never properly became acquainted with the American bluebird. I once saw one in flight, a flame of blue above the trees along Riverside Park, and I concluded that Central Park must be the bluebird sanctuary; but, perhaps because I was not observant enough, my wish to know the bluebird is still unsatisfied.

The American robin, on the other hand, seemed to know me very well. The English robin redbreast is a most daring and friendly bird. Its counterpart in New York is much bigger and is actually a species of thrush. It is very daring too, doing just what it liked in my presence. Late one afternoon I was loitering round the Mall of the Park. After crossing several foot-paths I landed on the border of the Green, where two beautiful old trees grew. Darkness was near, hiding in the woods. But the Green lived up to its name, looking like an enormous emerald carpet. A number of American robins strutted about almost at even distances from one another, their big red breasts stuck out as if on parade. They made the ideal decoration for a green carpet—a typically American carpet, without the complicated pattern of a Persian one. I wondered if Mr. Arthur Urbane Dilley, the leading American authority on oriental rugs, had ever made a study of the pattern.

There were always seagulls and pigeons perched on the Maine Memorial whenever I entered the Park from the Broadway entrance. They looked very well-fed; even the pigeons did not seem to be greedy and incessantly pecking the ground. Once I watched them settling themselves along the marble edges of the monument, where they waited and gazed for a while, and then, at some signal unseen by human eyes, rose on the wing and made a circle round before settling down again. They repeated this several times as if practising some performance for presentation on an open-air stage.

I remember best the mallards or ducks round the little pool

on the west side at 101st Street, where I often went with bread
to feed them. As soon as they became aware of my approach
they would greet me with a loud quacking. But the morning
after the heavy fall of snow, the pool was frozen and there was
no water for them to swim in. They looked helpless, and
although they quacked their greeting, it was feeble and
depressed. However, they ate the crumbs I threw them, and
then waddled across the ice to the tiny island in the middle
of the pool. I made a number of sketches of them. Once I saw
three or four of them fly from a rock into the stream when I
was standing near a willow facing a small stone bridge behind
which were several tall buildings on the Fifth Avenue side.
They gave a lively rhythm to the scene and I decided to make
a picture of it.

I used to stand by a small rock near the Pond overlooking
the south edge of the Park, with its surrounding trees and
shrubs in soft colours and the twin towers of a tall building
faintly visible in the background. One morning in early May
I found there in the trees and shrubs a great variety of colour—
pink, red, white, dark green and yellowish green, intermingling
with the bluish black of yews and brown maples. Suddenly
a little shower made everything look different. The colours
were less sharply defined, and the drizzle made them seem
further away. The pond looked bigger and the twin-towers
building more distant and loftier. Two or three wild duck
skimmed the water as if urging other birds to come down and
take some exercise. By chance I spotted a fine white dot in the
distance facing me. Moving nearer it I found it to be an Ameri-

A sight in Central Park

can white pelican standing motionless on a small rock at the water's edge, its long bill sticking upwards.

Dogs are not common sights in this park. Perhaps it is difficult to keep dogs in the apartment houses which are the commonest form of New York dwelling. Certainly I did not see nearly so many as in London parks. On the other hand, I do not remember seeing Londoners taking their rabbits or cats out for an airing as I saw in New York. I noticed that the rabbit or cat was usually kept in a beautifully-knitted woollen bag and set on the bench beside its owner. The rabbits' lips would move and nibble incessantly; the cats just dozed in the sun. Once—only once— I saw a stout lady walking slowly on

Taking the cat for a walk

the grass with a long lead in her hand, to which was attached a bright red satin ribbon round the neck of a black cat. In fact, the cat was leading the way and taking the lady along. Though the cat was as large as any I have ever seen, I felt it so horribly small in comparison with its owner, that I thought I was seeing one of the unbelievable shows in the circus in Madison Square Garden.

The creature I met oftenest in the Park was the grey squirrel, a native of North America. I read that five or six pairs of grey squirrels were brought over to England in 1890 and released at Woburn in Bedfordshire. They multiplied at such a rate that many were given away as gifts for private grounds and public parks. In thirty or forty years' their numbers had increased so much that they were doing serious damage in highly cultivated areas of England, presenting a menace to bird life and exterminating the native English red squirrel. A public outcry arose and a national campaign was organised for their destruction. Fortunately or unfortunately they developed an epidemic disease of their own and most of them died in 1931. Mainly because of their love for the native red species, English people do not care much for the grey squirrel.

There are references to squirrels in old Chinese books, but I cannot be sure whether to red or grey ones. Our poets and artists had a great love for them, often writing about them or

Climbing rocks

painting them in connection with grapes and vines. The following is a humorous poem by Kung Hsin-chih of the thirteenth century:

> The squirrel boldly shows no sign of fear of man,
> Perched high up a tall tree as if forgetting itself.
> Greedy people are always like this.
> Mark my word, gardeners, don't scold it extravagantly.

This poem does not apply to the grey squirrels in Central Park, for they would climb on a man's hand to eat their fill. New Yorkers feed squirrels as Londoners feed pigeons. Once I saw a man standing between a tree and a rock and holding peanuts in both outstretched hands. There were ten or more grey squirrels round him, climbing all over him as if they thought him a kind of tree. An elderly lady spoke to him and the squirrels did not run off as she approached. He spoke of their friendliness, demonstrating it by stepping forwards and backwards with the little creatures all following him as if they were his own. Another time I saw a girl lying on her back on a rock, eating peanuts idly. She had scattered a number of peanuts on her chest and about the rock. A grey squirrel sat on her right knee pushing a nut into its tiny mouth with its forepaws. Two or three others ran about her body as they might have done on the rock. The sparkling eyes of the squirrel are full and black, indicating alertness. I loved to watch the whimsical quick-nibbling lips, the acrobatic manner of holding the nut or fruit, the swift movement, and the bushy tail.

There are no cattle or sheep in Central Park, as there are in Kensington Park or the Bois de Boulogne. Horses do appear frequently, though very seldom in their own interests. But there are slow-moving carriages, with drivers in top-hats, in which sightseers sit at ease. The unusual slowness of such motion usually makes New Yorkers quite silent. Young ladies on horseback wearing brightly coloured riding habits and trotting and galloping along the riding track often enliven the Park scene. Once I was inspired to write the following few lines:

> All the way a delightful wind is blowing;
> Both sides are lined with spring trees in green.
> The slender hand brushes back the temple hair,
> While many falling petals are confusing the horse's hooves.

The skyline of the tall buildings to the south of the Park was a source of endless fascination to me. Once I saw it after a heavy fall of snow. Most of the buildings are of white stone or concrete which merged with the grey snow-laden sky, so that from a distance their little windows seemed to be stuck on the face of the sky. Another time, on an afternoon in late April, thinking to take another look at this view, I had crossed the riding track and climbed a mound when a mounted policeman rode towards me and shouted to me to come down. I told him that I only wanted to get a good view of the skyline. He suggested that I could see it equally well from somewhere else, though he did let me stay for a while. He was quite right, for I later had a better view of it from the top of the

Summit Rock near the American Museum of Natural History, at sunset, when the evening mist covered the tree-tops in the foreground. The façades of the buildings then cast aside their artificial man-made appearance and looked like something tranquilly alive.

> The spring water is quite still in the brimming lake;
> There are many rugged rocks standing in this Park.
> I love best watching the sunset sky near dusk,
> When the towering skyscrapers appear in a hushed row.

The natural rocks in Central Park are one of its most attractive features. I admired the designer's courage in leaving them. In a park in China they would have been usual. Apart from our principles of using a natural setting in garden planning, we *could* not have removed or levelled such huge rocks even if we had wanted to, without terrible labour. But in New York nothing seems impossible. If someone wanted to pull down all the skyscrapers and put up a huge mountain instead, I would not say that it could not be done. To flatten a few hundred rocks and plant a lawn on the site, therefore, would present no difficulties at all. The designer of this interesting park had the foresight to leave many rocks, large and small, in their natural state as ornaments and special features, though I do not suppose he foresaw my coming to appreciate them.

The Ramble is one of the many natural rock formations. It stretches a good way round the edge of the lake; the narrow gorges, the splashing waterfalls, a rather gloomy cave, and many thickets and small winding footpaths inside the woods all became familiar to me. Each time I was there I met many children, for whom it was clearly a favourite haunt.

In China, poets and artists like to give names to rocks either according to their shapes or because of some incident connected with them. As I had been brought up in this tradition, I gave the name ' Tung-hsin Shih' or 'Twin-heart Rocks' to two small ones standing together near the road between the Green and Heckscher Playgrounds. This came to my mind when I saw a couple sitting on them on one of my evening walks. The silhouette of their slender figures and a tall white building in the distance, suggested a peaceful world within everyone's heart, so unreal yet so real.

Apart from the Ramble, which only occupies a small

Twin-heart Rocks

portion of the lakeside, there are many more natural rocks left along other sides. Once I entered the Park after a long tour of the Museum of Natural History and walked straight towards the lake. I found an interesting rock which I had not noticed before, stretching into the water, I sat down on it. It was a sunny afternoon in early April. Many trees were just about to have their looks changed by new leaves. I began to feel drowsy, and presently relaxed and went to sleep. When I awoke I composed a picture as well as a poem:

> There is a strange rock by the lake side;
> I sat on it to enjoy the spring light.
> The skyscrapers reach upwards to the edge of Heaven;
> The distant trees wear their new fashions.
> Gone in a flash are the rowing boats;
> Flying at will the light seagulls.
> The warm wind seems longing to intoxicate me,
> Blowing over my face and causing my thoughts to wander
>   vaguely.

The rocky side of Harlem Meer received me very well many a time. I seemed to meet more children there than elsewhere. On a cold and snowy morning of February I went to see Harlem Meer which had become a solid block of ice. Two or three red-painted notice boards said 'Danger warning'. Suddenly a loud whistle sounded and a fat policeman, who had apparently just enjoyed a good breakfast, walked down to the edge to chase away a few youngsters. He then walked to and fro beside the Meer. I bade him "Good Morning" and he gave me a sharp look but said nothing. A policeman in London, I thought, would undoubtedly have replied, adding a comment on the snow, the ice and the weather in general. There were a few tall trees on the west side of Harlem Meer near Cathedral Parkway, and their dark trunks and long interlacing branches against a background of pure white snow, with the little red-painted bridge on the rocky side of the Meer, suggested an attractive composition for a picture.

The natural rocks are great attractions for youngsters. One morning while I was sketching, three boys and two girls were climbing about near me, and presently the girls came to watch me. Soon the youngest boy came along too. I was surprised to find them so quiet. They made no comments and I wondered if children in New York were used to watching artists sketching. Then the biggest boy shouted to the others: "Leave him alone" and they immediately responded to the call and ran away.

I had nearly finished when two more boys came along. They seemed to know something about art and we were soon chatting together. The older boy, who told me he was ten years of age, asked if he might see my sketch book. I never make detailed sketches and only aid my memory by a few very rough lines, but the boy looked at one of these and confidently pointed out this and that building in it to his companion, who was eight. Then he told me that his family came from France and that his mother and father had been sending clothes and food to France for some time. He looked physically tough, but of a gentle disposition and he showed no inclination to run away from me. The younger one, who had very healthy red cheeks, seemed content to linger too. These two little fellows were very friendly. They were not like the children of my generation in China, who were always very shy and would run away at the *sight* of a foreign face. Nor did they resemble the children

I used to meet in London, who tried to find out what language I spoke by asking me: "What's the time?" These two took me for granted. I asked what they would like to do when they grew up. The older boy told me that he wanted to be a sailor and the young one that he was going to be a soldier 'to kill the Japanese.' "But the war is over," I remarked. "You don't want to kill anybody now, do you?" He looked downcast and declared that he first wanted to be a boxer. Jumping up, the boys started to wrestle then and there to show what they could do. I complimented them and then moved on, but they followed me as if we were in the same party. So we chatted and presently sat down on another rock by the pond. For some reason I then said that when they grew up they might like to

Two boys wrestling

go to the cinema and to take their girl friends out dancing and that they would forget boxing and such things. At once the older boy unexpectedly replied: "I've got a girl. I have a photo of her in my wallet. Do you want to see it?" Before I could answer, the wallet was in my hand and the photo was before me. The two youngsters had been taken together by a street-photographer like a pair of young lovers in a film advertisement. The boy went on to tell me that his girl-friend was ten and a half, and that he did not want to marry her when he grew up, for, though he liked her, he did not love her. I could only say: "Oh!". Then the younger boy took out his wallet in which there was also a photograph of a young lady—his mother! I apologised for not having the same kind of wallet to show them. An American friend once told me that everybody in New York carried a wallet with a photo in it.

Apparently he was right. I felt I must try to get one before leaving.

There is a very small pond inside the Conservatory Garden. I went there once to have a look at the bronze statue of a girl holding a bird bath and a boy blowing a flute. The notice on a stone reads:

"Fountain group given to the children of the City in the name of Frances Hodgson Burnett, 1849-1924".

Three little sparrows were taking a bath in the bowl held by the girl and they seemed to make the carved sparrow come alive too. I was making a rough sketch of the scene when a little boy of about three unexpectedly appeared and asked what I was doing. Without waiting for my answer, he vanished. Perhaps he was the boy of the fountain group!

I do not claim to know much of what goes on inside the Park after dark, but I was interested in the following story told to me by a friend. There was once a lady who lived in a big hotel facing Central Park. She used to go out every morning in her luxurious chauffeur-driven car, and on several occasions she noticed a poorly-clad man lying on one of the public seats by the Park, and gazing longingly at the hotel. She felt curious about him and wanted to find out what was in his mind, so one day she crossed the road and asked him. The answer came: "Dear lady, I'm a penniless person and sleep on this seat whenever the cops don't chase me. But I dream day and night that some day—just once—I will spend a night in that mighty swell hotel across the road." The lady was amused by this and said she would make his dream come true that very night by paying for the best room in the hotel for him. The next morning she had the man in while she breakfasted and asked him how he had slept. To her great surprise, he said: "Never again, dear lady. I sleep better on the seat in the

Park". Amazed, she asked if the bed had been uncomfortable "It wasn't that," he explained. "You see, over there I can dream I'm in the hotel. Up here, I kept dreaming the whole night that I was on the Park seat."

I once left a dinner party rather late and taking the wrong bus arrived at 100th Street and Madison Avenue. Not knowing where to catch a crosstown bus, I thought it would not be a bad idea to walk through Central Park to 103rd Street West, where I was staying. It was very dark in this part of the Park, but I felt well and happy, perhaps because of a little stimulant I had had at the party. For some distance I met nobody. At a point where several roads met I was puzzled to know which to follow, and was afraid I might find myself downtown again. After a little hesitation I decided to take the path through the woods. The thick foliage and branches hid all the lights and the darkness became intense. I could only see the big tree trunks. I began to feel a trifle chilly, but was soon warmed by the sound of someone running. Suddenly this someone bumped right into me. I could not see what sort of person it was, but I laughed and said: "You must have had a little more drink than I had." The fellow answered: "Sorry soor," sounding, very young indeed. He went on to say that he was chasing his girl who had just left a cinema with him. Before I had properly grasped his meaning, he was off. I realised that as I had no hat on, I had been mistaken for a girl. I seem to become all sorts of things, a deity in Wall Street, a country-cousin in Times Square and now a girl in Central Park. Anything seems to be possible in New York.

I made a personal link with Central Park on May 19th, when the Mayor of New York City held a grand celebration of 'I AM AN AMERICAN DAY' there. Though I am not an American, the date happens to mean more to me than any other in the year, and I had kept it entirely free. When the time came, I made for the main entrance to the Park, leading to the Mall. Masses of people were there already and many more were streaming in. The biggest attraction was to be the personal appearance of some of the most popular film stars, whom the Mayor had asked to come and take part. For cinemagoers this was an opportunity not to be missed. I cannot call myself a cinema addict but I was anxious to see how the girls and boys would react to the stars. I went with the crowd. Many of the people were holding blue or yellow cards. I had none, but just the same I went on with them into the enclosure where there were hundreds of rows of seats. Outside a number of policemen were patrolling. Everyone was smiling and laughing. Yes, it was a very happy day for all Americans and particularly for those who had just completed their naturalisation papers and become American citizens. I could not get near enough to the platform to see what it looked like. The singing was

'I am an American Day' celebration

relayed by microphones, but was either too loud or too low for my unmusical ears. I spent most of the time gazing at the many coloured wheelbarrows selling ice-cream, chocolates, sweets, puff-corn, peanuts, paper hats, and coloured balloons. One balloon-vendor was inflating his wares most efficiently by means of a machine like a used shell. The barrow salesmen must have enjoyed themselves more than anybody else at this celebration. I was standing among a big crowd just outside the enclosure when a roar of laughter was caused by a fat policeman patting his 'corporation' and saying in a sing-song

voice: "I am . . . an . . . Ameri . . . can . . .". Suddenly a tall
dark-faced fellow in a smart grey suit with a dark-red rose in
his buttonhole stretched out his arm and said smilingly:
"You *is*, yeah, you *is*!" Indeed, you *is*, he *am*, but I *are* not
an American. Yet on May 19th forty-three years before, I
happened to be born into this amazing world in an amazing
age and enjoyed this big gathering in Central Park even though
it was not to celebrate my birthday!

"Yeah, you is !"

IX

ALONG FIFTH AVENUE

I AM no window-gazer and very seldom go to see places simply because of their fame or historical associations, but while I was in New York, I soon found it impossible to avoid Fifth Avenue.

Fifth Avenue has been referred to as *The Street Called Straight* and also as *The Lane that has no Turning*, but I do not care for either name. I would like to suggest instead *The White Satin Rope Fastened at Both Ends*, with the idea that we humans are the rope-walkers. The attraction of Fifth Avenue is

One of the rope-walkers

irresistible, but I always felt a certain tension in my heart while walking there. There are things to see which can benefit one's mind, broaden one's outlook, call forth one's admiration, increase one's desires and force one to smile, to cry, to hate; even, I fancy, to die! There are many noble churches, important museums, a Public Library, art galleries, big bookshops, famous buildings and skyscrapers: all call forth one's admiration. Fashionable objects displayed in the shopwindows increase one's desires: if one can afford them, one smiles; if not, one cries. But useless longing to possess results in hate; that is the way of life, whether the year be 1946 or 100,000. The rope-walkers fall off and are replaced. I was one of the rope-walkers, and I always felt disturbing stirrings.

Some of my walks on the white satin rope, however, are linked with cheerful and memorable little incidents. The first of them happened near that end of the rope which is fastened at Washington Square. A very impressive building called 'Hotel Number One Fifth Avenue' marks the starting point. Outside are tables and chairs neatly arranged along the wall, with a large coloured canopy above. It reminded me of pavements in Paris. I had no reason to go into the hotels but I conceived a childish whim to take some refreshment on the pavement, in order to mark the first step of my walk. But it turned out that it was not the hour for service, so I crossed the road and had a meal outside a restaurant opposite.

One day a friend and I sought the house where for some years Mark Twain lived. My friend, a student of foreign literature, knew much more of Mark Twain than I did. He is, moreover, characteristically Chinese in his persistence. For an hour and a half we roamed Washington Square and its neighbourhood, but no one could guide us to the house. A smart young policeman we thought looked knowledgable, but he seemed never to have heard of Mark Twain. Another half-hour brought us upon the same policeman again and he asked us if we had found the house yet. On hearing that we had not, he looked very pleased, took out his notebook and directed us a little way along Fifth Avenue. He had made enquiries after we left him. It warmed our hearts that he should have taken the trouble.

The house, a red one, has an occupant, and we could not

go in, but we found a copper plate on the wall with bas-relief portraits of Mark Twain and Washington Irving, both of whom had lived in it. My friend happily copied the inscription under the reliefs, wiping the sweat from his forehead while he did so. I tried to cool him down by saying mischievously: "You are excited at the prospect of being able to boast to your friends and pupils how much you know of Mark Twain."

Mark Twain and Washington Irving

Among the many notable religious edifices in New York, I visited each of the three big ones on Fifth Avenue: St. Patrick's Cathedral, St. Thomas' Church, and the Temple Emanu-El of the City of New York. There are three other Fifth Avenue churches—the Church of the Ascension, the First Presbyterian Church and the Brick Church—but I got no further with them than reading the names in the porches. How I found the 'Little Church Around the Corner' was purely accidental. I was rope-walking one morning and it suddenly began to rain. I have never minded rain of the English drizzle kind, but here my newly acquired light flannel suit soon began to look limp, so I moved to the shelter of a shop window. The goods displayed attracted me and I sidled along till I found myself taking a turn in East 29th Street. There, in a noticeable gap between the usual tall buildings, stood a little church.

It was named, I was informed, by ' Rip Van Winkle' Joseph Jefferson. When an actor named George Holland died in 1870 and the pastor of a neighbouring church declined to bury him, Jefferson heard that this little church would perform funeral services for strangers and remarked, "God bless the little church around the corner". It is said to have become the church of the theatrical profession from that day, just as St. Paul's, Covent Garden, is the church of the theatrical profession in London. The green grass and the young leaves on the trees in the churchyard, mingled with the sculptural ornaments and statues, appealed to me. The gateway, with its emerald roof and reddish walls, did not look like the churches I had seen in Europe, but the small spire and tower made the building's significance unmistakable. Inside, everything was beautifully polished and clean. There were a number of people in the nave but not a sound could be heard. I was greatly impressed by the stillness so near to the heavy traffic of Fifth Avenue. A young priest came in. He made no enquiry concerning my presence. Then two ladies and a girl in beautiful dresses entered, and one of them asked me where the wedding was to take place. I realised that she mistook me for a guest, and I decided that it was time for me to go. Outside it was now drizzling, and I went up the steps of the house opposite to get a general view of the church. The silver lines of the top of the Empire State Building above some tall darkish masonry behind the church shone in the rain and made a bright and unusual scene only to be found in New York. A passer-by stopped, unasked, to tell me that this was one of the oldest churches in New York, its first services having been held on Mid-Lent Sunday 1850 by the Rev. George Hendric Houghton. I thanked him wholeheartedly. It is rare for anyone in a New York street to be able to spare the time to chat. I wondered how the little church had managed to survive for a hundred years in such an expanding quarter of Fifth Avenue. Its members must have been very full of faith. As Robert W. Service (a poet not well thought of but one who said, I think, many true if not exquisite things) wrote:

"Yet somehow life's not what I thought it,
And somehow the gold isn't all."

The two lofty spires of St. Patrick's Cathedral between 50th and 51st Streets, and the spire of St. Thomas's at 53rd Street, stand out unmistakably as replicas of ancient architecture in direct contrast with the modernity of the rest of the great street.

I had a look at the interior of St. Patrick's because I had been told that the Cathedral was Gothic, and similar in style to Cologne Cathedral. I noticed the Italian marble altar and the Altar Tabernacle which are richly decorated and inlaid with sparkling precious stones. Many candles were burning and people were praying or meditating. I moved round as noiselessly as I could. When I came out at the back, on Madison Avenue, I was pleased to find two fine magnolia trees in bloom. Flowers always give me pleasure. These two trees, with their purplish-white blossoms shining in the bright sun like the candles inside the Cathedral, should be a delight to anyone who happens to pass through this neighbourhood where there is otherwise nothing but steel, stone and machines.

One morning I found myself behind a group of photographers in a crowd outside St. Thomas' Church. I thought an important wedding must be about to take place. Two photographers were arguing hotly. One said: "There's a big shot just coming out of the left door. He's got a lot of potatoes. I'll get him." "Never heard of him," said the other, "better wait." "I can show him the picture," replied the first. "You won't get much out of that guy," said the second. The first then squeezed away and was lost to my sight. The exceptional mobility of their faces as they talked fascinated me. I felt I should now understand better the dialogue in stories by O. Henry and Damon Runyon. All kinds of people in their best clothes came streaming out of the church. Most of them paused a moment on the church steps. I hope I was not uncharitable in feeling that they were aware of the photographers. Every one held a long piece of yellowish-green grass, and these went well with the brightly-coloured dresses and fresh faces of the young people. It was Palm Sunday.

Another morning I went to look at the Temple Emanu-El, which I had heard was the third largest religious structure in the City. It is in early Romanesque style showing Byzantine influence. I was particularly impressed by the great recessed arch with the rose window on the Fifth Avenue side, but the whole interior is colourful and interesting. A very amiable fellow-visitor walked towards me and remarked in a manner I did not feel able—even if I had felt inclined—to contradict, that this was the most beautiful building in the world. His chest was nearly double the breadth of mine and his very prominent nose made me conscious of my little flat one. He smiled incessantly, stood by me while I looked my fill, and

H

accompanied me when I left. I was sure he must be the director of some big concern. When he learned that I came from England, he said that he knew London and Paris very well and before the war had visited them nearly every year. "Hyde Park is very good in June," he continued. . . . "Plenty of nice girls!" I was, in Boswell's phrase, 'a good deal stunned' by this remark and did not know what to say. Whereupon he laughed and left me.

I have dealt separately with my visits to the Metropolitan Museum of Art, the Frick Collection, Museum of Modern Art and other galleries in another chapter. The displays of new books in the many fine bookshops and big publishing houses along this Avenue astonished me each time I saw them. I felt constrained to crane and stare to read the titles and authors, most of them to me unknown and unpronounceable. I could not look away from the glossy wrappers with their attractive and in some cases startling coloured designs, and I was also amazed at the enormous size and thickness of the books. I did enter a few shops to browse but I felt rather embarrassed at not buying anything when smartly dressed, and even perfumed, young assistants came and stood by me.

With so many books on sale, it is astounding that there should be four and a half million persons visiting New York's Public Library annually. There are, I was told, about three million books and pamphlets in the Reference Department, more than one million in the Circulation Department, and nearly twelve millions are lent every year for home use. New York should be called 'the most read city in the world'. This Library is as arresting in its solidity as the Empire State Building in its height. Perhaps I am more conventional than progressive as far as architecture is concerned, for I find this white marble building, which is neither highly polished nor over-decorated with carving, very simple, dignified and satisfying. It has only four storeys and is clearly distinguished from the adjoining premises in this busy shopping quarter. Strangely enough, the few skyscrapers near its east wing, with the Empire State Building in the distance, seem to frame the library into a picture. The founders could not have chosen a happier site. The library serves as a reminder of mental refreshment to people otherwise given over, in this part of the city, to the satisfaction of material needs and comforts. I visited it on many occasions, and never walked in with my eyes closed, though I was told that there is a special Department for blind readers, containing more than 20,000 books and 6,000 music scores in Braille, as well as magazines in several foreign languages. I had a look there and was informed that most of the blind readers came unaccompanied. I marvelled how they managed to pass unscratched through the New York traffic. To me, with excellent eyesight, the charging yellow taxis, which look like tigers and hoot like maddened beasts, kept me on the jump.

Inside the Library there were always plenty of people; the revolving doors clinked incessantly. But I noticed once or twice someone dozing on a marble seat at the corner of the hall and even snoring gently. Unlike the British Museum there are many reading rooms, each given over to the study of a particular group of subjects. The Photographic Department was always full of people looking through millions of photographs in search of—what? I should so like to have asked them. I was told that for a very small charge one could get a copy of any picture in a day or two. As the author of a few children's books, I spent a good while in the Children's Department. That there should be such a Department at all in a national library appealed to me.

I was attracted, too, by the great wealth of Americana, one of the Library's most interesting sidelines. The American Indian Department contains all kinds of books and material relating to the American Indians. Once I was taken there to look up some legends and folklore about the dogwood tree and the American robin and was courteously accorded much help by one of the assistants. Had I been able to stay longer in New York I should constantly have been found delving in the books in this Department, for I have a private belief that my honourable race had some connection with the ancient American Indians.

I was fortunate in meeting at a friend's party, Mr. Karl Küp, Curator of the Spencer Collection and the Print Room. He showed me round his Department with its many beautiful 16th and 17th century illuminated manuscripts in French and English. Though I have never made a study of these illuminated books, I am always interested to see specimens of calligraphy. This meeting with Mr. Küp reminded me of the great joy I had

when my good friend, Mr. Strickland Gibson, formerly keeper
and sub-librarian of the Bodleian Library at Oxford and author
of *Some Oxford Libraries*, showed me many of the most valuable
manuscripts there. Mr. Gibson has retired now, but he still
goes to the Bodleian every day. He says that he just can't part
with the books which have been with him nearly all his life. I
think I should be attached to books in the same way if I had
been with them for forty years. Books may yet empty my purse
and bring me to bankruptcy! Mr. Küp showed me a number
of old Chinese books with woodblock illustrations, some in
colour. He said that he was proud to have secured so many,
but it was I who felt the greater pride.

Monument in Bryant Park

On the walls of the long corridor outside the Print Room
are coloured prints of New York landmarks and scenes. One
that particularly interested me was a panorama of the Hudson
River from New York to Albany, drawn from nature with
words indicating individual places and mountains, and
engraved by William Wade in 1845. It reminded me of the
famous Sung painting, 'A Thousand Miles of the Yangtse
River' by Hsia Kwei, though there was of course no similarity
in the artistic rendering. I indulged for a few minutes in
fantasies of the romantic mountains up the Hudson River so
well described by Washington Irving. Another interesting

The morning look of the Civil Service Building

feature of the Library was the Lenox and Stuart art collections. Here I found works by Reynolds and Turner, but I was more attracted by the exhibits executed by Stuart and Copley, for they were American artists. The other countries of the world that I have seen have a long way to go before they can compete with the United States in the efficiency and enterprise of its public libraries, museums and art galleries.

On the west side of the Library lies the charming Bryant Park. Spacious, without being big, its trees, flower-beds and lawns are a little above the street level. Half of it is surrounded

Evening noises round Bryant Park

by tall buildings. Many readers come out of the Library to rest or stroll in it. I often spent a little time here before entering the Library. I shared the seats on the steps of the Bryant Statue, watching the pigeons being fed. Sparrows flutter about and enjoy any crumbs left untouched by the pigeons. Here is peace in the midst of the busiest quarter of New York.

There are many skyscrapers in New York which have called forth much admiration. I endorse that admiration. Two of the tallest—the Empire State Building and the Rockefeller Center—are on Fifth Avenue; but nearly all the buildings on both sides of the street are tall enough to rank as the highest building of any city in China, if not also in Europe. I once discussed with my friend Alan White why skyscrapers came to be built in New York. We neither of us believed that "New York is built on rock" was a sufficient explanation for them. We even doubted whether they were altogether convenient. Alan thought they are tall for the same reason that Gothic churches are lofty: because the builders like them so. The great builders of the eleventh and twelfth centuries meant their cathedrals to soar above, and dominate, the surrounding towns; whereas New York builders meant their skyscrapers to emphasise the importance and grandeur of the city of all cities. Seen together, each skyscraper and tall building contributes to the magnificence of the "White Satin Rope". It is the *streets* of New York, we thought, that are wonderful rather than the individual buildings in them.

The 'Flatiron' Building at 23rd Street, though far from being a skyscraper, is one of the most startling landmarks along Fifth Avenue. It has the shape of a flatiron and stands at the intersection of Broadway with Fifth Avenue, a most conspicuous site. I once saw it in morning haze, the dull dark-brown of its walls appearing soft and rather mysterious, instead of hard and resistant as in the noon-day sun. The lack of heavy traffic and people in the early morning increased this impression. It is unlike any other tall building in New York, whose lower storeys are always mixed up with other buildings. As a single building complete in itself, the 'Flatiron' has no match, but I cared little for it on clear, bright days.

Facing the 'Flatiron,' at some distance, stands the statue of 'Eternal Light', a war memorial in honour of American men who fell in the First World War. It contains a 125-foot shaft of Oregon pine on a base of pink marble, surmounted by a heavy glass star inside which electric lights are kept burning perpetually. I gave this 'Eternal Light' a deep bow, for the memory of the Second World War is poignantly with me and I have been amazed at the speed with which many people seem to be forgetting it. I think a new medium for memorials is needed, otherwise—on present showing!—in another thousand years or so cities like New York will be so full of them that there will be no room for houses. I was brought up in an ancestor-worshipping country, so I naturally feel concerned about my descendants. If in times to come they have no place to live, how can they worship me? The only solution will be higher skyscrapers. But then if everybody lives half way to heaven who will bother to look down at memorials? The answer, I suppose, is that they—those unborn generations—should worry!

The 'Flatiron' Building was one of the first achievements in steel frame construction, I was told. Was it, when it was first built, the tallest building in New York? Probably not, for the creator did not think of providing a sight-seeing roof, as did his successor who built the Empire State Building. This towering structure, at 34th Street, is the tallest building in the world. I wondered why the word 'Empire' should have been used for the tallest building in New York. My friend Paul Standard explained that just as Connecticut is called the Nutmeg State, New York is called the Empire State. 'The title is a tribute to its historic importance, its wealth and its enormous resources—in short a state whose combined features suggest a grandeur imperial rather than merely regional or local.' The statistics about this building make me feel dizzy: 102 storeys; a height of 1,250 feet from the street level to the tip of the mooring mast, which is covered with glass, chrome-nickel-steel and aluminium, and illuminated from within; a rentable area of 2,158,000 square feet which can house over 25,000 people. To me, the Empire State Building seemed to stretch out its invisible strings, like a giant maypole, to hold on to me wherever I went on and around Manhattan Island. The further I went the more prominent it became; all the other skyscrapers are subordinate to it, though one other is almost as high. It is the optical center of the skyline: and New York's skyline is its most characteristic feature. It is what you immediately think of when you recall the city.

To climb up a mountain of more than a thousand feet requires determination and energy and brings the satisfaction of achievement. I anticipated a big thrill in the lift of the Empire State Building as it soared from the first to the 86th floor; but I did not get it. The lift is so well-constructed that there is no vibration or noise, only a necessity to swallow every few seconds to clear one's ears. Apart from that I should not have known we were climbing if the indicator had not moved from 1 to 34, then to 50, 60, 70, and so on. At the top I was rather concerned at the number of people; I had the sensation that we might make the building top heavy; but I was assured that the floor could accommodate 500 persons.

From the roof of the Astor Hotel I had thought cars were beetles and people ants: from here they all looked like dust. The surrounding buildings together with the infinitesmal people and things stuck up from the ground like something familiar. What was it? Eventually I got it. Bamboo-shoots in a Chinese grove in early spring.

A large group of visitors, mostly young, were rushing from one corner to the other, to look through the telescopes which a nickle will operate for a specified time. The youngsters shouted out what they had seen and the girls, I noticed, were noisier than the boys. Cameras were clicking on every side. A group of girls were lined up to have their photo taken by a professional cameraman who clung alarmingly high up the wall of the writing room for the purpose. In the high wind, the girls' long hair was blown or tugged in all directions and they tried vainly to control it with their hands. Their varied gestures were charming, and I was delighted at the sight of so many graceful hands and arms, white, pinkish or brown, mingling with golden, red, or dark hair. I am greatly interested in ballet dancing, particularly in the movements of hands and arms. No choreographer could devise a ballet better than that which I then witnessed. The chattering and giggling of the girls provided the music. But the cameraman seemed to find his task troublesome.

Presently I moved on up to the 102nd floor. Here the observation platform is much smaller and can only accommodate 100 persons at a time. The visibility was so good that everything appeared as clear as from the 86th floor. More people seemed to want to come up, so I presently descended to the first observatory again. On the way I overheard the elevator man tell a woman that about two million visitors from all parts of the world came up this building each year. "We have no competition," he continued, "we are quite contented." I was interested in his use of the word 'contented'. Do the members of the company who run the building feel contented? Before it was built perhaps the owners of the Flatiron Building felt contented. Surely someone will now try to erect a building even higher than the Empire State? A friend assured me that this is unlikely, as already the offices in the higher floors have been difficult to let, and with the increase in flying, very tall buildings are considered dangerous. Yet I cannot help feeling that someone will try.

In the lounge people were indulging in the immemorial habit of collecting souvenirs. If only half of the yearly two millions of visitors buy a souvenir each, mass production methods are justified! And I saw some visitors buying more than one item. Picture postcards depicting the building, and posted on the spot, seemed to be the favourite form. Outside the refreshment room, in a large space filled with chairs and tables and glassed in all round against wind and rain, was a thick book on a table and a queue of visitors waited to sign their names in it. What a wise provision! How many thousands of defacing pen-knife scrawls it must prevent! For it is a natural human instinct to leave one's name in a notable place one has visited. The Empire State Building protects its walls by means of this book. How many volumes have already been filled, and what does the company do with them?

I went to lean on the balustrade. The half-oval-shaped crest of the Chrysler Building showed up most distinctively, being the closest. To the south three downtown skyscrapers rose against the sun. Central Park, which I had thought of as a vast and varied area, was revealed to me as a small lacquer tea-tray, inlaid with green and bluish jade, to represent trees and lakes. I took pleasure in the childish fancy that for once I was higher than any winged creature. One or two white seagulls, circling over some lower buildings, did not look like real birds in flight but like ornamental ones of white marble in fixed positions of suspense. Occasional bursts of laughter from the lounge were like unearthly voices near the gate of Heaven. The warm sun in this spot sheltered from the wind 'inclined my eyelids' and the haze in the distance contracted the horizon. The long, slightly twisted, white-silk-like Hudson River had no end. I murmured to myself how right our T'ang poet Li P'o was when he wrote the line 'Huang Ho Chih Shui T'ien Shan Lai," 'The waters of the Yellow River come from Heaven!' as he gazed at the Huang Ho from a lofty pavilion, or again: 'Wei Chien Ch'ang Chiang T'ien Chi Liu', 'I can only see the Yangtse River flowing near the edge of Heaven!' Both these lines could well describe what I saw of the Hudson River now.

My thoughts drifted to our own ancient pavilions. In a world history of architecture little needs to be said about the ancient buildings of China, for no important ruins of palaces or mansions are extant except the towers along the world-renowned Great Wall, built in the third century B.C. Most of our ancient palaces or mansions were not built of stone, and even the hardest woods do not last much longer than a thousand years. Nevertheless, there are clear and apparently authentic records in our ancient books of a good many lofty pavilions. It is said that in 115 B.C. the Emperor Wu of Han Dynasty felt well satisfied with his peaceful reign and desired to prolong his life. On the advice of his astrologers he ordered a pavilion to be built and sent his ministers up to wait upon the supernatural beings who could deliver to him from Heaven some elixir to prolong his life. The Emperor called his pavilion 'Tung T'ien Lou' or 'Pavilion for Reaching Heaven'. Another tall building, 'Fang Ch'en Lou' or 'Pavilion of Fragrant Dust' is said to have been built about A.D. 335 by the notorious, short-lived and self-titled emperor Shih Hu. It had a height of four hundred feet, and was decorated with silks, pearls, precious stones and many bells which rang in the wind. The Emperor ordered several hundred men to grind precious gems mixed with scents into minute particles and blow them down from the pavilion so that his subjects should smell the fragrance and be happy in their Capital; hence the name. It was a poetic name and a romantic act. How far would the scented particles have flown had they been blown from the top of the Empire State Building?

My first impression of the Rockefeller Center or RCA Building was that I was still on board the *Queen Mary*. The smoothness of the shiny metal floor, the huge murals by Frank Brangwyn, the electric-light indicators, the eating places, even the post-office windows, did not seem much different from what I had seen on board ship. I saw no earth, no bricks, nothing but metal with a very little wood ingeniously inserted. Furthermore the continuous movement of the people, most of them women, was a reminder of the two thousand G.I. brides with whom I had crossed the Atlantic.

A few days later a friend, Mr. K. C. Tsien, suggested that he and I should do one of the tours of the Rockefeller Center. We chose the one which we were told would include the broadcasting station. A black-haired girl in a blue uniform took twenty of us round, explaining everything we saw. She knew her words by heart, just like those white-moustached and bearded guides to be found in museums and other places of pilgrimage in Europe, particularly England. But unlike them, she made no reference to history, nor to great names and dates, which seemed to me an improvement. However, I found I missed the excited and pompous gestures of the old guides when they happen to know this or that duke or prince or to have experienced the war of which they speak. This girl showed us among other things how the sound instruments worked and the vibrations of various words in different languages. Then we entered a gallery where we were told to sit and watch a lady in evening dress apparently singing and a pianist apparently playing; we could hear nothing but the guide's explanation. Through the reflectionless glass of the studios the gestures and movements of the broadcasters made them look like inmates in a silent human zoo. I was enchanted. Nowhere else can one look without hearing. Some of our party were interested in the indicator boards. The guide showed how to open and shut a door by simply pressing a button and other similar wonders. Lastly we came to the television department and volunteers were asked to go on the stage. One elderly man, who had all along been ready for everything, stepped forward. His offer was accepted and he was immediately rejuvenated. The guide, though young herself, treated us all as children, continually saying: "Isn't that wonderful?" She was quite right. We were children in this connection. I noticed that she had a habit of putting her first fingers together in front of her chest. I sympathised with her difficulty in disposing of her hands while repeating the same explanations over and over again.

One evening I went round the concourses of the Center. They are lined with smart shops and show rooms and once you start gazing it is difficult to find your way out. This difficulty was repeated when I went up the building to the Chinese Consulate-General and the Chinese News Service, for the rooms on each floor are almost identical; it reminded me of the shrub maze at Hampton Court, Henry VIII's palace a few miles west of London. In the early seventh century, the Emperor Yang of Sui dynasty gave the name 'Mi Lou' or 'Mansion of Mystery' to a big house designed and built by Hsiang Sheng with hundreds and thousands of identical doors and windows so arranged that, once having entered, one could not get out in a single day. The buildings of Rockefeller Center are a 'Mi Lou' too, at least for me, despite the many clear electric indicators.

As I had been up the Empire State Building on a clear sunny day, I purposely went up to the 70th floor of the RCA Building in the late afternoon. The sun was about to set and I had great expectations of the sunset scene viewed from such a height. Pots of bright red geraniums, placed here and there on the roof and between the seats, breathed a cheerful air. The number of visitors was not great and very few seemed inclined to move. Though I had no sensation of being lower than when on top of the Empire State Building, I felt different. By degrees the visitors disappeared. Perhaps they had intended to stay for the sunset but were disappointed when the sky grew overcast. But I was not disappointed. The clouds were moving fast in the wind and an evening mist was rising quickly too. Soon many of the buildings below were blotted out. I felt like stretching out my arms to caress the clouds. The upper storeys of the Empire State and other tall buildings rose above them, fainter and paler than others. Then heavier and darker clouds enveloped them, distorting their outlines and changing them into a Sung painting of high peaks in China. It was an unforgettable sight for me. Presently some of the clouds cleared away and the tops of skyscrapers appeared again like masts. I felt I was sailing on a cloud sea, a Silent Traveller indeed!

At length it grew pitch dark and the wind was chilly. But I was not chilly at heart. Moist particles of cloud touched my face coolly, sometimes big drops of water. Was this the early summer dew?

My mind went back to the Emperor Wu of Han Dynasty in the second century B.C. After he had built the 'Pavilion of Reaching Heaven', he erected another tall structure in his palace grounds, which he called 'Ch'eng Lu Pang' or 'Dish to receive Dew', a huge dish in the shape of a hand, palm upwards. Dew collected near the ground was not thought to be pure, but high in the air it was not only pure but sweet and believed to have the power of prolonging life when drunk. There is evidence of similar practices by later emperors, with alleged good results; but I will not describe them in case I cause trouble to New York doctors.

Over the balustrade the sky was jet black, clouds could no longer be identified, mist having engulfed the whole city. Myriads of lights twinkled far below. Inspired by the sight, I composed the following little poem:

Fort Tryon under the moon

若　下　始　失　霧　如　雲
躡　憑　知　形　深　春　樓
群　欄　天　入　深　笋　聳
星　我　在　宵　各　煙　亙

Many-storeyed buildings stick up like shoots of
　　spring bamboo;
The clouds and mist grow dense and make them lose
　　their shapes.
As darkness falls I begin to know that heaven is down
　　below;
Touching the balustrade I feel I am treading on a
　　myriad of stars!

The shop windows of Fifth Avenue stirred me. In the main
the displays are aimed at the opposite sex, but men are
not forgotten. There was always attraction in the arrangements
of colour and light. In some windows a 'natural' background
emphasised a particular object; birds, flowers, even trees were
mingled harmoniously with the goods. Elsewhere lighting was
used to good effect in interior scenes. The object seemed to be
more to please the eye than merely to attract a crowd.

One morning I noticed some very original displays. In the
window of Bergdorf Goodman two wooden statues of the
sixteenth century Franconian School, representing St. John
the Evangelist and St. John the Baptist, flanked a clay model
of a girl in modern attire with a flowery hat, a leather hand-
bag, and that aloof expression usually thought appropriate
for lay figures. In another shop was the top of a Cyprian
limestone tomb, dating from the second half of the fifth
century B.C. In another, two wooden statues of St. Catherine
and St. Barbara. I think it was in Delman's window that a
limestone statue of an Egyptian youth, about 500 B.C., with
three white lilies, was displayed. Further along, a good example
of Chinese embroidery on red and black satin was shown with
a few small Chinese *objets d'art*. At first I thought that the
proprietors of the shops must be noted art collectors; then I
caught sight of a notice: 'Proudly New York observes the
75th Anniversary of the Metropolitan Museum of Art. Are you
doing your share to raise $7,500,000 to enlarge and improve

this Cultural Institution?' I had to confess at once: 'No, I have
not and cannot. Even if my share were no more than one
dollar, I should have to think carefully whether the currency
restrictions would allow it.' So I went away as quickly as I
could. Nevertheless I was interested to know that the Metropolitan Museum of Art could lend out its valuable exhibits
in order to raise funds. The British Museum is forbidden by
Act of Parliament to allow a single object to leave its care.

Inside a New York building one can judge neither season
nor weather, for central heating always adjusts the temperature,
and the interior decorations represent spring nearly all the
time. Only the goods in the windows along Fifth Avenue are
a guide to the time of year, and they are inclined to be a
little ahead of the season.

What fascinated me most was the inexhaustible variety of
ladies' hats. I saw many different hats in other busy streets,
but there was infinitely more variety on Fifth Avenue, as if a
perpetual hat show were in progress. There are always so
many people walking on both sides of the Avenue that it is
hard to distinguish face, figure or dress from a distance, but
one can always see the different colours and shapes of the
hats on the surface of the moving mass. It is one thing to see
beautiful hats fitted on perfect models in show-windows or on
the heads of mannequins in photographs or advertisements: it
is another to see hats actually being worn. But vast as is the
number of hat styles, it is not so great as the number of types
of head. The two together obliged me to revise all my previous
theories about personal adornment and beauty. For instance,
a little cone-shaped hat may sit perched on a big round head
while a wide-brimmed hat is set on a long, thin, narrow head
on a long neck. Or a gentle, docile face may be surmounted
by a huge, brilliantly-coloured flowery hat with a vivid lining,
while a strong face with penetrating eyes may look from under
a little hat dotted with tiny flowers. Some outlines resemble the
head of the crowned heron, others that of the umbrella bird,
and some are even like that of Scottish Highland cattle, whose
eyes are shrouded from the light. One fact which struck
me several times was that ladies with dark faces seemed to
favour dazzling white, rose pink, silver or gold for their hats. I
could not help staring at them. One night I was walking along
Fifth Avenue after attending a party, and as I approached

St. Patrick's Cathedral, where there were no shop-window lights, to my great astonishment I saw three or four white and rose-pink balls dancing in the air. They were, I discovered, hats worn by four dark ladies wearing dark dresses. At a distance the wearers' heads and bodies were invisible in the semi-darkness.

I used to be surprised that no two hats in London were ever quite alike, but the dissimilarity in New York is infinitely greater. A young English nobleman once told me that no woman could choose a suitable hat for herself. His theory was that if one saw the wrong sort of hat on a woman's head, it had certainly been chosen by herself; on some other head it might look charming. I have no means of judging whether his theory is right or wrong. Certainly he was himself quite ready to

Four white flowery balls dancing in front of St. Patrick's

choose hats for ladies. There is no doubt that it is a subtle job, highly valued. I was told a story of a lady of New York who was admiring some ribbons in a shop when a clever assistant approached her, picked up the ribbons and draped them round her head. Looking at herself in the mirror she exclaimed: "Isn't that wonderful? Isn't that beautiful? Isn't that cute?" She asked the price and, on being told sixty dollars, objected that after all they were only ribbons. The assistant unwound the ribbons from her head, and gave them to her, remarked: "With our compliments, Madam." To me this story is the more remarkable because in China women do not wear hats.

Next to hats in variety came cosmetics. I have no knowledge of them, and those shown in the windows of Fifth Avenue mostly seemed to have French names, so I became no wiser. But I thought of Sir Max Beerbohm's entertaining essay, 'A Defence of Cosmetics', first published in The Yellow Book, Volume I, April, 1894.

Quotations could not do justice to the essay; it should be read in full. "Cosmetics," says Sir Max, "are not going to be a mere prosaic remedy for age or plainness, but all ladies and all young girls will come to love them." The article provoked fury among pressmen at the time. Someone urged that "a short Act of Parliament should be passed to make this kind of thing illegal". But Sir Max must have foreseen what Fifth Avenue would be like half a century later.

Once I was nearly pushed off the pavement by a middle aged lady rushing up behind me with her arms stretched to the sky, crying "Isn't it cute? Isn't it sweet?" She ignored me, though I had thought she was talking to me. Bewildered, I watched her clasp her hands as if in prayer and murmur to herself ecstatically. I wondered if she was quite normal, but in a moment she walked on happily. I still could not understand what had excited her. Then I noticed, by a red traffic light, an old fashioned motor car, with a body like a cart, and so beautifully polished all over that it shone in the sun. Everybody was staring at it. Inside was a tiny old-fashioned lady, possibly over ninety, wearing a white flower hat and white fur coat, and sitting in a most dignified manner by the side of the chauffeur, whom I could not see very well. We Chinese have a traditional respect for old people and ancient things, and I could not but hold in admiration the owner of this car. I had believed that the New Yorkers were mad to own the most up-to-date type of car, and always anxious for next year's model. Now I saw that they can also admire an old-fashioned one. I overheard passers-by discussing it. One said that it had been running up and down Fifth Avenue for a couple of hours that morning. Another that the owner only came out for a drive once or twice a year; if so I was very lucky to see her.

In New York some people seem to become friendly on the slightest pretext; in London one can talk to strangers only about the weather. Once a man gave me a slap on the shoulder and laughed loudly while I was looking at an old coloured print of a short-horn bullock in the window of Kennedy & Co. The bullock was so fat, with shoulder and back in a straight line, that I knew it must be a prize-winner. I had learned this from my Scottish friends. The man simply could not stop laughing, and after a while he said: "That picture of the animal is out of proportion. There is a lot of beef in that." He then gave me another pat on the shoulder saying: "I would like to buy that picture to get a good laugh," and then went away still laughing. I thought he was going in to buy the picture. If a picture like that can make a man so happy, we artists are in for a good time!

The inhabitants of New York spring from many races, and, as each nationality tries to preserve the customs of its fatherland, some kind of parade or procession occurs nearly every day. I saw a number, but missed a lot too. Three in particular, impressed me very much. First, the Holy Name Parade, led by dark-faced gentlemen in shining silk toppers from Resurrection Church to St. Aloysius at 132nd Street and Seventh Avenue. Then there was the parade of three hundred Americans of Chinese ancestry in military uniforms through Mott Street, which formed part of the formal dedication

Peace in 59th Street at 5th Avenue

ceremonies of the first Chinese post of the American Legion in the East. But to my mind the St. Patrick's Day Parade along Fifth Avenue surpassed all the others. A girl working in the hotel where I was staying advised me, when she learned that I had been in Dublin and other parts of Ireland, to get my 'greens' for the parade. I had a lunch engagement with a friend, who afterwards drove me through Central Park and set me down at 72nd Street to watch the fun. There were many people in the Park, and even more on the pavements, but no traffic at all on the Avenue. The parade was already in full swing. Many of the spectators wore badges of green silk. Some of the men took off their hats whenever a flag or colour passed by. It was a very long procession and extremely well-organised. All the participants displayed pride and enthusiasm. There were even very young children prancing along excitedly in front of some of the groups. I was interested to see a number

I

of groups wearing tartans and kilts and playing the bagpipes vigorously. There were several girls' bands wearing brightly coloured satin uniforms; the leading girls with long silver staffs in their right hands looked like characters in some costly film. Each time one of these bands passed by, a number of boys shouted out the names of the girls, whom I suppose they knew, and then burst out laughing. I was moving northward inch by inch through the throng. Though some people were taller than me, I could see most of the procession quite well. Suddenly I saw the word RICE, the name of a school, embroidered in big letters on a yellow flag and also used on the badges of a large group of young men. It made me smile wryly for I had had no rice during wartime in England. One tall boy standing on the wall of Central Park with his hands clasped round a tree-branch shouted repeatedly "A Bowl of Rice". This probably meant more to me than to anybody else. Heads projected from windows all along the Avenue, and they were an interesting sight, too.

Fifth Avenue from 65th Street to 109th Street is the best part for morning walks, I think, if one does not wish to stray too far inside the Park and lose the feel of city life. It was in this part that one evening I attended a dinner party given by Mr. and Mrs. Hugh Bullock on their roof apartment at 1030 Fifth Avenue. The whole of Central Park was in view. The myriad of lights through the windows of the skyscrapers along Central Park South reminded me of Hong Kong with all the lamps lit up in the houses on the island hill when I approached it on a ship at night.

On the last morning of my stay I decided to find out where the other end of the 'white satin rope' was fastened and eventually reached Mount Morris Park, which, if not quite at the end of Fifth Avenue, is near enough. That characteristic Western mixture of attitudes towards the sun was apparent: some people were deliberately sunning themselves, others were shielding their heads with newspapers. Many dark-skinned children were playing and talking to each other in sharp tones as if they could never agree on anything. One of them was dressed in a most picturesque fashion with long feathers round his head, an outsize coat and a number of leather belts, a toy gun hanging at one side and a self-made bow in his right hand. He looked very solemn and the whites of his eyes shone. He was certainly an Indian chief, though without followers, and it seemed to me appropriate that I should find him guarding one end of the 'white satin rope.' I made a sketch and went away satisfied.

Indian Chief guarding one end of the White Satin Rope

X

AT BRONX ZOO

"IF a man does not make new acquaintances as he advances through life", said Dr. Samuel Johnson, "he will soon find himself alone. A man, Sir, should keep his friendships in constant repair." Wise advice, doubtless spoken from the Doctor's own experience. I have been fortunate in making new acquaintances based on some mutual interest or shared affection. In my book *The Silent Traveller in Oxford* I described

The main entrance of the Bronx Zoo

flowers as a 'Medium for Friendship'. In New York I gained a friend a new way, through the giant panda!

Mr. John Tee-Van, Executive Secretary of the New York Zoological Garden at Bronx Park, did not know my name until my book *Chinpao and the Giant Pandas* was published in the United States in 1943. He wrote to tell me that he had read and liked the book and its illustrations, particularly the silk painting of the giant panda. He also told me how he had gone to China to receive the unusual gift of two giant pandas from the Chinese Government and how the animals had since been in his care. We continued to correspond and after the death of Ming, the immensely popular giant panda in the London Zoo, just before Christmas 1944, I wrote to Mr. Tee-Van that as I was left with no model for my drawings, I might have to come to New York for one. Now, more than a year later, here I was.

Immediately after my arrival I sent Mr. Tee-Van a note, and he asked me to lunch at the Zoo to meet the surviving giant panda. I do not know how Mr. Tee-Van felt about our meeting; but for my part I felt more warmly towards him than if I had been introduced in the conventional way. On February 17th I reached Bronx Zoo in good time, as I thought, for my appointment, but to my astonishment it took me more than twenty minutes to find the administrative office. The Zoo is much bigger than the London one; in fact it is as big as Whipsnade, though differently planned. I apologised for being late, but Mr. Tee-Van seemed to be more gratified than displeased at my explanation. Perhaps he had tried in this artless way to impress on me its size. In any case it was very pleasant to meet after two years' correspondence. In addition I had the unexpected pleasure of being introduced to Mr. Fairfield Osborn, President of the Zoological Society. Then Mr. Tee-Van showed me a large number of photographs of the giant pandas which he had used during his lectures in many big cities in the United States.

It was a fine Sunday and the Zoo was already full of visitors. There was not a vacant seat in the restaurant and we had to line up. After six years' queue-ing in England this was no novelty for me. On the other hand it showed that Bronx Zoo must be very popular with New Yorkers. I liked the democratic spirit of the restaurant which gave no priority even to the Zoo's Executive Secretary. During lunch I was introduced to Mr. William Bridge, Curator and Publications Director, and others on the Zoo staff. Mr. Tee-Van and I talked about the giant panda a great deal, including its various Chinese names. Mr. Tee-Van had begun to learn Chinese and was interested to know the animal's correct name in that language. The natives of Western China call it *Pei-hsiung* or White-Bear. This not only led to confusion with the polar bear but is inaccurate, for the animal is not entirely white. Some of our scholars wrote the name Giant Panda as *Ta-hsiung-mao* or Big-Bear-

Cat, because it looks like a bear while the ordinary or lesser panda looks like a cat. I myself think this name unsuitable, for it calls to mind a hybrid animal between bear and cat. The giant panda is certainly something like a bear, but offers no resemblance to a cat. So when I began to write about it I decided to give it a name of my own. It is a common practice in China when two colours such as black and white are combined to describe them by the word *Hua* which means 'Flowery' or 'Coloured'. For instance, we call a black-and-white dog *Hua-kou*, a black-and-white cat *Hua-mao*, and so on. Thus it is quite simple to call the giant panda *Hua-hsiung* or 'Flowery bear' because it looks like a bear with a black-and-white coat. However, Hua-Hsiung is not scientifically correct, because the panda belongs to the racoon rather than to the bear family. The Chinese language has no alphabet and cannot borrow words from Latin or Greek or other languages, but the well-known ornithologist, John Gould, once said that the law of priority established by naturalists requires that the oldest name given to a species should be the one adopted, even if it was found inappropriate afterwards, so I think Hua-Hsiung is the best possible Chinese name for the giant panda. Mr. Tee-Van agreed and suggested that we should try to get it officially recognised. I have used it in my book *Chinpao and the Giant Pandas* which I call in Chinese *Chinpao Yu Hua-Hsiung*.

Mr. Tee-Van enquired how I began to be interested in the animal and when I started to paint it. I said that my interest was due to the innate love of Nature and all her creatures felt by my people, and particularly by our artists, to which I am no exception. My father was a noted flower and bird painter and I followed in his steps, with an additional interest in all kinds of animals and landscapes. I admit that I had not seen a giant panda in my own country and first met one in London in 1938. As this animal was not known in China in the old days none of our artists had ever drawn or painted it. As soon as the first giant pandas reached London and their photographs appeared in the papers, I could not resist going to see them. I fell in love with them at sight. With their comical black ears, the two black rings round their eyes, their four black legs and their pigeon-toed fashion of walking, as well as their friendly nature, the giant pandas proved tremendously popular and won the hearts of everyone, old and young. I found them a most suitable subject for my brush. In the first place I enjoy painting animals, in the second the giant panda comes from China, in the third its black and white colouring is particularly suitable for Chinese brush work, and in the fourth its chief diet is bamboo, a favourite subject for Chinese artists for a thousand years or so. I began to make studies of this new animal without delay and I also made a special arrangement with my friend, Dr. Geoffrey Vevers, Superintendent of the London Zoological Society, to enable me to spend an evening with the pandas in order to study their night life. The result was a hundred or more sketches. I think I must be the first Chinese artist to have painted the giant panda on silk.

Presently Mr. Tee-Van suggested taking me round the Zoo and showing me their giant panda. First we set out to see the children's Zoo, which, he explained, is uniquely arranged and extremely popular with the youngsters. But as it was locked we did not go in. From outside I could see a few huts and bowers, and a long winding track for pony-riders. At one entrance youngsters of five and upwards of all nationalities were lining up for a ride. As the ponies came round, the mounting and dismounting of the children proceeded as if by machinery. Each pony was led by a boy. A jovial old keeper kept crying "Yeah, Wee, Ah, Yeh," as he helped the youngsters on. He seemed to answer in every language at once, whether correctly or not I do not know. How internationally minded these American children are! Two small girls with black faces and plaits sticking out from their heads, looking unusually charming in brightly-coloured frocks, sat astride a pony which was being urged forward by a fair-haired boy. Such a sight is probably unique to the Bronx Zoo.

Passing the seals' pond, we came to the Birds' House, where Mr. Tee-Van said that he wanted to show me something special. I saw many lovely birds, which I had not seen before, such as birds of paradise, humming-birds, and toucans. He particularly pointed out the quetzal as 'the most beautiful bird in the New World', and also showed me the rare umbrella bird. We then entered the Jewel Room, which Mr. Tee-Van said was an innovation in the Zoo. Much time had been spent in working out the right background for the coloured plumage of the birds. It was dark inside. Each species was kept in a specially designed cage, inside which were arranged a small tree and other plants familiar to the particular bird. Perfect air conditioning, temperature and light no doubt contributed to their healthy appearance. Each of the cages had a circular or rectangular opening which reminded me of similarly shaped Chinese fans with paintings of birds, trees and other plants on them. Our fan-painters would enjoy seeing these cages; each movement inside would help them to a new design. I know that my father would have been delighted with them. Each summer his desk was loaded with fans of all shapes which his relations and friends had asked him to paint for them. I remember how he used to get up very early and wander round our little garden or outside the city wall seeking fresh inspiration. If my father and I could have stood together in this 'Jewel Room' I should have been the happiest person on earth, but he died more than twenty-five years ago, never having left his native land.

There was such a big crowd in the Reptile House that we moved on to the Tiger and Leopard Houses, where three young tigers were amusing everybody with their antics. After that we had a look at the Elephants, Monkeys and Rodents, and the African Plain. There is even a Question House in this Zoo, where any visitor can get an answer about any animal strange to him. This is an excellent idea. After visiting it, I was shown two of the rarest animals in the world, the bongo and the okapi. I had not seen the bongo before, but there is an okapi in the London Zoo, lent by the King of England, to whom it belongs personally. I have often watched it eating leaves high up in a tree. It has a beautiful, smooth, dark brown coat with white stripes round its legs and near its tail. It is said to be a cousin of the giraffe, and looks like a cross between that animal and a zebra. The bongo is the African forest antelope. Bronx Zoo has the only specimens of these two animals in America.

At last we reached the giant panda's quarters. As we approached, Mr. Tee-Van's face lit up. The fact that he had brought the animal to the Zoo had earned him the nickname of 'The Panda Nurse'. I was happy too: had not one English reviewer of my books called me 'The Panda Man'? This giant panda seemed to be particularly active, rolling round and round the enclosure with its famous pigeon-toed gait. The floor of the enclosure was on two levels and the panda climbed from one to the other by means of a tree-trunk. Under this was a small pool, in which it now and then took a dip. Then it lay beneath the branches and stretched its paws like a clown in a circus—as if it had fallen down purposely and was pretending helplessness to get up. I was touched by its clown-like welcome.

Mr. Tee-Van remarked that it was still very difficult to make generalisations about the giant panda's nature as no one had yet sufficiently studied it. When he first saw it drinking with its two forepaws wide apart, he had thought that it always drank that way. Later he found he was mistaken. He had also noted it plunging into the water and coming out without shaking off the water, but it did not invariably do so. Mr. Tee-Van must have planned specially to show me the giant panda last, and I much appreciated his thoughtfulness. I did not want to keep him from his office work too long, so I said good-bye and thanked him for a perfect afternoon, adding that now 'The Panda Nurse' and 'The Panda Man' had met at last.

Very soon after this visit to the Zoo, I received an invitation to dinner at the Tee-Van's home. There I had the pleasure of meeting Mrs. Tee-Van, who, I learned, used often to put on a diver's suit and go down into the sea to watch the movements of fish and study them in their true environment. It must be a thrilling experience. I told her that I had seen and admired her fine illustrations, particularly of fishes, in the *Encyclopedia Britannica*. After dinner Mr. Tee-Van showed his guests the film he had taken of his trip to fetch the two giant pandas from China. The development of the giant pandas from their younger days was clearly shown and I could see how much care 'The Panda Nurse' had taken of them.

I visited Bronx Zoo whenever I could. Whipsnade Zoo near London is surrounded by typical English fields, hills and patches of wood. The surroundings of Bronx Zoo are enriched by rocky cliffs and the gracefully winding Bronx River, which alone would attract people to this part of New York, without the additional attractions offered by the Zoo. I watched people rowing on the river and listened to the sound of the falls or rapids near the entrance.

The peacock greens and whites of the African Plain enchanted me many a time, and I noticed that zebras, deer, antelopes, and crowned cranes all lived together in harmony there. The lions were displayed without the usual encircling iron bars. The otters playing in the water detained me a long time. A Manchurian stork summoned me to its enclosure for information about our homeland, and two Père David's deer for news of the Peking Palace Park where their ancestors were reared. The pelicans peacefully floating on the huge lake near the main entrance did not escape my notice. I fed the wild duck in the ponds and watched the demonstration by the electric eel. And while I was resting on a seat I could watch little grey squirrels, which roam about everywhere, burying their peanuts in the earth in the most ingenious manner and

afterwards coming back to eat them one by one and never failing to find their hiding place again.

My first sight of the humming-birds and our many sub-sequent meetings remain perhaps the most memorable moments of all. My feeling for humming-birds sprang from the merest chance. Some eight or nine years ago I received a hand-painted New Year's greeting card, representing a 'Ruby-throated Humming-Bird'. I was struck by its minute size, its glossy plumage and its tiny wings. It was quite unfamiliar to me and I was curious to hear more of it.

Its name is derived from the rapid movement of its wings which produces a vibratory or humming sound while the bird is in flight and which can be heard at a distance of several yards. It has such a very small body that, in the rapidity of its flight, it almost eludes the human eye. It is extremely fond

Ruby-throated Humming-birds

of tubular flowers. Its only song is a single chirp, no louder than a cricket or grasshopper, generally uttered while passing from flower to flower. It is exceedingly susceptible to cold, and if long exposed to it weakens and soon dies.

The following description of the humming birds by Audubon is fascinating to read:

No sooner has the returning sun again introduced the vernal season, and caused millions of plants to expand their leaves and blossoms to his genial beams, than the little humming-bird is seen advancing on fairy wings, carefully visiting every flower-cup, and, like a curious florist, removing from each the injurious insects that otherwise would, ere long, cause their beauteous petals to droop and decay. Poised in the air, it is observed peeping cautiously and with sparkling eye into their innermost recesses, whilst the ethereal motions of its pinions, so rapid and so light, appear to fan and cool the flower without injuring its fragile texture, and produce a delightful murmuring sound, well adapted for lulling the insects to repose. This is the moment for the humming-bird to secure them. Its long delicate bill enters the cup of the flower, and the protruded double tongue, delicately sensible, and imbued with a glutinous saliva, touches each insect in succession, and draws it from its lurking place, to be instantly swallowed. All this is done in a moment, and the bird as it leaves the flower, sips so small a portion of its liquid honey, that the theft, we may suppose, is looked upon with a grateful feeling by the flower, which is thus kindly relieved from the attacks of her destroyers.

The prairies, the fields, the orchards and gardens, nay, the deepest shades of the forest, are all visited in their turn, and everywhere the little bird meets with pleasure and with food. Its gorgeous throat in beauty and brilliancy baffles all competition. Now it glows with a fiery hue, and again it is changed to the deepest velvet-black. The upper parts of its delicate body are of resplendent changing green; and it throws itself through the air with a swiftness and vivacity hardly conceivable. It moves from one flower to another like a gleam of light, upwards, downwards, to the right, and to the left.

Audubon was not only a great naturalist, an ardent ornithologist, and a very observant artist, but a sensitive writer with a rare choice of words to express his feelings.

"It was on the 21st of May 1857," wrote John Gould, the Bird Man, "that my earnest day-thoughts and not infrequent night-dreams of thirty years were realised by the sight of a living humming-bird. To describe my feelings on the occasion would be no easy task; I leave them then to the imagination of my readers rather than make the attempt." I proved to be luckier than he, thanks to modern educational institutions such as Bronx Zoo. In the cages of the Jewel Room I watched these tiny creatures lightly leaving the twigs, flying with incessant rapid wing movements like bees, and darting their long delicate bills into small glass tubes where honey was provided for them. I cannot describe how fascinated I was to see these birds in cages for the first time, yet I was left with a new desire to see them in natural surroundings. But it was too early in the season for that during my visit. Man is a greedy creature in every respect. Some men are greedy for wealth, some for food, some for clothes and some for fame. I was greedy for something that would delight the eye and the mind.

The body movement of New York women

XI

ON BEDLOE'S ISLAND

I TAKE the advice of the Roman poet Martial:

> So, Posthumus, you'll live tomorrow, you say:
> Too late, too late, the wise lived yesterday!

Though not particularly wise, I certainly 'lived yesterday'. I do not know how I shall live today or tomorrow, because planning my day seems to impose a restriction on my spirit. I find it more satisfying to recall my past activities. I take real pleasure in recalling the happy time I spent at Liberty, by which of course I mean the Statue of Liberty on Bedloe's Island, southwest of Manhattan. I heard of Liberty before I sailed for New York, watched it from afar while approaching the City, and finally became on intimate terms with it, for I actually went through its body right up to the head!

It was a sunny, hazy afternoon, typical of early spring in New York, when I took a subway train to Bowling Green and thence went to Battery Place for a return ticket to the Statue of Liberty. The steamer was just about to leave and I mounted to the upper deck. Most of the space along the railings was already occupied, most of the seats too, and everyone was talking hard. Youngsters were violently running round the decks and shouting their heads off. Young couples were laughing and even wrestling without restraint; I suppose because they were on their way to Liberty.

I seemed to be the only person on the steamer without a companion, but I had perhaps a different motive from the rest in visiting Liberty. I watched the wharf slowly recede and the downtown skyscrapers diminish as we moved away. The sunbeams caught and gilded their windows through the bluish haze, and touched the shiny silvery wings of seagulls swooping astern.

The haze was not unlike that of the Thames estuary, but without its damp cold. For a considerable time I could not see the Statue, the steamer was still too far away. Gradually a brightly-lit vertical tube peered through the haze and I recognised the Statue. The general effect reminded me of Cleopatra's Needle in Central Park lit by flood-lighting. The colour turned out to be an illusion created by distance. The Statue was not now emerald green at all.

Passing a cheerful group of people waiting on the landing stage to be taken back to New York, I followed my fellow passengers through the gate in the base of the pedestal. We walked in line between thick ropes and entered a lift on payment of a fee. Someone gave a fifty-cent piece for change and the white-haired attendant remarked that he had not seen a silver piece like that for years. As soon as the lift began to go up, a mysterious voice began telling the story of the Statue; its remarks were conveniently timed to conclude before we reached the top. It gave a great deal of information in a very short time, most of which I could not hear. The 'top' turned out to be only the top of the pedestal, whence we had to climb flight after flight of stairs, each narrower than the last. Though we knew we had started from the foot of the Statue, there was nothing to indicate our progress through the body. Inside were huge metal beams and machinery, awe-inspiring to my unmechanical eye. Breath began to be short and legs to ache as we mounted, but no one was daunted, and we all reached the head. At least twenty of us were able to move about freely inside the head. We looked through the apertures round the crown. There were maps above each hole, but I could see very little through the thick haze. Many expressed disappointment, but I knew I had chosen the right day. I had wanted to see Liberty in the original meaning of the word and here I was—in space! Suddenly I overheard someone say triumphantly "It's reducing anyway. It's reducing. I think I've lost five pounds!" Another use for Liberty!

The descent was easier and I got out of the building quickly. Before I did so, I glanced at the photographs of the Statue on the wall and read the long poem entitled *The New Colossus* by Emma Lazarus. I liked its last stanza:

> Give me your tired, your poor,
> Your huddled masses, yearning to be free.
> The wretched refuse of your teeming shore.
> Send these, the homeless, tempest-tossed to me.
> I lift the lamp beside the golden door.

From a paper giving the dimensions of the Statue the detail which struck me was that the length of the finger nail is thirteen inches. It reminded me how, in bygone days in China, some gentlefolk of both sexes used to wear very long finger nails as a sign of gentility, an indication that they did no manual work. Those were the days! No Chinese of to-day can afford such an affectation. My young compatriots probably do not even know that there were ever such people. But I, with one foot in that bygone age, saw one or two of them in my youth, and it pleased me now to fancy that the Statue of Liberty was a Chinese lady of great virtue and purity, chosen as a symbol because she possessed a strong free will of her own, despite the bondage laid on her by tradition.

I went into the island café for a coca-cola. A few tables were spread outside under yellow sunshades, and many people were having meals. Others were busy writing postcards and buying souvenirs. Later I strolled round the star-shaped base and then approached the water. A few small fir trees are grouped here and there, and the whole island is well laid out with cement bricks and green lawns. The water's edge is as straight as if cut with a knife.

I was surprised at the lack of natural features. I had never come across before a piece of land *entirely* remade by man. The architectural achievements of New York fill me with wonder, but give me no feeling of stability. New Yorkers—and probably other Westerners—seem ever eager to alter the whole face of a landscape. I should not be astonished to hear one day that the little islands round Manhattan had been removed altogether. To me, the smallest Pacific atoll has the permanent look of all natural things, whereas Bedloe's Island I should suppose to have been *built* in the sea by Americans had I not been told the truth. Aerial photographs of Ellis Island, Governor's Island, Welfare Island and Bedloe's Island make these whims of Nature look like marvellously well-made, scale-model toys. They suggest, too, the house-rafts of bamboo or logs which float down the Yangtse River from Chungking, occasionally remaining stationary in the middle of the river for a while, with the local folk taking no notice of them, and presently drifting silently on their way. I often saw them outside my native city Kiukiang. The 'sailors' lived just like people in the city. If the upright hand of the Statue of Liberty held a long pole instead of a torch, I should expect Bedloe's Island to move gently away one day like a raft. But I dare say it is more likely to be towed away by tugs to 'a more convenient site'. . . .

A certain man of Ch'i one day, some 2300 years ago, began to dread the fall of Heaven. As he knew no way to prevent this calamity, he worried over it day and night, forgetting to eat and to sleep. But Heaven did not fall. And probably Bedloe's Island will remain very much where it is today.

I confess I never understood how Frederic Auguste Bartholdi, the originator and sculptor of the Statue of Liberty, came to conceive such a fantastic scheme. It is a piece of *Occidental* inscrutability to me. None of the many lovers of liberty before Bartholdi thought of such a way to proclaim their faith. In addition to his artistic ability and technical achievement, Bartholdi's powers of imagination must have been exceptionally great. Visitors to the Statue of Liberty should remember not only its name and colossal size but also the man who made it.

The poem, *The New Colossus*, expresses the effect of the Statue on a poet's mind. So far I have not found anything dealing with its artistic merits, which I doubt if we can judge adequately from the small reproductions in metal or pottery which are on sale as souvenirs. Perhaps its gigantic dimensions prevent it being judged at all from the artistic point of view. Size alone can impress but can also minimize artistic effect. Too small dimensions will tend to confuse the spectator, while too big ones are beyond his grasp. For instance, I admire Frank Brangwyn's mural paintings inside the RCA buildings, but I prefer to look at postcard reproductions of them rather than at the originals, which are so high upon the huge walls that my eyes cannot take them all in at once. Similarly I find it difficult to appreciate the artistic merit of the enormous sculpture of Atlas outside RCA Building. Pressed by the crowds moving along the pavement I have to stand too close to it to see it properly. The placing of an outsize work of art presents serious difficulties. Bartholdi's choice of Bedloe's Island for his Statue of Liberty was perhaps the happiest part of his work. He wanted it to be, above all, *impressive*, and it impresses every visitor to New York. I read somewhere that Bartholdi began work on the Statue in 1879. The building of skyscrapers was a much later development. I am no student of the history of architecture and have no urge to trace the origin of skyscrapers, but clearly the impulse which made Bartholdi build his 305 foot statue must have been the same which later prompted the solving of the technical problems involved in building skyscrapers three times that height.

Possibly the Temple of Isis by King Nekhtnebf about 350 B.C. on the Island of Philae in the Nile, Egypt, which was protected by a stone quay all round with the necessary staircases, etc., had something to do with Bartholdi's thought on his gigantic project at first. Or he had in mind the Egyptian Pyramids and Sphinx, and the colossal monuments and statues of the Greco-Roman world; but to me his Statue seems more akin to the early Chinese colossal sculpture of Buddha on the rocks of the Yun-kan and Tun-huang caves. These huge stone representations of Buddha still rouse onlookers to veneration and faith. I regard the Statue of Liberty not merely as a Statue but as a symbol of a faith, and meditating in front of it I tried to visualise what Liberty has meant for mankind. There have been grand words uttered about it by the great thinkers of the past, but the following poem by William Lloyd Garrison (1805-1879) appeals particularly to me:

High walls and huge the body may confine,
    And iron gates obstruct the prisoner's gaze,
And massive bolts may baffle his design,
    And vigilant keepers watch his devious ways;
But scorns the immortal mind such base control;
    No chains can bind it, and no cell inclose.
Swifter than light it flies from pole to pole,
    And in a flash from earth to heaven it goes.
It leaps from mount to mount; from vale to vale
    It wanders, plucking honeyed fruits and flowers;
It visits home to hear the fireside tale
    And in sweet converse pass the joyous hours;
'Tis up before the sun, roaming afar,
    And in its watches wearies every star."

Though no actual word or term for Liberty is to be found in the ancient Chinese Classics, 'to be one's absolute true self' is the principal Confucian teaching, and 'to keep one's soul free' the chief point of the rhythm of life advocated by Lao Tzŭ who originated Taoism. Chuang Tzŭ, the sage and disciple

K

of Lao Tzŭ, was once angling in the river P'u. When messengers came from the King of Ch'u asking him to take up a high administrative position, he replied that he had heard that a holy tortoise which had died three thousand years before was kept by the king in a golden casket in the great hall of his ancestral shrine. Supposing that when this tortoise was caught it had been allowed to choose between dying and having its bones preserved and venerated for centuries, and keeping itself alive with its tail dragging in the mud, he enquired of the Court messengers which fate they would have preferred. Their answer being the latter, Chuang Tzŭ told them to go away and let him drag his tail in the mud. And he was at once left alone, for, fortunately, his regard for liberty was appreciated by the messengers.

But the idea of liberty has not always been so well understood. In modern life its meaning has become more and more obscured. I do not refer to politics, which I cannot pretend to understand; what I deplore is that we human beings seem to have lost the sense of liberty in our daily life. We 'tighten our belt' to order; we follow every fashion; we listen to what we are told; we are bound by convention. I know that there are many who are happily married, but I am inclined to think that in every country there are some husbands like the one in the following Chinese story:

"One night a much henpecked husband began to smile in his sleep. The wife gave him a punch to wake him up and asked what had made him so happy in his dream. The answer was that he dreamed he had taken a small wife (concubine). This made the wife furious, and adopting her usual method, she punished him by making him kneel beside the bed and giving him a good beating. The husband begged her not to take it seriously, saying "Dreams are only illusions." She retorted that he could dream on any subject but this one. He promised to do so. However, the wife was not sure how she could know what he was dreaming about. "It will be easy," replied the husband, "I shall be safe from temptation if you let me sleep quietly until I wake in the morning."

The poor man was not even accorded liberty in his dreams. But can we really declare that any one of us today possesses the *feeling* of liberty? To regain this priceless sense and preserve ourselves from further degeneration, what could be better than to use the Statue of Liberty as a centre of pilgrimage?

New Yorkers seem to be fond of notable processions: why should there not be an annual procession to the Statue? Husbands like the one in the story, anyhow, would gladly participate!

Pilgrims' Procession to Liberty

XII

ALONG EAST RIVER

THE unforgettable month of my stay in New York was May. It was on a May morning that I first saw the panorama of the great city complete, when I took a round-Manhattan steamer trip. I very seldom plan my 'silent travelling' even over night, but it so happened that I had read a notice about the date of the season's first trip round Manhattan Island in the evening paper, and I did not lose a moment.

The steamer was not due to start until after ten o'clock,

Ferry boat, Manhattan to Staten Island

but I thought I would take myself early to the Battery to see something of Lower Manhattan in the early morning. I had seen it in daytime often enough and also in the evening and at night, but never in the early morning. I entered the IRT subway about 6 a.m. to find myself already rather late. The downtown train took a full load without me. Into the next train I managed to squeeze, but with so many others that we were like sardines in a tin. Many passengers got off at Times Square but as many more jammed themselves in. Each time the train stopped I felt the pressure renewed. My intention was to get out at Bowling Green but so many of my fellow sardines got out at South Ferry Terminal that I found myself with them.

I emerged from the subway as from a dream. A dense morning sea-mist hid all the buildings, high and low, and the scene was so unlike any other part of New York I had seen that at first I thought I had overshot Manhattan altogether. Not until I recalled the elusive beauty of three skyscrapers, which now loomed through the mist, did I recognise the outlines of the New York I had seen as the *Queen Mary* approached it. I realised that, early in the morning at least, New York could be lost in mist every bit as much as London in a winter fog. "But London fog", wrote Mary Howitt, "consists of something more than vapour of water partially condensed. Every house contributes a number of little fiery volcanoes, which are busy all day long supplying to the air vapour of

Morning rush near Battery Park

water, sulphur, carbon, as well as sulphurous, nitrous, and pyroligneous acids, and some other matters, all of which become to a great extent mixed with the vapour." No doubt this formidable scientific explanation accounts for the greater freshness of the mist over Manhattan. I found it inspiring.

Lingering in the subway exit, I was brushed aside by the storm of passengers, who rushed out into the mist and moved away at high speed, like rice-husks out of a polishing machine. The process continued endlessly. Presently another throng poured off the ferry boats and mingled with the crowd, moving along in a similar manner.

I moved back a few paces. I seemed to be facing a cinema show on a huge white screen. None of the faces was clear and many of them were rather distant; heads and bodies joined into jigging blackish blobs like figures in an ancient silent film. Seen thus, they suggested, above all, struggle and determination. I never saw a great mass of people like this in London. Not that Londoners do not work as hard as New Yorkers, but they do not appear to *strive* so greatly to succeed. New York is reputed to be the gayest city in the world; but that is later in the day. In the morning it works.

Presently I came to rest near the edge of Battery Park, facing the U.S. Custom House and a large group of skyscrapers. On the ground the mist had lifted, driven up (it seemed) by

Paper-stand near Bowling Green

the mass movement of people, but it still hung over the upper parts of the skyscrapers. Minute particles of vapour drifted around in varying degrees of concentration. It was as if gauze scarves were being twitched through the air by invisible hands.

Moving a little nearer to Bowling Green, I stared up the great misty canyon of Broadway. Everything was vague but I identified the Singer Tower and the tower of the AT & T Building, and fancied I discovered the faint image of the Woolworth building beyond. Mist is not always white; here it was pale brown and pale blue, soft colours mysteriously imparted by the buildings. In the distance yellowish and reddish tints showed where the sun was trying to break through. The growing day had reached its boyhood and it was time for me to begin my trip.

The steamer was anchored at Pier 1. My hurrying steps disturbed the pigeons, who rose and circled overhead like a lady's dotted veil, through which I could see, behind some old little weathered reddish houses on Washington Street, a yellow and a grey skyscraper. I believe these small houses have been uninhabited for fifty years or more, but are unlikely to be demolished until the owners find a buyer willing to erect another skyscraper on the site. They did not look happy, these little houses, squatting there beneath their towering neighbours. The morning mist, however, harmonised the scene, and I decided to make a painting of it later on.

No sooner had I embarked than the steamer moved off. To my great satisfaction it turned left—I do not know the nautical term—and took me up East River first instead of right up the Hudson, which I had seen from the *Queen Mary*. In a few minutes the mist, with all its charming deceptions, dispersed, disclosing a typical balmy New York May morning. The steamer glided by the water front, moved into the Bay, and then turned northward. Not much of Battery Park was visible, for it was walled off for the excavation of a tunnel under the East River to Brooklyn, but the South Ferry wharves were clear; I knew them well, having crossed the Bay from there to Staten Island three times already. From East River the mass of soaring buildings of lower Manhattan on the left and of Brooklyn on the right were uniquely impressive. No other city in the world can afford such a sight. Each cloud-topping obelisk stood clear in the hygienic atmosphere as if dressed for a parade. I wanted to congratulate someone, in military fashion, on the men's smartness and fitness!

A frivolous story about skyscrapers slid into my mind. I had heard that most downtown skyscrapers have no thirteenth floor, the number of storeys being therefore one less than that claimed. Everyone in this part of the city, it was said, dreads bad luck and will have nothing to do with thirteen. How, I wondered, do they count their money when it adds up to thirteen dollars? Leave one out? I remembered a story about the building of a skyscraper in Shanghai. An American architect showed a Chinese contractor a picture of the Empire State Building and jokingly asked him how he would like a contract to put up a building like that. "What a chance", said the contractor (who had a sense of humour). "I could leave out a whole floor in these skyscrapers, and no one would be any the wiser!" Well, American contractors have actually left out a whole floor in these skyscrapers and no one is any the wiser!

Someone on the steamer was trying to point out to somebody else the site of New York's earliest dock. My eyes followed his pointing finger. The shore was lined with docks and piers as far as the eye could reach. With the countless docks on the Hudson for ocean liners and the other chain of them along the water fronts of the east side of lower Manhattan and of Brooklyn, it seemed hardly credible that New York should ever have had but a single dock. Every kind of vessel—steamers, tugs, and boats I could not name—pottered and trotted about or lay inert in dock. Numberless ants swarmed over the motionless ships loading and unloading merchandise. The docks were what Walt Whitman once described ferries as being, 'inimitable, streaming, never-failing, living poems.'

Presently I was recalling walks I had taken along South Street. There are many nicely weathered houses here similar to those on Washington Street. They are not particularly small; they only seem so by comparison with the skyscrapers. In colour they are mostly red, and having been built long before skyscrapers were thought of, they offer a picturesque reminder of the early days of New York.

The Fulton Street Fish Market I had seen in full operation. It is so large that, but for the fish of every description being packed in barrels and boxes with large quantities of ice I should have supposed it was intended for cattle. Sweet's Restaurant, established in 1845, is situated here. While eating there I heard of what was called the Dead Area, where stood one of the richest organisations in New York, the Sailor's Snug Harbour, a big building surmounted by a carved stone cross. One of the best things on South Street, near Depeyster Street, is a lane so narrow one would suppose no one ever entered it, yet it usually contains a few smart cars parked beside demolished houses. On both sides the buildings are derelict, their doors and windows blocked with wood. At the far end stands the slender column of the Cities Service Building, intensifying the narrowness of the lane. Leaning against a wall, when I was there, was an elderly fellow without a tie feeding the pigeons with peanuts. He wore an innocent carefree expression. The well-blent harmony of old and new, rich and poor, busy and idle, appealed to me, and I made a sketch for a painting.

A buzz of excitement among my fellow sightseers on the steamer drew my attention to the fact that we were approaching Brooklyn Bridge, the first and oldest of the world's great suspension bridges. Perhaps because of its age I have a stronger attachment to this bridge than to any of the other grand

Fulton Street Fish Market

structures of New York. With their great wealth and limitless energy, New Yorkers can, and do, make changes in their city which they may not like after a while; very little seems absolutely secure. But Brooklyn Bridge is famous as well as important, and it will be preserved if anything is. I had walked over it a few times. I liked the pattern of the steel work, and still more the view of the downtown skyscrapers seen through it; the landscape was improved, just as a black silk veil may add charm to an already beautiful face. At night, when the lights were on, the giant steel net was even better.

After Brooklyn Bridge came Manhattan Bridge, and then

the Municipal Buildings commanded the scene, fine-looking and properly aloof.

Approaching Williamsburg Bridge I remembered its striding silhouette when seen in the fish-white light one evening from East River Park, near Lillian Wald House. I was sitting on a bench close to the river's edge. In the still, dusky air there was hardly a ripple on the water. The clear reflection of lights from the opposite bank and from a boat anchored near by intensified the tranquillity. Faint whisperings and gentle laughter reached me, along with the agreeable rustle of leaves. I wrote a poem:

聞 在 不 清 燈 江 江
脂 風 覺 光 倒 宿 色
粉 過 春 渾 影 長 澄
香 微 遽 然 吐 珠 明

The river's colour is pure but the river-night seems long;
Pearl-like lamps reflected in the water glint clear light.
I am carefree and forget that spring is still here,
After the wind breathes I vaguely smell the faint perfume
of face-powder.

I had a new view of Williamsburg Bridge when the steamer passed under it, a brilliant, unmysterious daytime view. Now the river became wider and calmer. Silvery-winged seagulls flew round us like escorting aircraft. The Midtown skyline was now on parade. The Empire State Building was in charge, supported by the Lefcourt Colonial, Lincoln, Chanin, Chrysler and News Buildings and the Rockefeller Centre; I could even detect faintly the gilded roof of Grand Central Building. My eyes, narrowed by the hard light, drank in the intoxicating sight.

While I gazed to the left of the steamer, my fellow-sightseers suddenly dashed to the right, to see the aircraft-carrier *Franklin Roosevelt*. I followed. The vessel was in a dock on the Queens side near the riverlet which divides Queens from Brooklyn. Its enormous size diminished all the steaming vessels in the neighbourhood. Workers were busy on the huge flat deck as well as over the side. They appeared to be breaking up the ship, and

I guessed that its task was ended. The passengers' talk was of how big a part the *Franklin Roosevelt* had taken on D-day and afterwards.

Next, as the steamer headed towards Welfare Island, I tried to locate Beekman Place, where I had been on several occasions. Mr. Karl Küp, Curator of the Spencer Collection in the New York Public Library, whom I have mentioned in a preceding chapter, happened to mention my arrival to Miss Edith Wetmore, and next morning I received an invitation to tea at One Beekman Place. I reached the spot half an hour early to have a look round. There was absolute stillness on Welfare Island under Queensboro Bridge. One or two persons were sitting on the public bench before the massive hospital buildings, but neither the trees nor the grass showed any signs of wind. What an ideal spot for a big bird sanctuary! Doubtless however, there are better reasons for using it for hospitals and charitable institutions. In Beekman Place the lift took me to the topmost floor and discharged me directly into Miss Wetmore's apartment. Miss Wetmore's family has a long association with China and she is herself very much interested in things Chinese. I was greatly flattered when she told me that she had a copy of almost every one of my books, including even *Chinese Calligraphy*, which, she joked, she did not know why she should have since she could never hope to understand it. While we had tea she showed me the wonderful views from her windows, in particular of the East River along which I was now steaming.

I had uncommon luck in making friends in New York, and more of them lived on the East side than on the West. Gazing at the lights of the midtown skyscrapers from their apartments became a habit. The roofs of skyscrapers are too high to be used as architectural features, as in Gothic or Renaissance buildings; they are usually flat, and generally anyone living in a building can make use of its roof. Apartments within easy reach of or directly below the roof are let at higher rentals than the rest. In the dry New York climate roofs can be enjoyed through most of the year. In London that would be out of the question, and besides, who would want to study chimney-pots however varied?

Once when I was enjoying a panoramic view from a high building roof on East River Drive, my companion produced a pair of binoculars and kept giggling while looking through them.

"There can be some exceedingly strange views from these roofs!" he remarked. "Especially in summer. You never know when you are being watched." No, indeed! In Edinburgh, when I visited the old camera tower at the end of the Royal Mile, and the guide moved round the enormous instrument naming the different parts of Edinburgh reflected in the lens, we saw at one point a girl trying to get over a fence. The back of her skirt got caught high on a bush, and the guide remarked pleasantly: "Just think of it. Ye never know when ye are being watched. Ye must behave well at all times."

At an open-air dinner party in another roof-apartment on

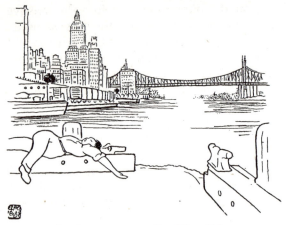

An afternoon nap at East River Side

the east side I found myself standing, glass of wine in hand, with a number of other guests, in a corner of the roof round a very small tree in a pot. Our host was relating how fortunate he had been to secure this tree. It stood about two and a half feet high and had a good many leaves but no flowers, and was presumably rare. We could not see it properly in the dusk, but we lingered round it for some time as if unable to tear ourselves away. The thought of so many people lost in admiration of a single small plant on the top of a skyscraper suggested a humorous drawing I might make on the lines of one I had seen in *Punch* of a large group of ruin-hunters contemplating one tiny lump of stone in the Scottish Highlands.

By this time the steamer was passing under Queensboro Bridge, and the New York Hospital and Cornell University

Medical College were coming into view. I found this enormous edifice very pleasing. It has a stability and feeling of permanence generally lacking in modern buildings. Its pure white stone showed up cleanly against the darkish surroundings. I had seen it at night from another angle: from York Avenue when visiting my friends Paul and Stella Standard, whom I have mentioned before and who live near Franklin D. Roosevelt Drive. Stella is not only a good cook but a famous one, being the author of the successful book *More than Cooking* as mentioned

New York in the blackout

before. Such was the pleasure of her company and her cooking that I seldom left the Standards before eleven o'clock and even so was often the first to go. Waiting for a bus on York Avenue my eyes were inevitably drawn to the New York Hospital. It looked like an illustration in a book of fairy stories.

Paul was an Air-Raid-Warden on York Avenue during the war. His patrol brought him a treasured series of night-views of the park-like grounds of the New York Hospital and Cornell University Medical College. "Like all city streets," he told me, "York Avenue is never in darkness. Two sets of green-and-red traffic lights are mounted on ten-foot posts set diagonally at each intersection, and are destined to blink their two colours at short intervals through eternity, while bright arc-lights illumine all streets after sundown. But in the war's blackouts the whole city felt again the effect of total darkness, for perhaps the first time since its early days as a metropolis. Thus for brief periods the city's streets and parks again had the night appearance of woodland anywhere in the world. It took a Second World War to bring this unscheduled boon, and the region gained (or rather regained) a loveliness which may not soon again be visible." I could not but admire Paul's inveterately aesthetic outlook even when on duty of such an unaesthetic nature.

I spent every minute of the six war years in England and I knew what a complete blackout was like. Quite a few friends of mine were wardens and on several occasions I walked round with one or other of them. But when the siren sounded, I was abruptly ordered, even driven, to shelter. I grew quite accustomed to being disturbed by some warden's loud knocking at my door to tell me that a pinprick of light was showing from my window. But it is a fact that not until enemy airplanes actually appeared over England and bombs began to drop, did the blackout really become complete. No doubt the New York blackout system was efficient, and I dare say Paul did not have to irritate anyone by pointing out tiny gaps in curtains—I certainly hope so. But those nights of utter darkness had their beauty; and I could imagine New York in similar conditions. By moonlight, unassisted by other illumination, the New York Hospital and the Cornell Medical College must have looked wonderfully ethereal.

After picking out Carl Schurz Park in the distance, a small but tastefully planned space, I crossed the deck to look at Triborough Bridge, which spans two islands, Ward's and Randalls, to connect the three boroughs of Manhattan, Queens and Bronx. Its construction is very different from that of the other East River bridges. Hell Gate Bridge, too, has a different design again. I remember feeling, while being driven over Triborough Bridge, that the skyline of midtown and downtown skyscrapers was one of the most impressive views in New York.

I was now at the end of East River, and the steamer was entering Harlem River, the second of the three great water courses which together circle Manhattan like a moat. Harlem

River is but a great canal, and so narrow that I felt as if by stretching my hand I could touch the warehouses and industrial buildings on either side. In the Harlem River Driveway I recalled having seen a boat race between the Naval Club and Columbia University. I had not realised till then that the English love of a boat race existed also in New York. But the atmosphere of the Thames banks on Boat Race Day was missing. Some people ran along the Driveway, but it was plainly not a traditional national event.

The steamer 'shot' more bridges, including the Henry Hudson and the George Washington, and reached the Pier 1, where it started, just before one o'clock. A little over two hours for the 32 miles trip. I treated myself to a substantial and tasty lunch while my mind chewed the cud of its impressions.

Scene along Harlem River

XIII

IN BROOKLYN BOTANICAL GARDENS

A FRIEND and compatriot, Peng Shinwei, was in New York as correspondent for a Nanking paper. I knew him well when he lived in London two years before the war; we used sometimes to visit Kew Gardens together. He was busy at the U.N.O. conferences nearly every day, but we arranged to spend a Saturday together, and I suggested we should visit Prospect Park in Brooklyn. This Park might have escaped my attention had I not been taken by two friends to an exhibition of Chinese Furniture at Brooklyn Museum. There were a few good specimens of our old furniture, well arranged behind the central hall, but I wished there had been a detailed catalogue to guide visitors. Afterwards we walked round the Far Eastern Department where I found two small Han stone bas-reliefs with unusual designs which interested me very much. On leaving Brooklyn Museum I noticed the great Civil War Victory Arch at the main entrance to Prospect Park. It was because I could not at the time go in and stroll round that the present visit was planned.

Peng Shinwei had been in New York for two years, but no business ever took him to Brooklyn; he did not think that he had been in any part of that Borough before. Neither of us knew how to get to Prospect Park, so we took the first subway train marked 'Brooklyn'. It was a long ride. When we finally got out I could not see the Civil War Arch and presumed we were at another entrance. We were about to move towards a group of trees when we saw a crowd of people of all ages coming towards us. Curious to know where they were going, we turned to follow them. No sooner had we caught them up than we all streamed through the main entrance of the Brooklyn Botanical Garden. There was no admission fee. The visitors were in high spirits, laughing and chatting as they went along, and many of them carried baskets for picnics. We went down a footpath beside a low wall. A number of small flowering shrubs were in bloom. Some of them had masses of yellow flowers on their branches but very few leaves. To me they

The wind in the willows in Brooklyn Botanical Garden

looked like *Fathesia,* which is a native shrub of China. The sight of them made me feel happy.

On leaving this enclosure we came to an open space kept more or less in its natural state. A group of tall, thin-trunked weeping willows held my attention. They stood near the centre of the open space and were very conspicuous by reason of their great height.

I have seen many tall weeping willows in my own country, but generally with thick trunks which become hollow and rugged as the trees grow old. The slender branches of these trees swayed in the wind; their trunks, too, moved in unison, like Hawaiian dancers in slow motion with their long grass skirts swirling about them. They looked extraordinarily graceful. As it was only mid-April, the leaves on the branches were still greenish yellow and not very big, so the movement of the trunk of each tree could be seen clearly. Though still growing, the shortish, slender upper branches were like golden tassels when the sun shone on them. The lower branches were long enough to ruffle the hair of the few youngsters who were playing around some of the exposed roots. Nearby many large stones lay scattered. At one moment the youngsters appeared to be puppets, each attached to a long string; at another their happy chatter revealed them as the merriest and liveliest little fellows, fastened by ribands that fluttered in fantastic knots round a Maypole. Many thick bushes seemed to support the queenly willows, and at the same time brought out the contrasts of the bright reds, yellows, greens, and whites of the dresses worn by the visitors. Behind these bushes I detected some magnolia trees in bloom. From far and near came the sound of happy laughter. The whole scene stimulated and rejuvenated me, and I made a sketch for a painting to be finished afterwards. I was also inspired to compose a little poem:

傳 去 笑 情 綜 拂 作

木 一 向 腮 楊 面 意

筆 路 花 游 柳 來 春

開 爭 間 久 亂 綜 風

L

> The purposeful Spring wind sweeps across one's face;
> Numerous silky-long willows entangle one's love-sick temples.
> Visitors laughingly move towards the flowering bush
> And all the way vie with each other to shout
> "The magnolias are in bloom !"

Shinwei and I continued to follow the crowd. After passing through a gate in a low brick wall we arrived at a greenhouse, outside which a long queue was lined up, so we joined it. In front of us a young couple filled in the time by exchanging increasingly long kisses, reminding me of a passage in a book called *Round About My Peking Garden* by Mrs. Archibald Little:

"And then comes a mystery. A little American girl was among the guests at one of the Empress's parties, and the Emperor Kuang Hsi at once took her up and kissed her, till the child, looking at her mother, said: "He does like me, mother, doesn't he?" After that he followed the child about, and kissed her again and again. She was a round-faced, rosy-cheeked little child of five. But how had the Emperor of China ever learned to kiss? How had the very idea of such a thing even been suggested to him? No Chinese man throughout the whole length and breadth of the vast Chinese Empire ever kisses wife or child, unless he has been taught to do so by a foreigner. No Chinese mother ever kisses her child. The nearest she gets to it is lifting her child's face up to hers, as if smelling at it. Yet here was the Emperor of China evidently versed in the practice, so that directly he saw this foreign child he took her up and kissed her, as if it were the most natural thing in the world, whilst to the everyday Chinaman this would be a most unnatural, and indeed repulsive, process."

This book was published thirty or forty years ago and was very successful; Mrs. Little was considered a great authority on China, about which she wrote seven or eight books. I do not know how people in England or America would react to the above passage, but I, a Chinese, could not help wondering how Mrs. Little got to know that no Chinese man 'throughout the whole length and breadth of the vast Chinese Empire' ever kissed wife or child. She must have been a fairy with magic powers to make her invisible and enable her to hide inside the curtains of every Chinese bed (these invariably have curtains, either of plain cloth or silk, to hide the rather uncivilized poses within from the eye of Heaven). It is interesting to know that Westerners who went to China in those early days, went simply to teach the Chinese to kiss! How did they teach? What a profession!

I have read a good many other books on China containing similar passages. And ten years or so ago I had an unusual experience myself. I had become friendly with an English family and stayed with them for weekends. Their little daughter and I became friends. One evening at her bed-time I was asked to read her a story. I then bent to kiss her 'Good-night' and she turned her nose to my lips, saying "Mummy says Chinese don't kiss but rub noses instead." She insisted on having my nose put against hers.

Now the girl is practically grown-up, and I wonder whether she will pass on the knowledge about China which she received from her mother to the next generation.

The truth is that kissing is something which we Chinese—at least our forefathers—considered to be 'sacred, secret and rare for special occasions.' 'Rarity makes precious', says an old Chinese proverb.

Presently we reached a red-roofed building with white-washed walls bearing the words *Darwin-Linnaeus*. No one bothered to see if they could go inside or not. Many people were already there: some were sitting on the steps, some leaning against the wall and some walking along the terrace and the footpath. But the eyes of all were upon a group of well-grown and profusely blooming magnolia trees. Each bloom stood up stiff and solitary, like a great purple electric-bulb on a huge candelabrum. What a grand show they made!

The cloudless blue sky and the clearest white sun enhanced their beauty. It was no wonder that I had heard so much talk of the magnolias a moment before. I was struck speechless, and moved a step nearer to one of the trees.

Graceful and refreshing were the newly-opened buds bursting forth from their fragile stems. They were all smiling as if they were in a beauty contest. Their rich and blushing countenances were inexpressibly delightful to behold. This must have been a special day for the magnolias in this Botanical Garden, and we had come to enjoy them at just the right time. Unexpected meetings with friends often bring pleasant surprises.

There are many species of magnolia in China, and we have always attached ourselves to this flowering tree with a special feeling unconnected with its beauty. My own preference is for a species called *Magnolia Conspicua*, which we call Yulan or the Lily tree, and of which I wrote the following little story in *The Silent Traveller in Oxford:*

"During the last year of my college life in Nanking I had a friend whose father, a famous man of letters, lived in a large and beautiful old house in the southern part of this ancient city. My own home being far away, I was often invited to this house, and one day I received an invitation to an informal gathering of friends to celebrate the full-blooming of the yulans in the garden. Time in those carefree days was unimportant, and such a gathering would generally last the whole afternoon and evening. I arrived early, and when eight or nine guests joined us, we all went into the garden. My friend, his young brother and myself were the only three young people there. Our elders in those days enforced their position of seniority very heavily. The existence of the younger generation was completely ignored, and we youngsters had to behave in a timid and subdued manner in accordance with the teaching of Confucius.

"There were five yulans, all covered with white jade-like flowers and extremely beautiful. The elders shouted, laughed, joked, and sang, but the silence imposed on me gave me time to enjoy the magnolias. At about five o'clock hot rice-cakes, wine, dried-melon seeds, preserved lichih and lungyen, and green tea were served on the table in the middle of a small thatched bower. There were also papers, inks, brushes and books placed within easy reach. It was incredible what mess and noise those supposed-to-be-stern-faced elders made! After dark, dinner was laid on the table in a room facing the garden, where from the windows the masses of white blossom were visible. Eating and drinking went on interminably. . . .

"There came a time when our host, my friend's father, left the party, probably to go to his study. Reappearing suddenly, he urged us with a broad smile to gather round the dinner-table again, in the middle of which he set a large round dish of valuable porcelain. The lid was removed, and a warm gush of steam rose. We all dipped our chopsticks into the dish and brought out a delicately-flavoured morsel of food. Speculation arose as to the substance of the food, and our host eventually told us that he had been in the garden picking yulan petals. Coating them with a thin layer of batter he had fried them in deep cabbage-oil until they turned a crispy yellow. How delicious they were!—And what an imaginative and thrilling idea! We raised a hearty cheer, and several new poems were written (most of them rubbish, of course!) in honour of this special dish. Someone declared that he had read about it in some book and was glad to have tasted a dish with such a wonderful flavour and texture. I too was glad. It was such an uncommon dish, more suited, perhaps, to the vegetarian. In all my forty years I have tasted it only this once, and I cannot help wondering if I shall taste it again."

I don't know if yulans grow in America, but I saw many purplish magnolias in Washington, Massachussetts, Connecticut and New York, and I regarded them all as Chinese trees. I discovered that there are two groups of magnolias cultivated in widely separated areas, one being native to the eastern United States, the other and larger one native to Asia, particularly China. I like the names of two American species, *magnolia Acuminata* popularly known as the 'Cucumber Tree' from the shape and colour of its fruit, and *magnolia Tripetala* known as the 'Umbrella Tree' from the radiating clusters of large downward-curving leaves at the apex of the shoots.

The name Magnolia was given by Linnaeus to this genus of deciduous tree in honour of Pierre Magnol, a French botanist of Montpelier, who died in 1715. It is very likely that the magnolia was discovered in China earlier than in America. I am not a student of botany and could not say whether the many magnolias I now saw were American or Chinese; I preferred to regard them as the latter. It made no difference to their beauty. Their glowing, smiling faces had intoxicated me entirely!

Rudyard Kipling wrote "Scents are surer than sounds or sights to make our heart-strings crack." Suddenly a scent pervaded the air. Peng Shinwei noticed it first, but I soon detected it too. It was not like the clear scent from some flower-bed, nor could it be from the magnolias, which have no perfume. I thought perhaps there might be one or two of the highly scented yulans nearby, but I could see none. Then, at the foot of a small mound where daffodils were growing round some shrubs, I noticed a crowd. There lay the solution to the problem of the scent. It was being wafted from the persons of two young ladies in modish bathing costumes, who were being photographed. Obviously they were models posing, and the photographs intended for advertisement purposes. I do not know whether 'bathing-costume' is the right term for their garments, which consisted only of two scraps of gaily coloured material, above, below and between which their bodies gleamed in the sun. We watched them don summer frocks in the newest styles and be photographed again. Summer, however, was still some time ahead. One of the things which has struck me most forcibly since I came to live in the West, is the degree to which things here are planned in advance. Here was an instance. Time seems to control Western life. But what is Time? Pieces of it are given such names as morning, day, evening, night, today, yesterday, tomorrow. The idea of time passing seems to appal people, yet apparently there are some who cannot make it pass quickly enough. I had seen people in New York waiting late at night to buy the next morning's papers to read before going to bed!

We strolled on round the garden. Many rose and peony buds were only waiting for warmer weather to burst into bloom; irises were already flowering.

I had a good look at the section of native wild flowers; a number of them, I found, came from South America and were unfamiliar to me.

Presently we came to a small Zoo, the third I had seen in New York. At the entrance there is a good sculptured tiger, probably in bronze. Some children had climbed upon it and were roaring happily. The Zoo itself was uncomfortably crowded, so we moved on to a little hill and I leaned against a large tree trunk to rest, remarking to my friend that though we had come out specially to see Prospect Park, we had spent our day mostly inside Brooklyn Botanical Garden. "What does it matter?" Peng Shinwei asked. "We have enjoyed ourselves, and that is what we came out to do."

A game at the entrance of Brooklyn Zoo

XIV

APPOINTMENTS WITH ART

Rome, Florence, Venice, Paris and London are generally considered the world's art centres and are the goals of art students. But there are in fact more museums and art galleries in New York than in any other single city in the Western world. I managed to visit a good many of them.

One of my first excursions was to the Hayden Planetarium where I saw all the images of the heavenly bodies projected.

Scene near the American Museum of Natural History

The dome of the building is wonderfully constructed, without pillars, so that the light is in no way obstructed and the illusion of depth and space is perfect. A special apparatus is used to light the stars. To me they looked both real and unreal, so, lest the only illusion of the mystery of heaven left in my earthly mind be shattered, I hurried away as soon as the presentation was finished.

I also visited the American Museum of Natural History. Like the Planetarium, this is not directly connected with art, but its exhibits can stimulate an artist's mind and give him subjects for study. It lies close to Central Park, the great recreation ground for New Yorkers, so it is much visited. Each time I was there there was a big crowd moving round, laughing and exclaiming "Boy, O boy!" "Gee Whiz!". Women and girls chattered round the huge cases, each of which contained several specimens of each species, old and young, stuffed and grouped in natural positions among trees and plants such as would be found in their native surroundings. They were all admirably arranged with good lighting and an appropriate painted background. One woman visitor would say exuberantly: "O, that is the kind of fur I would like to have for a coat"; another might remark: "What a lovely feather! Wouldn't it be cute for a hat?" Possibly some people come to the museum to study the psychology of the visitors, particularly women and girls, as revealed by their taste in furs, feathers and colours. For my part I studied the layout from different angles and noted the plants peculiar to the various animals. Chinese art is renowned for its artistic representation of Nature in every form and mood. More than a thousand years ago our best artists began to specialise in the painting of birds and mammals in their natural settings. It is unlikely that the director and curators have been influenced by Chinese masterpieces, but I can imagine how delighted our old masters would be if they could see this museum applying similar principles to their own.

I most enjoyed the section in which sea-life is displayed. The colours of several unfamiliar fishes and of many sea-plants were a revelation to me. In the Hall of the Natural History of Man, where I tried to find out how we reached our present state, there is, if I remember rightly, a board with diagrams and illustrations of the development of Man compared with that of fishes. I understood that it is a new theory that Man and the fish have a common origin.

At the Cooper Union Museum, I saw many famous paintings, pieces of furniture, and decorative art of various periods. This museum is chiefly concerned with the applied arts and must be a great help to those who want to make a systematic study of decorative art or to get ideas for new designs of their own.

A unique museum is the Children's Museum in Brooklyn. I had not realised before that there is so much to be seen, discussed and learned about children. The simplicity of a

child's mind has always fascinated me, and I find it a matter
of regret that the modern child tends to know too much and
easily loses simplicity and spontaneity. But if they must know
so much, it is good for them to learn it clearly and syste-
matically. This Children's Museum has given a lead to the
world.

   I had often heard of the Museum of Modern Art on 53rd
Street. In London there was before the war a movement to
establish a similar museum, but the outbreak of hostilities and
the continuing post-war austerity have hindered its development. I visited this museum as soon as I conveniently could,
and I was greatly impressed by its spacious rooms and the
way in which the numerous exhibits were displayed. Each
work was arranged to the best advantage with regard to
position, light and frame. There was no hint of overcrowding.
In many cases a whole wall was devoted to a single picture.
This is admirable, for if many works of art are crowded together on one wall, their merits tend to be obscured, for the
eye cannot wholly exclude surrounding objects.
   In China, as far as I can remember from my artist-father's
practice, it is usual to hang only one picture on a wall, very
seldom more than two. Ever since the time of the great Sung
masters 'Space' has played an important part both in our
pictorial composition and in the arrangement of works of art
in our homes. The result is a tranquil atmosphere in rooms,
which helps the onlooker to become absorbed in a picture.
Instead of framing our pictures, we mount them on silk or
paper, which can be easily rolled up and unrolled; for it is
not a good thing to look at the same picture all the time, so
we hang one on the wall for, say, a month, then roll it up and
replace it with another. I myself do not think mounting pictures
on silk or paper is altogether satisfactory, because the frequent
rolling and unrolling is apt to damage them, but it does save
the trouble of finding the space in which to store a large collection of framed pictures. Of course, there is the additional
problem that one does not want to hide away a picture which
has considerable value, nor does the artist like to have his
work stored. Still more difficulties must confront the directors
and curators of a museum or art gallery. Nevertheless, the
director of the Museum of Modern Art has arranged the

exhibits so artistically and agreeably that I feel hopeful that more may be done in future to do artists justice.

As a matter of fact, in this museum—the only one, incidentally, which charges for admission—I saw more people than in any other. It has a friendly atmosphere. Round it is an open space decorated with trees and plants in pots and a few big pieces of sculpture well placed. The visitor can sit in a deckchair and gaze at these at his ease, and enjoy a light lunch or other refreshment at the same time. I was told that the aim of this museum is to assist the average person in the understanding of art; perhaps it would be better to say in the understanding of modern art, for the exhibits I saw were all confined to this style. I saw the original of 'Guernica' by Picasso, and I was interested to find works by Henry Moore, the English sculptor, and Ben Nicholson, the English painter, whose creations have become familiar to me during my residence in Britain. Two big sculptures, 'Kneeling Woman' and 'Standing Youth' by Wilhelm Lebumbruck, impressed me very much.

I must here say something about the Museum of Non-objective Paintings. I have mentioned it before, but I was not able to visit it immediately. Later I made a special point of going there. It appeared to be housed in temporary premises. The paintings exhibited were mostly very large, in bold colours, with huge plain gold or silver frames about seven or eight inches wide. Many paintings took up nearly the whole of a wall. Among the chief exhibitors were Wassily Kandinsky, Rudolf Bauer, and Hilla Rebay. After a careful look round, I went up a staircase, along which were a good many examples of the work of Paul Klee, who exhibited in the National Gallery, London, during the war and aroused much controversy in the press.

The recollection of that controversy made me wonder whether it is really necessary to explain art at all, dividing it into 'schools', such as the Abstract School, the Surrealist School, the Futurist School, and so on. Puzzled by the name 'Non-objective Painting', I bought two pamphlets, one called *Public comments made in the Museum of Non-objective Painting in New York*, the other *The Power of Spiritual Rhythm* by Hilla Rebay.

After reading the pamphlets I went round the exhibits

again. Many of them bore such titles as 'Growing', 'White Edge', 'Improvisation', 'Open Green', 'Glowing Up'. This conveyed little to me and I wondered why they should have titles at all. The larger pictures seemed to catch my eye from wherever I stood in the room and I tried to imagine how they would look if they were much smaller. After a while I approached a girl and a young man who were there to help visitors. What I wanted to know was the difference between 'Non-objective painting' and 'Abstract', 'Surrealist' or any other painting. We had a good talk but never got to my point, beyond agreeing with a laugh that *size* must count. Afterwards I wrote to my friend Herbert Read, the English poet, essayist and art critic, who told me that Kandinsky is a 'colourist', which brought to mind the following passage:

"The family of emotional colourists can never be satisfactorily described. Colour makes a more insidious attack on the emotions than form. Moreover, *form* can be described. Words like 'jagged', 'suave', 'bulbous', do convey a mental picture to the reader's mind. But to say that a picture entitled 'Nursing the Rumps' owes all its meaning to an astringent harmony of dusty pink and pale malachite green, interwoven with accent of dark wine colour, is to say practically nothing. One might as well attempt to convey the meaning of the Parthenon by tabulating its measurements".

I have always wanted to get to the bottom of things that I could not at first understand, but the more I tried to fathom Non-objective art the greater was my bewilderment.

I should really have started this chapter with my visits to the Metropolitan Museum of Art.

I was introduced to the curator of its Far Eastern Department, Mr. Alan Priest, at a dinner party arranged for us by a mutual friend. I had read a number of works on Chinese art by Mr. Priest and at our first meeting found him most congenial. He had spent many happy days in Peking and told me humorous anecdotes of his sojourn there. He had learned to sing some Chinese opera and actually took part in stage performances once or twice. Later when our famous opera-singer, Mr. Mei Lan-fang, came to give performances in the U.S.A., Mr. Priest helped with the sets. When I visited him in the museum, he gave me a copy of the catalogue of the *Exhibition of Chinese Royal Robes* and showed me many colour plates of them. His knowledge of Chinese silk, sculpture and bronzes is very extensive. He had taken the trouble to have assembled most of the collection of Chinese paintings for me to go through. We agreed on many points and in particular we both liked the long scroll, 'Enjoyment of Wine' by Kung Tsui-Yai of the Sung dynasty. I also liked the album page 'Fish at Play' by Chao Keh-hsiung and 'The Moaning of the Monkey' attributed to Wen Hsien. Mr. Priest told me that the museum had now bought A. W. Bahr's collection of early Chinese paintings, which have been reproduced in book form. I know this collection well and wrote a review of the book which appeared in the London Burlington Magazine. The best picture in this collection is I think 'A Section of the Vimalakirti Sutra' in gold which I discussed fully. Unfortunately they were not on show while I was in New York; but I hope many other visitors will enjoy them.

I also had talks with Mr. Hobby, who is in charge of the Chinese section of pottery and porcelain in the same department and who kindly showed me some rare pieces. He mentioned the names of English collectors of Chinese porcelains and we exchanged opinions. In his Section I often met my compatriot, Mr. S. S. Han, who has been in the department for a number of years. He always wears a gentle smile and is very popular with his colleagues. His face struck me as remarkably like both the sculpture of the Head of a Woman, Sung dynasty, No. 30, 130, and a wooden sculpture of Kuan Yin, Sung Dynasty, No. 33, 116, while the bronze statue of a monk, Wei dynasty, No. 28, 122, Rogers Fund, bears perhaps an even greater likeness to him. This likeness interested me very much as it was not a mere coincidence. The early Chinese artists moulded their works from the facial structure of the Northerners, not the Southerners like the Cantonese, etc. Mr. Han was born near the old capital, Chang-An, of the Wei and T'ang dynasties. Eyebrows close above the eyes and a rather long nose making a good space between the eyes and mouth—these seem to me the most characteristic features of the people in the North-west of China, and most old Chinese sculptures show them.

All the exhibits in the Chinese sculpture room in the Metropolitan Museum are well displayed and I could study them one by one from almost every angle. Mr. Han told me that the arrangement was strictly supervised by Mr. Priest, who made changes from time to time. While I was examining the exhibits, I suddenly thought of the shops along Madison Avenue where they sell mass-produced pottery and wooden statues claiming to be Chinese art, some of which must have been copied from these very exhibits. The modern method of copying is so expert that the layman's eye could hardly detect the difference. It is of course a good thing to bring beautiful works of art within easy reach of everybody, but there is a danger of thereby lessening the regard for a work of genius. I have seen many of these machine-produced statues, horses or vases, for example, in use as lamp-stands, and they are certainly very decorative. But I feel that some means of adapting the electric bulb to go with such lamp-stands should be devised. In a vase, for instance, lamp-shade and lamp could be made like an inverted lotus leaf or a big peony; a T'ang horse could have with it a rugged tree or a man with an old Chinese processional umbrella. The following are a few designs that I would like to suggest.

Rough designs for lamp shades

The Frick Collection at 70th Street, Fifth Avenue, gave me great pleasure. As soon as I entered this fine building, I realised how beautiful the interiors of some of the houses in New York could be. It displayed the same wealth of artistic and literary taste as is to be seen in many of the big houses in

London and other European cities. The arrangement of the Collection is somewhat similar to that of the Wallace Collection in London, though the paintings differ greatly. I had a good look at the painting of St. Jerome by El Greco, for there is a similar one in the National Gallery in London. I found three Vermeers: *'Girl interrupted at Her Music'*, *'Mistress and Maid'*, and *'Officer and Laughing Girl'*. I was rather surprised to see two Constables: *'The White Horse'* and *'Salisbury Cathedral from the Bishop's Garden'*; and five Turners: *'Antwerp'*, *'Cologne'*, *'Fishing boats entering Calais Harbour'*, *'Mortlake Terrace'* and *'The Harbour at Dieppe'*. I had heard that works by Constable and Turner could not be sold overseas; perhaps these had come to New York before that law was passed. The Gilbert Stuart portrait of George Washington held my attention; I had seen so many reproductions of it. The last find in my round was six characteristic Whistlers. I know him well through two books, *The Gentle Art of Making Enemies* by himself and *Whistler as I know Him* by Mortimer Mempes, his successful pupil. His own book throws light on his quarrel with John Ruskin. Whistler established himself in London and ended his life there, and his best works are to be found in Britain.

It is remarkable that several of the most renowned American artists—Mary Cassatt, Sargent, Whistler—made their names outside their homeland. I asked myself what these artists would have created if they had remained in America, and I decided that their talent would have been bound to bear fruit anywhere. But their example made me wonder what the T'ang and Sung masters would have created if they could have travelled to Europe and seen Greek and Roman art: or what Venetian artists would have created if they could have travelled to China. Nowadays the whole tendency of world culture is towards fusion, for we see so much of each other's art. But I wrote in my book *The Silent Traveller in Edinburgh* :

" The modern urge towards internationalism tends to kill every form of provincialism. For artistic value and for beauty I prefer to retain ' provinciality ' and local colour."

I was glad when I heard my friend, Mr. John Walker, chief Curator of the National Gallery of Art in Washington, say:

"I am convinced that there came to be a native flavour in our painting, something that is not derived alone from subject-matter, costumes or scenery. It is a quality which we also find in American literature. There is a parallel between the hard colloquial vividness we find in the paintings of such American realists as Bingham and the writings of Mark Twain; or the shadowy, symbolic beauty, apparent in the canvasses of our imaginative artists like Ryder, which is very similar to the poetry of Poe or the novels of Melville and Hawthorne. Though this indigenous quality is difficult to describe except by such analogies, it is apparent that we have developed a native style distinct from Europe."

I did my best to study this native style of American painting. I had heard of the Hudson River School and wanted to see works by Thomas Doughty, Asher Brown Durand, Thomas Cole, John P. Kensett, and others, but could not find any. I did not find much at the New York Historical Society, though two scenes of 'Skating in Central Park, 1865', by Ned J. Burns and the 'Pushcart Market on Rivington Street, 1934', interested me.

The Whitney Museum of American Art proved to be the best place for my purpose. It is comparatively new, and the founder, Mrs. Harry Payne Whitney, must have foreseen that there would be people, including one from China, wanting to see American art by itself. The Museum contains many oil paintings, water-colours, drawings and sculptures by American artists. The names were new to me, and the pictures had a novel local flavour. An exhibition called 'Pioneers of Modern Art in America' invited me to make a tour of it. It was said to be a second exhibition following an earlier one by the same artists, who, between the turn of the century and the outbreak of the First World War, developed a movement dedicated to aspects of everyday life. The present exhibition showed works executed by those artists in the first twenty years of the century. I was struck by the extent to which many of these painters were influenced by the great movement of modern art in Europe and also how far each artist had evolved a characteristic style of his own.

I often made expeditions to some of the galleries in 57th Street and very seldom finished a tour without being struck by something new. After my years in England, I know what to look for in galleries in Bond Street and other parts of London. But in New York I never knew what to expect in any one gallery in 57th Street. Many of the shows that I saw there were mainly concerned with exploring the use of lines,

curves, planes and colours to represent life and ideas internationally rather than within the limits of any particular
country or way of life. But the few works by Hovsep Pushman
in the branch of the Grand Central Art Gallery in 57th Street
gave me a hint. Though Pushman does not usually depict
American subjects, he has developed a highly accomplished
technique of his own and his use of colour seems to me to be,
consciously or unconsciously, typically American. Or perhaps
I ought to say Whistlerian.

My meeting with Miss Marthena Barrie at the above-
mentioned branch of the Grand Central Art Gallery was
unexpected and unusual. The first time I went there I exchanged a few words with the branch manager, Mr. Claude
Barber, saying that I had just arrived from England and did
not know what to look at yet. He asked me if I knew
Mr. A. W. Bahr. I was greatly bewildered and said "Yes,
why?" He then introduced me to Miss Barrie, who has known
Mr. Bahr since childhood and who was having a few of her
embroideries shown in the gallery at the time.

Miss Barrie's brother, Mr. Erwin S. Barrie, is the manager
and director of the whole gallery. I was soon introduced to him
and he was kind enough to ask me to lunch with him and his
sister, and later invited me to his gallery on several occasions.

The Grand Central Art Gallery, being situated on the top
floors of the Grand Central Station building, does not have to
rely on artificial lighting. This gallery, I was told, was established under the auspices of the American Artists' Association
and its exhibits are chiefly works by American artists. Mr. Barrie
told me how he had met Lady Eve Tennyson and had helped
her to collect works for the exhibition of Contemporary
American painting in London in 1943. I said that I had also
met her when she organised the United Artists Aid to China
exhibition. We agreed that Lady Tennyson had done a great
deal to widen the appreciation of international culture. I saw
many good shows in this Grand Central Gallery, where there
are separate rooms for oil paintings, water-colours, and
sculptures. The walls, I was told, are repainted to suit the
exhibits at each show. The staff seemed to be busy all the time,
starting preparations for the next show as soon as the current
one had opened.

My excitement was keen when I was invited to attend the

Sunset over Washington Square

opening ceremony of an exhibition of '*Three Progressive Sculptors*', Messrs. Oronzio Maldarelli, Hugo Robus and Warren Wheelock. As soon as I had seen a few of the exhibits I said to myself that they looked familiar, and then I realised that each of these sculptors had been represented in the Whitney Museum of American Art which I had visited. Mr. Barrie introduced me to all three of them. As they were the centre of attention and many visitors wanted to shake hands with them, and as the central hall of the gallery was packed with people,

C.Y.   Maldarelli   Barrie   Wheelock   Robus

we did not exchange many words. Each of the sculptors had a distinctive style, yet the works were so well arranged that they seemed less to contrast than to harmonize with each other. This must be a rare achievement, and I offer my humble admiration to those responsible. The arrangement of sculpture needs even more thought than the arrangement of paintings. Every sculptor has in mind a particular setting for his work. Even to arrange several pieces of sculpture by the same artist is a difficult task, but to arrange works by different sculptors requires very great skill and taste.

Most of the exhibits on this occasion were in the central hall of the gallery round a pond with fountains playing and sur-

M

rounded by green plants in pots. The vivid green added charm
to the show, while the colours of the ladies' dresses and the
endless chattering made for a lively atmosphere. Miss Barrie
introduced me to many of her friends. One, hearing that I had
been in Dublin, talked about the things in Phoenix Park.
Another insisted on my telling her how I had climbed up
Ben Nevis from Fort William, because her grandfather was a
Scotsman who had come to the U.S. from Inverness. Two ladies
kept asking me to say something because they liked my English
accent! This reminded me that I had been rebuked by an
English friend in New York for acquiring an American 'twang'.
I found them both amusing, for after all I am still a Chinese.
Later I had a chat with Mr. Barrie and the three artists.
Someone cracked a joke and the five of us roared with laughter. The whole gathering was a happy one. Mr. Maldarelli's
work is full of vitality and strength, Mr. Robus's of imaginative
power; Mr. Wheelock's outstanding quality is his simplicity,
or rather his ingenious capacity for simplification. Each
breathes an air of America.

My last appointment with art was at the *American Academy
of Arts and Letters* where the *National Institute of Arts and Letters*
Ceremony was held on a Friday afternoon in May. I was taken
by a friend. We met at the Academy entrance at 632 West
156th Street. The auditorium was almost full when we reached
our seats. Soon the processional orchestra and organ began to
play the American national anthem. The President of the
Academy, Mr. Walter Damrosch, made a short and amusing
speech in which he said that the audience would not be able to
see all the notable personalities on the platform as they had done
on former occasions because the orchestra had replaced them.
Then came the induction of new Institute members by the
Secretary of the Institute, Mr. Henry Seidel Canby, followed
by the induction of new Academy members by the Secretary
of the Academy Mr. Van Wyck Brooks, who received the Gold
Medal of the Institute, a high award only made once in ten
years, for his essays and critical works. Many 'Arts and Letters
Grants' were given to those who had distinguished themselves in
art, music and literature. An award of Merit Medal of the
Academy was presented to the dramatist, Mr. John Van Druten,
and another, for good diction on the stage, went to Miss Ethel
Barrymore. I was very interested to see the Institute Award

for Distinguished Achievement given this year to an eminent English poet living in America, Mr. Ralph Hodgson. The whole ceremony went well and I found the atmosphere most congenial.

After the ceremony tea was served and we all proceeded to the art gallery for the art show of the year. It was packed with people and it was difficult to get near enough to the exhibits to see them. I caught enough glimpses to realize that they contained plenty of local colour. It reminded me of the Private View Day at the Royal Academy, London, which I attended the year before. The ladies had on their best dresses and jewellery and large groups gathered round famous figures. Whenever I came across some friends, I was separated from them almost immediately. One suddenly grasped my hand and exclaimed earnestly: "Please help me find my wife. I have lost her". I was surprised at the request at first but soon realised that they were parted by the crowd. We squeezed resolutely through the crush, but we got separated ourselves before long, and when we re-met an hour or so later, his wife was standing beside him. By that time I was sweating freely and I decided to come away. It was all rather fun.

Flower Push-cart

XIV

IN WASHINGTON SQUARE

I NEVER tired of lingering in Washington Square, however often the Fifth Avenue buses, especially the open double-deckers, insisted on putting me down there. Times Square is a show place which forces one to gaze at this or that. There my ears were always trying to listen to something I could not understand. Washington Square, on the contrary, has a free and friendly atmosphere. I went there to relax.

Before visiting New York, I had the notion that the people living there were somehow different from the rest of the world. In Times Square, along Fifth Avenue, in Wall Street, I still felt that this might be true, but in Washington Square I realised that human beings are the same all the world over. The surroundings and the atmosphere of the Square might easily be mistaken for somewhere in London or any other European city. The Victory Arch, with two statues of Washington on the columns, is a copy of a monument in Europe, and, apart from the Number-one-Fifth-Avenue Hotel, there are no skyscrapers. Some buses and cars do run into the middle of the Square, but somehow they do not seem to me to travel as fast or as noisily as elsewhere. Perhaps the drivers were tired of sounding their horns.

After listening to the constant clatter of the elevated above and the subways below and to the frequent sirens of ambulances and fire-engines, I could not help drawing a deep breath of relief when I stepped off the bus into Washington Square. Even the pedestrians seemed to move in more leisurely fashion, and the public seats were always full of people looking as if they did not intend to move for hours. There are many more public seats in the streets of New York than in any other place I know. Most of them are always occupied, but people who sit on those in the middle of the streets are lost to sight in the moving throng; those who sit on the benches in Washington Square are conspicuous by their appearance of ease and peacefulness.

In the middle of the Square, near Washington Arch, is

the large concrete circle where there are always people playing some ball game while others watch. The players seemed less rough than those in the recreation ground in Central Park, and I watched them with pleasure. I got the impression that anyone interested could go inside the ring and join in the game. Once a passer-by in khaki uniform stopped to watch. He threw back the ball several times when it came outside the ring, until finally, taking off his coat and tie, he jumped inside. There were no arrangements to be made. The game continued amicably without a break. After a while he put on his coat and tie and went on his way. Others did the same. There was constant laughter from the players, many of whom were students of New York University, which is on the east side of the Square. On one occasion, when I had been watching a flock of homing birds fluttering above the top of a big elm tree, with the greyish Washington Arch and the pale brown hotel building as background, my attention was recalled to the ring by loud laughter. A stout fellow with a body like Bacchus in a Rubens painting had just split his shirt all the way up the back while throwing the ball. He was laughing himself as he tried to throw the ball again. This time it knocked my hat off and a young woman player rushed to pick it up and put it on my head with a wink and a smile. In New York, particularly among women, the wink seems to have some democratic, comradely significance.

Students' Dormitory of New York University

If I had not seen so many young men and women with bundles of books under their arms coming out of the building on the east side of the Square I would not have realised that this was New York University, for it has not the conventional appearance of a University, but rather do its lower floors

resemble business premises. The chatter and swift movements
of the young people seemed to me indicative of the particularly
happy and free life of university students on the west side of the
Atlantic. I noted the bright-coloured and variously fashioned
dresses of the girls, and the very loose coats of the young men,
inside which their slender bodies moved like the pendulum in
an English grandfather clock. Some were coatless, displaying
their shiny silk shirts and muscular hairy arms. Some carried
their coats slung over their shoulders. Many sat on the railings
of the Square, with their feet curled round the bars, talking
and joking. Now and then a scream arose when one of them
lost his balance and fell over backwards to the ground. All this
contributed a great deal to the cheerful atmosphere which
I sensed in Washington Square. Walking slowly and gazing
non-objectively I could observe the different types of people—
some reading idly, some chatting leisurely, some dozing, some
cracking peanuts and throwing the nuts into their mouths one
at a time. There seemed more men smoking pipes than
cigarettes or cigars. To my surprise I saw one man wearing
a black bowler hat, which is an even rarer sight in New York
than in present-day London, but New York is not always as

ultra-modern as I had imagined. The
mothers here were busy gossiping about
their domestic troubles, the young girls
discussed their shoes and hair-styles, and
the small children ran to and fro round
the ice-cream sellers. Not once did I see
a hot-dog seller inside the Square and this
probably gave me the feeling that I was
not in a new world after all. The essence
of life remains always and everywhere
the same, though it may assume different
outward semblances.

The copper-green statue of Garibaldi
never failed to attract my attention, not
because I am specially interested in Garibaldi, nor because I admired this statue
more than those I have seen in Trafalgar
Square and Whitehall in London, but
because its colour was almost my favourite
emerald green in the strong New York

Pigeon and Garibaldi

sunshine and because there were always one or two pigeons standing on Garibaldi's head. The pigeons recalled to me my remarks 'About Statues' in *The Silent Traveller in London:*

"I always feel there is a great bond between pigeons and statues. Those statues which were erected without columns are generally very friendly to pigeons. Sometimes I have looked up and noticed something on the bald head of a statue. I thought first that the person was coming to life or something was amiss with him. But it was only a pigeon strutting about, proud of itself for standing on such a prominent place—the very top of an important monument! And those people sitting, standing or riding on their pedestals, perhaps drawing the attention of visitors for a little while, but always ignored by the eyes of ordinary passers-by, always the same year after year, must be very pleased to have the friendly pigeons jumping up on their laps, hands, shoulders, and heads to make a change for them. But I read in the newspaper one day about a certain place where a statue of a famous man was going to be erected and how this man declared he did not want his statue put up because he had no wish to provide a seat for pigeons. He is really very sensible, but when I think of the Society for the Prevention of Cruelty to Animals and Birds, I am afraid he might be summoned for lack of consideration to pigeons. . . ."

Garibaldi had no chance to state whether he wished to provide a seat for the pigeons or not. But the sculptor, Giovanni Turini, had depicted Garibaldi with his face tilted upward, and looking into the distance, as if he were annoyed with the pigeon on the back of his head and trying to shake it off. I might not have noticed this, if it had not reminded me that the statues in Trafalgar Square and Whitehall show many prominent persons in gowns with their heads bent, as if acquiescing in the persistent presence of the pigeons. Turini had unconsciously shown that Garibaldi did not wish to provide a seat for the pigeons and this, I ventured to imagine, might have hindered him in getting further commissions!

Now that the second World War is over, people will soon be thinking of putting up statues of those who by their great services helped to win the victory. Many of these people are still alive, and while I do not expect them to share my views regarding statues, I think it is up to them to say whether or not they want to provide seats for pigeons, and whether they prefer to be represented in Cubist or Surrealist style.

Washington Square is not a place of national importance in America, as far as I can judge, and has no space for further commemorative statues. After gazing at Garibaldi for a while, I used to move on slowly. Sometimes I joined one or two older folk in feeding the pigeons, for it is easy to buy peanuts in New York. Sometimes I went to watch the photographing of mannequins wearing the latest fashions. This is a favourite place for such photography, on account of the many flowers, such as tulips and irises, growing on the west side of the Square. And sometimes I would watch two people playing draughts on a bench or overhear discussions and unusual conversations. If I have been eavesdropping I never deny it, and I guess that some of the talks in the Square were designed to be overheard.

One sunny afternoon I was sitting on the end of a long bench beside an elderly person who kept knocking the ash from his pipe. To distract my mind from this irritating noise I became absorbed in a conversation between four or five people on my left. A young fellow did most of the talking; he was dressed in the prevailing attire of a two-coloured coat and creamy-chocolate trousers. The talk passed from politics to art and eventually to modern life in general. The speakers' mode of expression was unusual and I was naturally interested in finding out what they were driving at, though I could not always catch the phrases they used. I must have unconsciously craned my neck from time to time and my neighbour must have noticed this. Soon they moved away, and to my surprise my neighbour suddenly spoke, though without looking at me. "Fool," he said, "She is a witch. She is a woman. Nobody knows what she is talking about." I began to enquire further. "I know it", was the only answer. He then went on knocking the ash out of his pipe as before. I was interested to know that the young fellow was a 'she' and not a 'he', though nothing in the dress or voice or manner indicated that. It was a success-ful disguise, but I wondered why she had adopted it. Was this part of modern life? I then remembered a post-war incident in England in which a young woman, successfully posing as an ex-service officer, had gone through a marriage ceremony with another girl. I remembered, too, hearing of young men in New York who disguised themselves as women in order to lure victims to be robbed, and I had seen photographs of them which made the deceptions seem credible.

With the scientific development of modern stage and screen technique, one can understand how a man can be disguised as a woman. But modern physical training and tailoring in the West do not help much to disguise a woman as a man. In Chinese literature and legend there are many instances of young girls posing as men in order to elope with lovers or take a long journey alone. This was because owing to Confucian moral teachings any young couple travelling together in China would arouse suspicion unless they were a married couple or sister and brother. Alone, it was easier to travel as a man. The old Chinese fashion of big, loose garments for both women and men simplified the disguise. For me it was interesting to find that unusual, and even apparently impossible things happen similarly in all parts of the world. But if women attired in men's dress are to be a feature in the modern life movement, I cannot see how this will succeed, especially in New York, where so many of the big businesses are chiefly concerned with feminine fashions. I was about to probe the question why a peacock and peahen should wear different plumage, and why zoologists still have difficulty in determining the sex of the giant panda, when my neighbour knocked out his pipe with particular violence and stood up to move away. This put an end to my whimsical meditations.

Presently three women sat down on my bench. They were soon engaged in animated conversation. I did not catch one intelligible sentence, though I tried hard. One of them sat with her right leg stretched out and her shoe set on a small wooden-stool to be polished. I had seen a number of shoe-shine men in Washington Square, but this was the first time I had see a woman's shoes being shined.

It was a constant surprise to me that New Yorkers should pay so much attention to their shoes. At nearly every street corner there is a shoe-shine stand or someone, grown-up or youngster, holding a small soap box of shoe-shine materials, leaning against the wall and crying for customers.

I found myself studying the different types of shoe-shine stands and soap boxes and the methods of carrying them. Some of the boxes seemed to be made of a few odd pieces of wood, others were attached by shiny leather belts round the neck or shoulders of their owners. Occasionally I saw in Washington Square a couple of shoe-shine men walking together with jitterbug steps while their boxes swung to and fro on their backs. The men took no notice when the sharp edge of the roughly-made box hit them in the back. The most comfortable shoe-shine stands in New York are the rows of big soft red-leather armchairs in the basements of Pennsylvania Station and Grand Central Station. When I was very tired after a full day I just sank into a shoe-shine armchair and hoped that the shoe-shiner would not finish his job too quickly. I often saw customers coming in twos and threes, to talk over business in these armchairs while their shoes were being shined. To have

Hot-dogs and Outdoor Art Show

my shoes shined in Washington Square was also very pleasant because I could enjoy the open air and gaze round at the same time. I understand that the population of London is bigger than that of New York City and that London buildings become blackened after a time while New York buildings do not. Why then is there such a continuous demand for shoe-shines in New York? I don't remember seeing many shoe-shine stands in Paris either. Yet surely Londoners and Parisians take as much care of their shoes as New Yorkers? The latter must have their shoes polished twice or three times a day otherwise the shoe-shine business could not have grown so extensively. The lady on the bench suggested that no one wants to do anything for himself if he can get it done by someone else. This is a common human weakness all the world over. The only peculiarity about New York is that there is always someone who knows how to turn it to business advantage.

Another reason I went to Washington Square was to see the Outdoor Art Show of which I had learned from a friend connected with its preparation. The opening day was May 25th and it was to last for a fortnight if weather permitted. It was the twenty-ninth semi-annual Show, and occupied the south and west sides of the Square and also both sides of Macdougal Street. I read in the newspaper that it contained works by a hundred and twenty five artists, six of them being wounded soldiers. This at once reminded me of the art show organised by the American servicemen which I had seen in Edinburgh when they were stationed there two years ago, though Edinburgh weather did not allow it to be held out of doors. On entering the show room I was given a small piece of paper on which to write down which picture I liked best. The room was packed with visitors, and I immediately began to wonder whether I had not better come some other time instead, but I was unable to get out. I was pushed on and was hardly able to see any of the exhibits. On the way out many people in front of me dropped their slips into a wooden box near the gate. Suddenly I overheard an elderly man say with a smile to his wife: "This is the American method of saying what you think of their pictures!" He looked like an artist himself. They both dropped blank papers into the box. I followed suit.

In Washington Square I had no trouble of this kind and enjoyed glancing at the works at random. The crowd was already big and fresh people kept coming all the time. New Yorkers must be very much interested in art, I thought, though I later reflected that a crowd speedily gathered round anything happening in New York. The constant stream of tourists from other parts of America must form a great part of most of these crowds, yet I was unable to see how passing tourists could spare the time.

There was great variety of artistic

Shoe shine!

expression in medium and technique, but I was astonished that so few of the exhibits were in the modern idiom. In fact, this was not a single show but a number of separate shows arranged together. Each artist was allocated a certain space in which to arrange his works in whatever way he liked. Most of the pictures were on the walls and some on the fences, but, where space allowed, some artists had devised means of hanging their works on a line supported by two poles. Some pictures were framed, but many more were unframed. I was interested in the way each artist displayed his work. What a job they must have had arranging their works every day! I do not know how spaces were allocated, but I paid three visits to this show and found that the artists did not all display their works on the same spot every day. The best space, to my mind, was the east wall of New York University Dormitory, opposite an open site where a house had been demolished. There seemed to be more people here than anywhere else, except along Macdougal Street. Several artists' works were displayed on the open site. Sometimes a strong wind upset the pictures and visitors lent a hand in putting them up again. Each artist looked after the sale of his own works. Some of them sat on stools either leisurely smoking a pipe or gazing round in search of prospective patrons. They were all ready to talk and to interest the onlookers in

Sketching in the Open-air Exhibition

their work. When I paused to look at a few paintings in rich bright red and yellow oils, the artist, who wore a Fairbanks moustache, got up and told me how he had caught those colours just right, as if helped by God, when he was painting the scenes in South America and that he could never paint them again like that if he tried.

I found myself a place behind an artist who was busy sketching a sitter. Quite a few others were doing the same, for there was no lack of sitters at the moderate charge of one or two dollars. The remarks casually made by some of the onlookers about the pictures were very entertaining, those made by the friends of the sitters were even more so. Once I was watching an elderly artist sketching a lady. He spent some time on her hair. When he finished the ear a lady's voice shouted in ecstasy: "He has got her ear all right!" Then another voice said "He has got her nose right too!" Later both remarked at the same time that the artist had substituted someone else's mouth. I could not help peering at the sketch. It reminded me of a story about a Chinese portrait-painter. When he had finished his portrait, the sitter quarrelled with him because in his opinion the portrait was not a good likeness. They agreed to ask the opinion of others. The first person to be asked thought the scenery in the background very beautiful. The second enthusiastically described the exquisitely-painted drapery. These remarks were not to the point, so the artist told the third to pay more attention to the bodily characteristics. After looking at the portrait and the sitter this way and that for a long while, he finally said: "The beard is extraordinarily like". The artist was quite disheartened and declared he would never paint a portrait again. Afterwards he became famous for flower and bird paintings. I was not sure if the elderly artist in Washington Square had heard the remarks about his sketch, or, if he had, whether he would change his subject-matter. Making a living has to be taken into consideration.

I remember seeing an exhibition of works by Robert Brackman at the branch of the Grand Central Art Galleries at 55 East 57th Street, for which Mr. Malcolm Vaughan wrote the following introductory words:

"Of the sixty thousand artists in the United States, there are some two hundred who possess considerable talent. Yet only a dozen among them have the technical knowledge and skill of hand to bring their talent to full fruition. The circumstance is unfortunate, for if a larger number of our artists could but fulfil their gifts, could but turn their rich imagination and bold inventiveness to account, we might have in this country in short order a golden age of art".

I knew that nearly half of the sixty thousand artists in the United States lived in and around New York, and I wondered how many of these one hundred and twenty five exhibiting in Washington Square were included in Mr. Vaughan's two hundred, and whether anyone was included in his dozen. To try to fulfil his gift and turn his rich imagination and bold inventiveness to account is what every artist wants to do. Whether he achieves something or not may depend on how hard he has to fight for life. Less strong-willed artists can be lost without ever fulfilling themselves. I do not mean to imply, however, that all artists have equal gifts of imagination and inventiveness, nor that an artist can fail to make the most of himself intentionally. An artist's life is often a hard struggle for existence. The general indifference towards art among a public easily swayed by adverse criticism has helped to kill many artists. But many others, including my humble self, struggle on. I salute the indomitable spirit of these fellow-artists who displayed their work in Washington Square.

Columbus Monument near St. Paul Chapel

XVI

AMONG THE LIGHTS OF BROADWAY

When G. K. Chesterton faced the blaze of lights on Broadway for the first time, he exclaimed: "How beautiful it would be for someone who could not read!" Personally I was more often dazzled there by the sparkling of jewels on the persons of ladies than by the brilliance of electric signs.

In my book *The Silent Traveller in London* I wrote of plays and films: "Though I do not go to the theatre often, I am very much interested in the queues standing outside London booking offices. They are a typical sight in London, and one we never see in China. These cheerful crowds are extraordinarily merry, unusually patient, and remarkably strong in the legs! An American friend told me there were no queues in her country either, except occasionally for the opera. I can well understand that, for I doubt whether any American has time to stand still for a couple of hours on end." In New York I was soon to learn that I had been misinformed. There may have been no queues there years ago, but day after day and night after night I saw people standing in interminable line round Radio City. I went there with two friends to see the film *The Green Years,* and it took us about an hour, moving on yard by yard all the while, to reach the doors of the cinema. This enormous theatre seats over six thousand people, and if the Rockefeller Center (the building of which it forms a part) cannot claim to be the tallest building in the world, at least the Radio City Music Hall is the largest of its kind in the world. And there is a chandelier in the Center Theatre which weighs over six tons, which is another record. There is a big difference between queueing outside a London theatre or cinema and queueing outside an American one. In London one is invariably beguiled by street-entertainers, but this is either not allowed or not desired in New York. A thick rope kept the queue within bounds, and elaborately uniformed attendants were on guard all along it. My companions told me that these 'N.C.O.'s' were necessary; on one occasion a riot had occurred among the

queuers outside the Paramount Theatre on Broadway on the
first day of Frank Sinatra's appearance there. The 'rioters'
were nearly all girls. Next day policemen, policewomen and
even mounted police, as well as a large number of detectives,
had to be provided to patrol the queues.

Having at last bought our tickets, we went up to the Grand
Foyer, which I was told was 140 feet long, 45 feet wide and
60 feet high. It certainly looked it. But there were so many
precisely similar entrances to the auditorium on each floor
that I began to feel lost. The house was practically full when
we took our seats. We were a long way from the stage, though
there were many who were still further back. It did not seem
to be the *picture* which attracted the enormous audience,
because that could be seen a little later in other cinemas much
more cheaply, but the stage show, which on this occasion was
called *The Easter Festival*. While the picture was being shown
I could see no difference between this and any other cinema;
but when the lights went up the innumerable heads, swaying
like waves of long grass on a gusty day, made the size of the
place into something quite peculiar.

Radiant figures appeared on the stage in the glitter of the
most dazzling light that modern science could make. Along
both walls of the auditorium elegant figures in white satin
slowly approached the stage, the front of which was decorated
with white lilies. An orchestra, hidden from sight, accompanied
what I took to be hymns sung by the characters on the stage.
There then came forward a company of 'angels' in coloured
garments who danced to the music. A second company
followed, then a third. It was a long show. I can make no
comment on the meaning of all this. I am afraid its emotional
effect was lost on me. My mind was pre-occupied with reflec-
tions upon the technical problems of stage presentation in so
gigantic a theatre. From where I sat, neither the characters
nor the settings and costumes could be seen clearly enough to
be *interesting*. My neighbours evidently shared my difficulty.
The figures were so small as to resemble slightly animated
statues.

I have had some slight experience of stage-designing. In
1942 I did the décor and costumes for a Sadlers Wells ballet
by Robert Helpmann called *The Birds*. My designs aroused
some discussion at the time. I knew nothing then of the

scene-painter's technique and could only draw in my own way. The dancers in the ballet being all birds, I designed a leafy wood in much detail for their setting. When the leaves and trees were enlarged from my model, the bird dancers seemed to be in about the right proportions to them. But there must be a limit to enlargement. If my leaves and trees had been made to fit the Radio City stage they would have dwarfed the dancing birds. The function of stage-design, in my view, is to intensify the effectiveness of the drama, not to overshadow it. Human figures cannot be enlarged. The answer to the

Boxes in the Metropolitan Opera House

problem in such a large theatre would be symbolical, abstract or surrealist designs, which can be quite effective on a big scale. Realism is impracticable.

It was in the Metropolitan Opera House that I saw the finest parade of dresses and jewels since leaving my own country. Friends had told me that 'the Metropolitan Opera House is the thing *to see* in New York. It's a must'. I wondered why the words 'to see' had been emphasised, but I was to realise their significance. My predicament was how to dress myself, for, as I have mentioned in another book, the worst type of uniform I have to wear is evening dress. I have never even tried a top-hat, but I have had enough uncomfortable experiences with a high, hard collar and starched shirt. I must

N

differ from Westerners in figure as in face, because in evening dress my head becomes immovable and my body feels as if bandaged, and when I eat or drink it gives me acute discomfort to swallow. But evening dress has to be worn on occasion or one cannot 'go to the party'. In my early days in London I took heart from reading Thackeray's essay on *Men and Coats*, and endured my pains with pride and a (literally) stiff upper lip. Thackeray says:

"A man who is not strictly neat in his person is not an honest man. I shall not enter into this very ticklish subject of personal purification and neatness, because this essay will be read by hundred of thousands of ladies as well as men; and for the former I would wish to provide nothing but pleasure. Men may listen to stern truths; but for the ladies one should only speak verities that are sparkling, rosy, brisk, and agreeable. A man who wears a dressing gown is not neat in his person; his moral character takes invariably some of the slatternliness and looseness of his costume; he becomes enervated, lazy, incapable of great actions; a man in A JACKET is a man. All great men wore jackets. Walter Scott wore a jacket, as everybody knows; Byron wore a jacket (not that I count a man who turns down his collars for much); I have a picture of Napoleon in a jacket at Saint Helena; Thomas Carlyle wears a jacket. . . . I prefer them (jackets) without tails; but do not let this interfere with another man's pleasure: he may have tails if he likes, and I for one will never say him nay."

But during the war Hitler's aircraft destroyed my dinner jacket and tails—and had a good try to destroy me too. In New York I was constantly reminded of them since for nearly all evening occasions a dinner jacket seemed essential. I felt that I was no proper man without one. It was easy enough to buy a tuxedo, but I had to count my dollars. Fortunately my hosts seemed always willing to forgive me for appearing at dinner parties in morning dress. But to appear at the Metropolitan Opera House without evening dress would never do. Happily I was able to borrow an outfit.

Though neither a musician nor a student of opera, I had visited Covent Garden Opera House in London as well as the Paris Grand Opera. During the war I made the acquaintance of the Sadlers Wells Opera Company when they came to the New Theatre in Oxford, where I now live. It was in Oxford that I began to understand a little about opera and to enjoy it despite my ignorance of western music and singing. Nearly all Chinese dramas and plays are historical and are sung on

the stage with music in a way similar to Western opera.
Conversational pieces are a comparatively late importation
into China from the West. So it is not surprising that I felt
an instinctive interest in opera. I enjoyed *The Marriage of
Figaro* and also *The Magic Flute*. In Oxford, too, I was introduced
to English light opera by the D'Oyly Carte Opera Company. My
years in England enabled me to appreciate to the full *The
Yeomen of the Guard*, while *The Mikado* tickles me every time
I think of it. One Gilbert and Sullivan light opera, *H.M.S.
Pinafore*, I remember reading somewhere, caused a furore in
America when it was produced on Fifth Avenue in 1879. The
Metropolitan Opera House was not in existence then. Sir
Arthur Sullivan wrote about his experiences as follows:

"It is hardly worth while mentioning it now, perhaps, as American
views on the subject have changed so completely, but as an instance
of what I mean, I remember that, on one occasion, having accepted
an invitation to dine one night at one of the best houses in New
York, there was one vacant chair. It should have been occupied
by a woman who was noted for her good looks and her good social
position. I afterwards discovered that her husband had prevailed
upon her not to dine with us, as there was a distinguished professor
of Music with us. He thought it was so curious that she should be
asked to sit down to the same table with a musician! If I remember
rightly, the husband was a prosperous watchmaker in the Broadway.
    "Music in America in '79 was in a very backward state in
many important respects. When I went there in '85 a great change
had taken place, and everywhere much consideration was shown
to music—and to musicians."

How much more change has taken place since then!
Thousands of girls will sit all night to catch a glimpse of Frank
Sinatra on the stage of the Paramount Theatre, and certainly
no girl would refuse to sit down at the same table with the
composer of 'Oklahoma' while it was successfully running on
Broadway.

I am not in a position to refer to the history of American
music or that of the Metropolitan Opera House; nor can I say
anything about New York opera in general. I went to the
Metropolitan Opera House as *the thing to see* and I duly saw
it. It reminded me of the opera houses in Paris and London,
though I think it has more boxes. My friend pointed out various
celebrities to me as had my friends in London before the war.
Moving my head round in a half circle and then turning back

again I got a peculiar angle of vision such as has often been depicted by ultra-modern artists. The auditorium was so brilliantly lit with an indescribable array of lights, that my eyes began to play me tricks, and were still further dazzled by the jewels. After I had gazed round for a while all the audience appeared to me to lose eyes, nose, lips, and ears, so that black jackets seemed to be set off only by a single line of white head and gleaming white shirt front; while alternately there was the long white line of a woman's figure, the neck appearing elongated above white shoulders. When the lights were dimmed, these black and white lines became more distinct. I could see the white lines made by the women in the audience moving slightly from time to time, but curiously enough those which represented the males did not move at all. This experience helped me to understand some modern paintings. I might have had a similar experience in London or Paris, but the Metropolitan Opera House being larger gives the effect more clearly. Also the evening dress rule for theatres and the opera was relaxed in London in wartime and I doubt if even yet the full splendour has reappeared.

During the singing, the house was most appreciatively silent. Not a cough or sneeze broke the spell. I do not mean to imply that a London audience would be less appreciative, but London weather may be responsible for some unavoidable interruptions. However, I did hear a whisper here and there, which was the more perceptible in the otherwise profound silence.

My companion and I moved out with everyone else during the interval, or 'intermission' as it is called in New York. I was taken to look round the lobby and the exterior of the boxes. Then we managed to enter a packed bar for a drink. There were one or two cameramen trying to photograph society people with flash lights; they seemed to have no difficulty in penetrating the throng. I was told that had it been the opening night of the season the jam in this bar would have been much greater and that there would have been many more pressmen and cameramen about. In the bar and the lobby was the best dress parade I ever saw. I may have seen similar dresses in the windows along Fifth Avenue, but here they were on the right figures and enhanced by jewels. There were dresses of every colour, and personally I preferred those of a single colour to the mixed, fussy patterns, though a lot depends on the figure! I must admit that I did not realise there could be so many types of figure nor so many good-looking people in the world. A beautiful dress is a necessity for a beautiful face and figure and vice versa. As a Chinese artist, I have been asked now and then if I did not find Western women beautiful. To this I have found it difficult to give a straightforward reply, as I feel that there is a sort of preconception about Chinese women behind the question. So I have generally replied: "Why not?". The important factor of age is often difficult to discern. In the Metropolitan Opera House I was more than once deceived by a back view, because the wonderful soft voice revealed no hint of age.

I was not only dazzled by the women's dresses and jewels, but also by their talk and gestures, not to mention their manner of smoking and eating. One woman asked her escort to pass along a meat sandwich, which disappeared in a flash; another tilted her face to the ceiling after her cigarette had been lit without realising that her long hair was dipping into someone's glass behind her; several were talking, whispering or joking to each other, apparently unconcerned with the opera. Though the men wore their black and white uniform, they revealed their characters as they talked and laughed. One was doubled up with laughter and just could not straighten out again. Almost every man had a big cigar, while to my surprise I saw one delicately taking snuff. The whole scene seemed typical of New York society yet was at the same time familiar to me, for in many ways it reminded me of Sheridan's play *The School for Scandal.* I had no reason to suppose that this audience's talk was scandalous, but here were characters easily identifiable as Lady Sneerwell, Mrs. Candour, Lady Teazle; Maria too. Lady Teazle said: "My extravagance! I'm sure I'm not more extravagant than a woman of fashion ought to be." What more appropriate comment could there

be on the women in the Metropolitan Opera House? The man taking snuff might have been Mr. Snake, who was equally good at spreading scandal and truth, as when he spoke to Lady Sneerwell for the last time: "I beg your ladyship ten thousand pardons: you paid me extremely liberally for the lie in question; but I unfortunately have been offered double to speak the truth." I saw Sheridan's play revived in London, with gorgeous costumes, only a few years ago, and could well imagine that leisurely eighteenth-century life, full of gossip about fashions, drinks and minor grievances, from which present-day London seems so very remote. That sort of life seems to exist today only during the 'intermission' at the Metropolitan Opera House!

I did not manage to see many plays during my stay in New York, but three have imprinted themselves on my mind: *Life with Father, Hamlet* and *Lute Song.* Curiously enough these three plays represent three different nations with which I am happily connected. They are respectively a comedy, a tragedy and a morality play.

Life with Father had already had a long run before my arrival. I was urged to see it because 'it's just too funny'. So I went along one evening.

I much admired the actress who played Mother and who remained calm and charming in the face of all her husband's tantrums. The actor who played Father was excellent too, and the part must have been very strenuous, with so much shouting. I wondered whether the play would be equally successful in another country, where the actors would not have the same American accent. I enjoyed hearing the New York audience laughing, as it were at themselves, and was very glad to have seen this play.

It was by a mere chance that I saw *Hamlet.* I learnt that Dr. Hu Shih had not yet left New York to take up his new appointment at Peking University, so I rang him up and he answered in a very friendly fashion, saying that he had some real good tea left from pre-Pearl Harbour days and that I must drink a cup with him that day. On arrival I found his apartment filled with huge boxes of books awaiting shipment to China. Dr. Hu was very busy working on a book himself and was surrounded by stacks of volumes on his desk and chairs. He gave me a copy of his essay on a new discovery in the Chinese classics, and showed me a bust of himself and a portrait, both by American artists.

Later several guests arrived, among them Mr. Arthur Walworth, author of *Black Ships off Japan* and *Cape Breton: Isle of Romance*. Our talk soon centred on the play '*Lute Song*', adapted from an old Chinese play, which was running in New York with apparent success. After tea and talk, Mr. Walworth suggested that I might like to go and see it with him. I appreciated his kind invitation and accepted at once. First he took me to dinner at the Yale Club, where he was staying. He is a Yale man and we talked about the branch of Yale University which was established in Changsha, China, many years ago. I noticed a few Chinese paintings on the wall in the dining room and many porcelain vases on the tables. There was a prevailing atmosphere of prosperity. Mr. Walworth commented that in the big clubs in London there were mostly white-headed old men but that it was not so here. Afterwards he took me to see another dining room where ladies could be invited as guests. It interested me very much to learn that it was not only English clubmen who tried to enjoy a little rest in their clubs by inventing a rule to restrict the admission of women. Then we looked round the club library and peeped through a window on a much higher storey for a view of the lights of the skyscrapers.

All attempts to get tickets for the play having failed, Mr. Walworth took me to see *Hamlet* instead. He thought I might be interested to see this New York production by Maurice Evans, who also took the leading part. Many English actors have made names for themselves as Hamlet, and I have learnt of these through visits to the Shakespeare Museum at Stratford-on-Avon. Having made no special study of English drama, I can make comparisons between one Hamlet and another only from my own limited experience, but three have left distinctive impressions in my mind, those of John Gielgud, Laurence Olivier and Robert Helpmann. The last, with whom I had a happy connection over the production of his ballet '*The Birds*', was the first ballet dancer ever to appear as Hamlet on the London stage. Maurice Evans seemed to me to play the part remarkably well. The production was having a well-deserved long run. I learnt that Maurice Evans first produced the play when he was in the American services stationed in Britain. It was a great success with his own unit and was subsequently shown to other American units with equally good results. So he put it on in New York just after the war ended. The cast consisted mostly of the original players who had been in the services with him and had first helped him to produce the play. There were a number of innovations in the production. I noticed particularly the long army overcoats and Wellington boots and rather unconventional set. To my amusement, my limited knowledge of English helped me to detect the various degrees of American accent among the performers. Except for Maurice Evans, this English play wore a huge and beautifully made American cloak. From the great applause the play received I think I can say that New York playgoers are Shakespeare enthusiasts. I wondered what the results would have been if a company of my fellow-countrymen had put on an English production of *Hamlet* on the Shanghai stage. Mr. Walworth noticed that I had enjoyed the show. I expressed my thanks by toasting him in a glass of ginger-beer in a small bar nearby when we came out of the theatre.

One day I received a telephone message from Dr. Wei Tao-ming, who had come to deliver a lecture to a New York society and asked me if I would care to see the Chinese play, *Lute Song*, with him. I accepted. I had a dinner engagement with some other compatriots that evening but they were kind enough to let me leave early. My host had invited two other guests: Lau Sha, author of the best seller *Rickshaw Boy*, and Tsao Yü, one of China's leading contemporary dramatists. *Lute Song* is adapted from an old Chinese play called Pi-Pa-Chi, which tells the story of a young couple's life. The young man is newly married to a beautiful wife, but is reluctant to leave his aged parents to go to the capital for the imperial examination which would qualify him for his future career. The wife encourages him to go, vowing to do all she can to look after his parents for him until his return. After he has gone, calamity befalls his home. There is a great drought in the district and everyone is hunger-stricken. The wife manages to get a little rice for the aged parents and eats some of the husks herself. She gets a little more from the famine-relief officer but is robbed by other hungry people. Eventually the parents die of starvation. The wife sells some of her long hair to pay for their burial. Then she paints portraits of the old couple, takes the lute, and goes to the capital in search of her husband, of whom she has had no news since he went away. In the meantime, the young man comes first in the examination, is forced to marry a princess and is prevented either from going home or sending any message. His love for his first wife never lessens and the princess understands but is powerless to resist her obstinate father's will. Eventually the wife meets her husband in a Buddhist Temple on a thanksgiving festival day. They are happily reunited through the good nature and help of the princess.

It is a morality play, and most of our old plays are written more or less to the same pattern with a moral about filial piety and faithfulness. This may be the reason why Chinese drama has not been so well developed as in the West, where drama aims rather to portray real life than to point a moral. There is very little plot in the play. Its chief merit lies in its beautifully written verses, which were originally meant to be sung and cannot really be translated into English. However, the American adapter has made an agreeable version of *Lute Song* for the New York stage. Many parts have been omitted and others added. All who took part acted very well, except that the heroine's manner might have been a little less stiff and both her facial expression and that of the hero might have been livelier. No doubt they were trying to be Chinese! I think there are three reasons for the play's run in New York: first its Chinese theme; second the adapter's clever arrangement of some Chinese tune into a song which begins 'Mountain high, Valley low, . . .'' and which sounded agreeable not only to Chinese ears but also to a western audience; third the décor and costumes by Robert Edmond Jones. Though rather a mixture, the colourful Indian costumes for the deities in the Chinese Buddhist Temple blended very well with the costumes in the procession, which were based on Chinese paintings of the Han and T'ang periods. The grandeur and glamour of the setting obviously appealed to the taste of the audience, who applauded loudly. Many were humming the song as they went out. What impressed me most were the expressions on the faces of the two actors who portrayed the Prince, the obstinate father-in-law, and the Imperial Chamberlain; their eyes were hooded all the time, even when they were walking about. Their actions reminded me of *The Mikado*.

My companions had left their coats and hats in their car,

so they got out without effort. But I had to wait in a long queue for my coat and hat, and while doing so I heard much gossip about the play, mostly favourable. Soon I was bombarded with questions. After I had said that it was a fine production and that I had enjoyed the song and the stage designs, I was put in my place by an elderly lady in a white fur coat "He is a young Chinaman and does not know what a Chinese theatre is like," said she. "I lived in Peking for more than thirty years and have seen many Chinese plays in the theatres there. While the play was on, street-pedlars came in to sell their wares, and the audience ate, talked and made all kinds of noises. Masses of melon seed pods were scattered about and hot towels were thrown in the air. Oh, you should have seen it. That is what a real Chinese theatre is like. This is not a Chinese play. . . ." She seemed to have an endless amount to say. Everyone listed to her patiently. Eventually I managed to interrupt with: "Isn't it too much to expect the audience here to be all Chinese?" There was a roar of laughter. *Lute Song* is not a Chinese play. It is an American play on a Chinese theme, just as Fitzgerald's *Rubaiyat* is an English poem on a Persian theme. Neither is strictly a translation; but who—except the lady in the white fur coat—minds about that?.

Night club

XVII

IN CHINATOWN

CHINATOWN is a name more familiar than that of China herself. People who have neither been to China nor interested themselves much in her generally have only a vague idea of her. But any reference to 'Chinatown' seems to strike a chord at once. Here I offer my thanks to all those writers, playwrights, composers and sightseers who have helped to popularise the idea of Chinatown, though my compatriots, the permanent residents of the districts, have of course been the chief cause of their fame. How the name came into being I am uncertain. It is said that when eighty or more years ago Chinese labourers were recruited from Canton for railroad work by Charles Crocker, at that time one of the leading figures of the Central Pacific Railroad Company, they lived together in San Francisco and called the place 'T'ang Jen Chieh' or 'The Street of the People of T'ang'. The T'ang dynasty (A.D. 618-906) is considered the golden period in China's long history and the Chinese are proud to call themselves 'The People of T'ang'. The translation of T'ang Jen Chieh may perhaps be the origin of 'Chinatown'. No other nation in the world has its name prefixed to the word 'town' in this way. I think every Chinese regards it as an honour.

Long before I left my country, I heard that the San Francisco Chinatown was the largest in the world and the one in New York the next largest, but I did not imagine that any place called 'Chinatown' would be of interest to tourists, until I arrived in London. Then I learnt that there was a 'Chinatown' there, in the East End, better known as Limehouse. I was taken for a meal to one of the small Chinese restaurants there. The food seemed to me particularly good after a whole month of European food on a not very notable ocean steamer. Later I heard of people going there on sightseeing expeditions and I noticed a glint of interest in people's eyes when 'Chinatown' or 'Limehouse' was mentioned. I was astonished. Pennyfield, the street in Limehouse where most of the Chinese seamen and laundrymen are located, cannot be adequately described in any of the established architectural terms. I saw Chinese—mostly seamen weary after long, rough voyages—standing idly in small weather-beaten doorways in the otherwise deserted street, their complexions in harmony with the dull grey sky of London. During the Second World War Limehouse was

Tour of Chinatown

badly shattered by bombs, being uncomfortably close to the docks. Directly after the war Americans, including film stars, who came to London on visits, were heard to lament the changed face of Limehouse, as they found it no longer the place they remembered. I had no idea what picture they had in mind until I saw 'Limehouse Blues' in the film *Ziegfeld Follies*. The colour scheme of this part of the film was interesting and I marvelled at the inventiveness of the script writer, composer and director. I saw the film in New York and then I understood why Americans had been disappointed in the real Limehouse. The place never had much colour or drama. 'Limehouse Blues' is a wild romanticism of a not at all cheerful reality.

Being Chinese I made a point of visiting the world's second largest Chinatown. On this occasion too I went first of all for a Chinese meal. The dishes tasted even better than those I had had in Limehouse, both because I had by then been away from China for many years instead of only a few months and because war-time restrictions limited all tasty food. There is every reason for the food in New York's China-town to be good, for the ingredients of almost every Chinese dish are available in quantity and quality. The sight of many familiar but long-forgotten dishes made me behave in a way which would have surprised my English friends. My animal nature gained the upper hand for the time being. At the outset all I knew of Chinatown was the names of a number of restaurants. There is little unusual in its streets except for some shop-signs in Chinese characters and some little Chinese curios in shop windows. Only a tiny bower-like structure on the top of one building is at all distinctive, and that is easily overlooked. Nevertheless the many Chinese faces made me feel at home. The streets were always crowded with traffic and people, most of them my compatriots, who, I was pleased to notice, looked well-dressed, prosperous and happily em-ployed, unlike those weary seamen in Pennyfield.

Window-gazing is not a habit of mine, but I found it difficult to pass some of the windows in Chinatown: not those displaying *objets d'art* and curios, but those offering Chinese vegetables, such as sweet cabbage, silkstring-like melon, huge pumpkins, red pepper, and fresh ginger, as well as fruits such as dragon's eye, lichih, lotus-seeds, and figs. I learnt with pleasure that most of them were grown in the United States, where the climate is similar to that of South China; I had not seen such things since leaving China. They convinced me that I could get a more genuine Chinese meal in Chinatown than in other parts of New York, though they were probably also supplied to Chinese restaurants elsewhere. So, like an obstinate child, I used to go there whenever I could, which was not as often as I should have liked because of that most troublesome piece of paper, the American dollar. Sometimes I was reminded of the article *On Being Hard Up* by Jerome K. Jerome, which concludes:

"There are degrees in being hard up. We are all hard up, more or less, most of us more. Some are hard up for a thousand pounds; some for a shilling. Just at this moment I am hard up myself for a fiver. I only want it for a day or two. I should be certain of paying it back within a week at the outside, and if any lady or gentleman among my readers would kindly lend it to me, I should be very much obliged indeed. They could send it to me under cover to Messrs. Field & Tuer, only, in such case, please let the envelope be carefully sealed. I would give you my I O U as security."

Jerome was once hard up for a fiver in London, and I for two dollars in New York's Chinatown. He only wanted the fiver for a day or two; I only wanted my two dollars for an hour, so that I could go into a restaurant on Mott Street for a special dish called Kai-yiu-yu, 'Chicken-broth fried fish', to which I had been introduced a few days previously. I had been hard up many a time before, but the lack of funds at this particular moment seemed more bitter to me than on any of the previous occasions.

Each time I was in Chinatown, I met groups of people being conducted round the streets. They had not come to taste Chinese food but to listen attentively to what the guide said. I was reminded of those tourists and sightseers who are so common a sight in London, Windsor, Oxford, Edinburgh and many other places in the British Isles.

A Syrian Restaurant in Washington Street

I have always admired people willing to load their memories with dates and names when they themselves are neither historians nor archaeologists. I had not imagined that there would be similar conducted tours in New York, but I found it to be a big business, as well-organised as any other in New York, with Chinatown as one of the chief places of pilgrimage. I had often noticed men in Times Square, wearing a uniform with 'Chinatown' or 'Chinatown Guide' on their caps, and shouting: "See Chinatown" or "Chinatown tour here". Presumably there are several companies that run these tours, for all the men did not wear the same cap. I suppose there are always tales to tell about a place, no matter whether its past be long or short. Of course, relics of the early Indians and the Dutch settlers are abundant in New York, and these are of great interest. But I wondered why Chinatown should be singled out for inspection. If it were for exotic flavour or foreign customs, then surely the Syrian, Spanish and Slav quarters should be equally popular.

In the hope of discovering the particular attraction of Chinatown I decided to take one of these tours. A guide in Times Square persuaded me to join his party and gave me a paper of directions. In England I had noticed that if I entered a curio shop containing Chinese objects the shopkeeper often seemed embarrassed at showing them to a Chinese. But this guide seemed indifferent to my nationality, I suppose because I was paying the same for the tour as anybody else; or else because he thought that I had been born in the United States and so would have no idea what Chinatown was like. Perhaps he did not even look at me sufficiently to notice the oriental shape of my face, for he ceaselessly shouted the attractions of his tour. I was unable to catch his words, but he must have specially trained his voice to be heard above the general uproar of Times Square.

There were a number of different tours, one starting Downtown, another Uptown, one including Bowery, another Harlem; nearly all included Chinatown, which explained why so many guides had that name on their caps. I chose a tour of Chinatown only. I was waved towards a group of people, none of whom took any heed of me. Perhaps I was a little over sensitive about my nationality, but I feared that my presence might prevent the guide from speaking freely and giving the other visitors their full dollar's worth. I quickly realised, however, that the guide was one of the most straightforward fellows I had ever met. One need hardly ever consider others so long as one expresses one's true feelings. Personally I would shake hands with anyone who claims that 'standing on ceremony' is simply a waste of time.

There were more women than men in our group. It took me no time to learn that one came from Texas, one from Ohio, one from Florida and one elderly lady from California, where she had lived both in San Francisco and Los Angeles. At first

I could not see her face as she was standing a few rows ahead of me, but her soft, lively voice and accent charmed my ears. She did not need to be asked if she had ever been to San Francisco's Chinatown, for she explained at once that she wanted to compare it with New York's. She had come to New York to visit her daughter, who was employed in some shop on Fifth Avenue . . . In a few minutes I knew her whole family history. "Of course", she raised her voice and slanted her head towards a lady near her, "Chinatown in San Francisco is the real thing. I can tell you—that's the real thing." Anyone who showed signs of listening attentively became a 'Dearie' to her. "Oh, oh, oh," she continued, laughing with her head thrown back and her face towards the sky, or rather the top of the Times Building, "I tell you: those clever *Chinks* can really *make* and *do* some *incredible* things." She explained further that my clever compatriots could produce wonderful ivory carvings, colourful porcelains, beautiful embroideries as well as many other *incredible* things the names of which I could not catch.

As she began to relate legends about Chinese carved ivory or porcelain figures and figurines, we entered a coach in which no one could hear what anyone else was saying. We were set down in Chatham Square. The guide took us into the shop of the Tien Sang Company, Number One Doyers Street. Four young ladies with eyes and noses like mine, but with highly coloured lips and hair permed in the prevailing New York fashion, stood up to receive the visitors. The guide began his patter. Years ago, on the site of this popular Chinese shop, there had stood a notorious water-front dive known as '*Callahan's Saloon*', where wharf rats waylaid drunken sailors and shanghaied them to the skippers who paid the highest prices. After the sailors had been relieved of their valuables they were dragged through a trapdoor at the side of the saloon, and down into a dungeon-like cellar which led to an exit on Chatham Square. The original trapdoor is still in existence and was shown to us in the basement. There is a similar door in Brodie's Close, Edinburgh, where the original of R. L. Stevenson's character 'Jekyll and Hyde' once lived. My fellow tourists busied themselves hilariously with the objects on display; some of them bought things. "Yes, they are all very nice, but I have seen nicer ones in Chinatown in San Francisco."

The Upper Hudson River near Newburgh

That soft, lively voice from the Los Angeles lady always reached me above the loud accents of the guide. She was now explaining the significance of a figure in white porcelain. It was Kuan Yin, the Chinese Goddess of Mercy, she said. But in this representation Kuan Yin had a little baby on her right knee and had a special name 'Presenting-baby Goddess of Mercy' (I supposed it was 'Sung Tzū Kuan Yin' in Chinese). "If a Chinese woman has no babies and longs for one," she continued—" and they do all want to have babies, particularly

Explanations inside a Chinese Shop

sons, for they drown their daughters—she buys an idol like this, believing that a baby will then be presented to her by the Goddess of Mercy. The babyless woman takes this idol to bed and worships it and prays in front of it. I mean of course a huge curtained Chinese bed. The funny thing is that they can have small chairs and tea-services in their beds as well. I suppose, when a woman prays for a baby, her husband joins her in worship and prayer, too . . . then they would drink tea. . . ." She could not stop laughing and in the end she remarked chokingly; "You know . . . you know . . . afterwards they do *have* babies. . . ." When someone actually set about buying this Presenting-baby Goddess of Mercy, I expected

o

the manager of the Company to come out and thank the Los Angeles lady for her skilful saleswomanship; but he didn't.

As we moved on quickly from place to place the guide kept shouting his descriptions. The lady had gone on from her Kuan Yin story to some other tales. For a time I heard neither her voice nor the guide's as my mind was occupied with the idea of the Presenting-baby Goddess of Mercy, which was entirely new to me. I decided that the lady must have been somewhere in China where I have not yet been, for it is a very big country, and its customs differ from place to place. Other-

"Murder! murder, right here!"

wise I should surely have heard this interesting story before. I thought of the many masterpieces representing the Madonna and Child and wondered if any of my compatriots had ever ventured to give a new interpretation to one of them. The story about the Chinese drowning their daughters I have heard many times, since I left my country. Adam and Eve, I believe, never visited China so I really don't know where we Chinese came from. If the daughters of our remote ancestors were all drowned, we must have leaned heavily on the Goddess of Mercy. And as the population of China today is over four hundred millions, she must have been kept busy!

A horrified squeal from one of the group and shivers from the rest roused me from my thoughts. The guide was describing a murder in Pell Street which happened some years before. The case involved two 'Chinks' who were killed in a fight between two groups of 'Chinks'. I wished I could hear the story, but the guide rolled it off his tongue as quickly as a football match commentator. Then he jumped to some other murder cases full of names and dates and unbelievable motives, heightening the effect of his words by dramatic gestures. In England guides are fond of telling of murders among kings and noblemen in romantic or historical settings: here it was just murders. I suppose the site makes a difference!

Presently we entered a Chinese Temple and then a Joss House. Fifteen years ago I should not have minded the fumes of incense in the temple; now I found them a little over-powering. They certainly made the place more mysterious. Truly this was an uncommon world right in the middle of New York. I have been to many a Buddhist monastery and Taoist temple in China, but to find this temple on Mott Street was quite unexpected. Our guide pointed out the elaborate wood carvings, many in the form of shrines. "The most elaborate shrine," he said, "depicts the Confucianist idea of the great beyond and the earth beneath. This other is to encourage kind thoughts for people of the Western World. The small shrine by itself is dedicated to the dead: the eternal light in the centre burns to guide the departed spirits through the dark regions to the celestial realm beyond." This was all outside my knowledge of Confucius. It was also news to me that the big statue of Buddha on a pedestal in the centre of the room was the largest Buddha outside China.

Next we were guided to a portrait of China's great statesman Li Hung Chang, the man who introduced *Chop Suey* to America. What had Li to do with this temple? Perhaps to be an object of worship for caterers. The wall to the left of the giant Buddha was lined with miniature *Household Gods*, including the Kitchen God, who, it was explained, makes an annual report upon a household under his protection, causing Chinamen to put a little candy in his mouth to incline his heart towards a favour-able report. This may explain why we Chinese eat so much less candy ourselves than people in the West!

We moved to the second room, on one side of which was a huge embroidered umbrella with red silk tassels and gold lace fringes such as can often be seen in Chinese temples. It is a gift from worshippers and is carried in festival processions. Here it was described as a *Wedding Canopy*, for holding over the heads of those making betrothal vows. How that could be when, according to old Chinese custom, bride and bridegroom met for the first time on their wedding day I do not know! I was, however, the only member of the party who was bothered by this. The rest were fascinated by the embroidery and the legends attached to the designs, and also, of course, by the idea of making a vow beneath such an exquisite canopy. "They don't vow in words", said the Los Angeles lady, "but just give each other a good kiss where nobody can see them at it." There were giggles. I smiled myself. There were many other objects such as staffs made of teakwood carved with dragon designs, and an old seven-storeyed bronze pagoda.

The Joss House gave me the biggest surprise. We marched into it through a narrow passage behind the *smallest* Post Office in New York, eight feet wide and ten feet long and run by an elderly compatriot who was said to be the *only* Chinese Postmaster in New York City. He handles all the mail for the residents of Chinatown. But we only saw a young girl attending to the business. In the Joss House there were more things new to me, and the incense was still heavier. An elaborately engraved and gilded *Shrine of Good Fortune* was pointed out to us, said to have taken three generations to carve. Several objects are placed in front of it. I was unable to identify the figure inside it, for the guide was now drawing our attention to a fragile girl of Chinese appearance who was emerging slowly and gracefully from behind a silk hanging. She wore a long skirt of Chinese fashion made of embroidered silk. After burning some incense, she stood by the shrine and waited to serve. The guide asked if any one wanted his or her fortune told or to make a decision regarding an undertaking. To my surprise, someone did step forward. He was told to kneel on a rug and kowtow before the shrine. The girl then gave him two small pieces of wood which fitted together in the form of a peach, and these he had to throw on to the rug. The guide meanwhile, was busy explaining the procedure. I was amused to hear him call these small pieces of wood the *Lips of Confucius*. What an interesting name, at once strange and appropriate, and what an ingenious invention! I felt that the Chinese in China should know of it. "If both lips fall with the flat side down", continued the guide, "or one up and one down, you should go through with your undertaking. If both lips fall face up it is an unfavourable sign and you should wait three months before seeking advice again." I could not see how the pieces fell on this occasion. The advice-seeker was told to rise and invited to pick a bamboo strip out of a 'fortune telling' box. According to the number on the strip, a pink paper with a verse printed in Chinese characters was chosen to tell the fortune. This particular verse was translated by the girl as follows:—"You will be getting married in three months' time and your domestic affairs will not hinder you from receiving a large amount of money from your newly-deceased uncle, though he has not approved of the wife you picked for yourself."

After this satisfactory prophecy we saw the *Burning Light of Confucius, The Three Wise Monkeys* cast in bronze, and also *The Shrine of Heaven, Earth and Hell* carved out of darkly stained teakwood and supposed to be very old. As we went out of the Joss House, the guide began again: "There is no regular service here, no congregation; each individual drops in when he feels so inclined, usually to consult the spirit of Confucius for advice in daily affairs."

At the end of Pell Street there is a Chinese theatre beneath the metal bridge of the elevated railway. Its exterior and all the posters were in Chinese, with photographs and the names of the Chinese actors and actresses, as in some old street in Canton. It was not open and all we could see were rows of chairs and an empty stage. Nevertheless, the guide had a lot to say, with more local colour than ever. I did not take in what he was saying, for my mind was much too full of Confucius.

The guide went on with the party, but I detached myself. I felt I had had my money's worth. There is a Chinese proverb: 'If you don't go into the tiger's cave, how can you get the cub?' I had got what I wanted by joining this tour, and can understand why there are always people eager to pay Chinatown a visit. But being a Chinese myself, I think I ought to mention that in fact Confucius did not talk about ghosts and gods, nor have the Chinese ever been known to seek advice from his spirit. Confucius has been honoured and revered since the first day of the Han dynasty (202 B.C.-A.D. 219) for his thoughts and teachings on the right conduct of man, but he has never been worshipped as a religious leader and it is odd that he should have been made into one by overseas Chinese.

Confucianism is humanism or pure ethics. When asked about death Confucius replied: "I don't know life yet: how can I know death?" This clearly shows, I think, that he never intended to exercise any 'religious' influence. So such terms as *The Burning Light of Confucius* and *The Lips of Confucius* sounded comical to me. Such hocus pocus is not connected only with Confucius' name but also with that of Buddha and the House-hold Gods, whose origins are unknown to many Chinese. The reason for this confusion is that China has never had a state religion. If Confucius had set up a religion he would have prescribed ceremonies, services, rules and prayers as in the other great religions of the world. No established system of religion can admit of wild confusion over objects in its churches or temples, yet here was this misleading display, quite seriously presented. Who can say that we Chinese have no sense of showmanship? I think we can also claim a strong sense of humour!

I talked to a number of friends about this tourist business in Chinatown. Very few knew much of it and most of them laughed at the idea of people being willing to pay to be taken for a walk through the streets. I doubt if any of the New York Chinese who do not belong to Chinatown have ever gone inside the Chinese temple or the Joss House or even know of their existence. They are run entirely commercially. It is interesting to know that a living can be made out of others' ignorance.

The main obstacle to mutual understanding between peoples is, I think, language. The first of my compatriots who left their fatherland for the West did not acquire much know-ledge of the language of their new country. They were wholly occupied in physical activities. As they lived according to their native customs, but could not talk about or explain these, they naturally aroused curiosity. If they had been able to explain themselves, China and the Chinese might have been spared many a misinterpretation.

Though I have tried my best to learn the English language it still presents difficulties to me. In New York I was often bewildered. I have not been able to find in either the Oxford or the Webster dictionary, words such as 'Yer,' 'wus', 'hisself', 'gals', 'jest', and many others. Anna Virginia Culbertson's diction causes me the most trouble. For example: 'You bin knowin' I is a slow man, an' if I kain't git some help, 1 hatter say good-bye by'ud and' wattles.' Or: 'We lef' dat fer you, dat ain' ow' bizness, but we done fix him up so't you kin do de ketchin' yo' se'f.' There is also Damon Runyon's language. My friend Eric Underwood once explained it to me by omitting nearly all the vowels thus:—'F-U-N-E-M? S-V-F-M. F-U-N-E-X S-V-F-X. L-F-M-N-X.' The translation ran: 'Have you any ham? Yes, we have ham. Have you any eggs? Yes, we have eggs. Let's have ham and eggs.' Well, even in a widely-spoken language such as English there are barriers. How can anyone be expected to penetrate the difficulties of Chinese? It is quite understandable that most of those who write about China do not know the language.

After lunch I went for an independent stroll along other streets in Chinatown. I noticed on a building in Pearl Street a sign-board bearing the words Hua-Chung-hui, 'Chinese Community Club', and I stepped in. Nobody questioned me and I went upstairs, where I found a spacious room neatly furnished and decorated with Chinese carvings and pictures. Some youngsters there, three boys and two girls, jumped up and dashed into another room to play table-tennis. The noise of joyful laughter was very agreeable. While I was looking round, all the lights were suddenly turned on, and a well-dressed young man entered and announced himself as the Secretary of the club. We exchanged names. He gave his as Li Pei-ching or William Lee. I appreciated his friendly smile and warm welcome. He explained that the place used to be a Chinese Bowling Club and had changed to its present name only a year or so ago. There are about 35,000 Chinese in Greater New York City, 4,000 of them in Chinatown. This Club was organised for three purposes: first, to keep youngsters out of mischief by providing them with a place for amusement; secondly, to achieve unity among different Chinese groups within Chinatown; thirdly, to make a truly representative centre in the City. In order to check delinquency, the club runs a baseball team, a basket-ball team and a football team, providing the necessary equipment. Smiling with pride, Lee said that Chinatown's basket-ball team was the best in New York City, and showed me a photograph taken after its victory at Madison Square Garden on March 17, 1945. Another photograph showed the Chinese athletic team which won the 1945 championship of Greater New York City. In the adjoining

Girl Guides' room was a photograph of the Chinese Union in the American Women's Voluntary Services. More people came in and Mr. Lee had to attend to them. I was glad of the temporary interruption, for I did not want to appear to be a journalist or news-hound. I admired the work done by this Club and Mr. Lee's energy and efficiency, and particularly the public spirit of the community in contributing money for the work. I wondered if any of the Chinatown tours had ever

A game of Chess

come to see this Club! Probably not, as there was nothing strange or curious about it.

I made a rough sketch of two people who were sitting round a table playing chess, and two watching, with some carved panels for background. Lee was very helpful in keeping everyone occupied so that they took no notice of what I was doing. When I had finished, I had another chat with Lee. Our subject was then about marriage. He admitted that there was some difficulty about wives among the Chinese community for there were four boys to every girl. The trouble was that very few Chinese girls could enter the country and very few of the boys were willing to choose someone of another race for a life-partner. He told me about an American boy who was adopted by a Chinese woman when he was very young, refused to consider himself an American and married a Chinese girl, thus increasing the shortage for Chinese boys.

Lee expressed a high regard for this young fellow, whom Chinatown much respected for loving his foster-mother so greatly. Filial piety is one of the principles of Confucian teaching and nothing wins more respect among Chinese. No doubt this Chinese mother did all she could for the boy and her maternal love received its due reward.

Shoe-shine and pawnshop

XVIII

IN GREENWICH VILLAGE

A VILLAGE in the center of New York City sounds like a joke. When I heard of it a few days after my arrival, it reminded me of the time when, shortly after my arrival in England some fifteen years ago, I was introduced to a gentleman as 'the hermit of London.' Buddha once remarked: "Remember, my sons, there is nothing constant but change," and I find that this is even true of the meaning of a word which, while keeping its original idea, gains new significance in particular circumstances. Experience has confirmed that a hermit can live in the heart of London and that a village does exist in the metropolis of New York.

Greenwich Village today no longer looks much like a village, but its name is a pleasant reminder of its former appearance. Van Wyck Brooks wrote in *The World of Washington Irving:*

"Bleecker Street was a blackberry-preserve, and water from the tea-water pumps was sold at a penny a gallon from door to door. New Yorkers could remember corn-fields on Nassau Street. In those days, not too remote, fishermen drew their seines on the beach at the foot of Greenwich Street, and a mill at Coenties-slip was turned by a spring, and a line of palisades at Chambers Street cut straight across the island from river to river. Everything north-ward was still open country, with farms, thickets, swamps and market-gardens and the hamlets of Greenwich, Chelsea, Yorkville and Harlem. . . . There were pretty country roads that wound about the island, through little ricky valleys, groves and copses, and both the river-banks were lined with quiet country-seats, embosomed in gardens, vines and hawthorn hedges."

That was in the early nineteenth century, in the days of Peter Cooper and Jefferson. I never learned the origin of the name 'Greenwich', which is English, whereas the first settlers in this part of the world were the Dutch. I have read somewhere that 'the Indian village located here was named Sappokanican. Except the settlement of Fort Amsterdam, Greenwich Village is the site of the oldest settlement of white people on Manhattan

Island.' I venture to wonder if there was not another name, after Sappokanican but before the English established themselves in this neighbourhood. Perhaps among the earliest English settlers were some who remembered the Naval College in London; it is not impossible, for they were certainly fond of naming the towns they built after their home towns in England.

I first visited Greenwich Village the day after my arrival in New York. An American friend of my friend Hsiao Ch'ien

Jefferson Market Court

lives there, and as he knows New York very well, I decided to seek him out and avail myself of his offer to show me round. I assumed that the village would be a suburb of the city and I began to enquire how to get there. Very few of my compatriots who have been running restaurants and other businesses in New York for years had heard of it. I walked to Fourth Street, then to Eighth and finally to Tenth Street. On the way I asked three young fellows, one after another, for directions, but not one of them could help me. I never dreamed I was already there, for there was nothing resembling a village to be seen. It was much later I learnt that Greenwich Village is a quarter like Chelsea in London where many writers and artists live. I did not become familiar with it until a month or two after my arrival; then I was to be found there more often than in any other place in New York. And first of all I must express my gratitude to Hsiao Ch'ien's American friend, Mr. William Allen, who introduced me so thoroughly to the place.

The first house we entered did not strike me as in any way unusual until I had been urged up flight after flight of stairs; then I realised the strange absence of an elevator. On the

Oyster Push-cart

fourth or fifth floor we entered a studio apartment. It was just before dusk and difficult to judge the lighting arrangements. The walls were lined and the floor piled with oil paintings and other types of art work. The colour schemes delighted me. There were three rooms, each small enough to be cosy. In the middle one stood an old-fashioned stove with a long metal stove-pipe twisting out of a window. I never saw anything of this type in any studio in Chelsea or elsewhere in London. The living rooms in English houses are built with open fire-places which form the focal point of the room. This old-fashioned stove roused a nostalgic feeling in me, for the type was introduced into China some thirty or forty years ago, and there was just such a thing in my school room, of which I grew ever fonder during my school days. Out-of-date though these stoves are in modern cities, they would still be a luxury in many remote places in China. Is it any wonder that the races of the world do not yet live together in harmony when they share the necessities of life so unequally? I do not mean that there should be a uniform life for all; that is neither possible nor desirable; but the minimum standard of living should be similar throughout the world. Mr. Allen brought my thoughts back to the present by telling me that most of the apartments and studios in Greenwich Village have stoves like this, which, if not beautiful, are convenient when one wants to make a cup of tea or coffee or to warm up a meal.

Mr. Allen knew the Village in the utmost detail. As we walked along, he continually pointed out houses and told me of the famous people, writers or artists, who had lived there. Historically, New York of course does not go back as far as London, Rome, Paris or even Peking or Nanking, yet she seems to have more notable figures, events and associations for visitors to hear of than any other city. I was overwhelmed with names and dates after only a few days' stay. But New York is essentially a show place, where everything with an historic background is catalogued and exhibited. In London, Rome and Paris there are many places obviously full of historical interest which are not *displayed* at all. The same applies to Peking and Nanking. I have lived in London long enough to have absorbed numberless stories about its buildings and sights. I doubt if there is any part of London, particularly in the center, which has no tale to tell. Yet research is still going on and will certainly produce more discoveries. The Chinese of Peking and Nanking refuse—fortunately, in my view—to bother about what happened there in the past, and few Chinese writers have found ready sale for books of what in the West is called topography. It is no wonder to me that Western visitors to Peking and Nanking should be astonished at the ignorance of the inhabitants about their great cities. I was astonished, rather, to find so many things to see and so many names and dates to remember in Greenwich Village, which, though the oldest quarter of New York, is so much younger than either Chelsea or the Latin Quarter of Paris. But I suppose there would be anecdotes of some sort even about a brand new city sprung up overnight in, say, Antarctica. I pity the next generation, who will have to remember so much more. I touched my forehead apologetically to indicate the limitations of my memory, and Mr. Allen was quick to understand my gesture. We parted with a laugh!

With another new friend, Miss Mary Elizabeth Scott, I wandered in Greenwich Village and had my attention drawn to further points of interest. Near Christopher Street I was directed to read these words on a triangular plate, about two

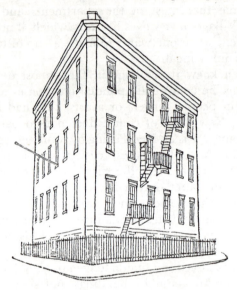

The house with one side on two streets
and two sides on one street

feet long on each side, in front of the door-step of a grocery shop:

"*Property of the Hess Estate which has never been dedicated to Public Purpose.*"

The stream of people entering and leaving the shop was so continuous that it took me some minutes to read and grasp these few words. I wondered if anyone had ever been prosecuted for infringing these rights.

The historic Northern Dispensary struck me as curious, for it is a house with two streets on one side and one street on two sides. It is built in triangular form and has red-washed walls. Nearby, Gay Street was pointed out to me as the scene of a recent murder film with the title '*Gay 13*'. My companion told me of a friend who lived at Gay 16 and who could not go back there the evening after she had seen the film. People say that films and novels are forms of entertainment, but it is not always so. I had a good look at Gay Street, which, though not gay in appearance, exudes a peaceful air like many small streets I know in London.

Londoners, I am sure, would feel as surprised as I to hear

Gay Street

that Cherry Lane Theatre, which we next approached, is the *oldest* theatre in the world still in use. Unfortunately the doors were locked. I resolved to come again, but it will have to be on my next visit to America.

As we approached Sheridan Park I saw the Sheridan Statue rising behind a hedge. A group of people was gathered outside the park near the entrance to a subway, listening to an orator. This was the first and last time during my stay in New York that I encountered the soap-box orator, so common in London. The speaker was a woman, who gave me a pamphlet bearing the words 'Unite, May Day, for Peace, Democracy,

Security.' My spirits sank at these all too familiar words, and I moved away. I recalled some words of Sir Thomas More:

> Learn one lesson hence
> Of many which whatever lives should teach:
> This lesson, that our human speech is naught,
> Our human testimony false, our fame
> And human estimation words and wind.

Have we learned them yet, I wonder?

During my years of residence in England something—probably the climate—has roused in me a longing for tea in the afternoon though this is wholly contrary to Chinese habit. But there is no tea-time in New York, and so it was perfectly understandable that we should go to Jack Delaney's Bar for drinks. The place has a queer horsey atmosphere, and my friend told me that the owner was a famous retired jockey. The bar seats were in the form of saddles, the telephone box in the shape of a horse-carriage, the lamps like those used on a carriage; there were horses' heads on the walls as well as on the floor, and a huge pair of red carriage-wheels hanging from the middle of the ceiling: everything, in fact was connected in one way or another with the horse, except the bar-tenders and the customers. I took a good look at myself in one of the many brightly polished brasses and was relieved to find that my face had not acquired a horsey shape. In recent years I have learnt to overcome my 'pussyfoot' preferences to the extent of taking small quantities of English beer and Scotch whisky. My friend now ordered a glass of rum-and-something, and suggested that I should have the same, which, she alleged, was no stronger than water. It did indeed *look* like water, but as it went down my throat I felt my face begin to burn. In the meantime a man with a bushy red beard had entered the bar. He had a hood on his head and his dress, though not particularly unusual, would not have been seen on Fifth or Park Avenue. I took him to be one of the celebrities of the Village and was enraptured with his fine beard. It reminded me of an amusing incident which occurred when I was teaching Chinese in the School of Oriental Studies at the University of London some years ago. Most of the students were employees of firms with branches in China, who wanted to know something of the language before going there. One young fellow, a Cambridge

Municipal Building in Summer Haze

graduate, was very happy at the beginning of the term but after two or three weeks became depressed. Nothing could stimulate or encourage him to get on with his work. I had him to tea in my flat and he told me that lately he had been reading some books about China and had heard stories from so-called 'Old China-Hands'. "I feel very sad," he sighed, "that I shall not be able to go to China after all, because of my red hair, which the Chinese do not like". I was astonished, for I could remember no special objection to red hair, and I tried to

Satisfied customer

convince him that he was mistaken. But he did not turn up the next term and I heard that he had left his old firm and taken a new job in Glasgow. There have been many books written about China since she came into contact with the West, but I think my readers will agree with me that no foreigner can claim to know everything about China any more than I can claim to know much about England even after fifteen years' residence. Tales concerning one corner of China are not true of another, but it is just such tales as this about red hair which may cause lasting misunderstanding. I have, for instance, often heard dog-lovers say that they will never go to China because they have read that the Chinese eat dogs, forgetting that Pekinese and Chows have been pets of the Chinese for centuries.

It is true that in Chinese temples and many old religious pictures, demons or evil spirits are painted with red hair and beards, and this may have caused such hair to seem of evil omen to illiterate country folk. But there have been Chinese whose hair and beards were not jet black and who felt proud of the novelty of possessing lighter coloured hair. There is also a story told of a Chinese man whose beard was yellow and who was in the habit of boasting to his wife what fine fellows were men with yellow beards, declaring that no one could withstand them. One evening he came home after being badly knocked about in a fight. His wife could not resist reminding him of his claims and remarked smilingly that she supposed on this occasion the other man's beard was bright red. Gazing at this fine red-bearded man in Jack Delaney's, I remembered this anecdote and started to laugh. My friend thought the rum was taking effect and I let it go at that. Before we left, a bar tender gave me four postcards showing different angles of Jack Delaney's face and my friend said that they would be posted to any part of the world free of charge if I cared to write something on them. I put the cards in my pocket, admiring the enterprise of the proprietor.

We next went along Macdougal Alley. My head was a little confused by the rum, but cleared when I was told of the protest made by the inhabitants of this alley when it was proposed to discontinue the gaslighting. Here were citizens of an ultra-modern city who yet adored old things. Gas-lighting was in fact still in use in the Alley.

Nearly all the houses were painted red, and by the doors of some were green shrubs in wooden boxes. When I stepped back a little so that I could see the pale brownish building of Number One Fifth Avenue Hotel in the background, I had an admirable colour scheme for a picture.

When we came to the Jumble Shop in the Alley, we stepped through the entrance of one accord, for we were both hungry. A small pamphlet printed in red lay on the table near the staircase where we sat. It announced the 25th anniversary of the Jumble Shop. What a bit of luck that I should have come for that! Childishly I expected a good meal for such a special occasion, and I was not disappointed. The pamphlet kept attracting my eye, until at last I picked it up to read. It contained a number of names, most of which I did not know and found difficult to pronounce. However, two had recently become familiar to me—Daniel Chester French and James Earl Fraser. I had seen French's seated figure of Lincoln in the Lincoln Memorial at Washington, D.C., a few days before, and Fraser's statue of Benjamin Franklin in Philadelphia. Fraser had a close connection with the Jumble Shop, for its main dining room was originally his studio, a converted stable, where he entertained, among others, King Albert of the Belgians and Theodore Roosevelt, and modelled 'The End of the Trail' and the 'Statue of Hamilton'. After the meal we had a look at the Louis Bouchè painted windows, and the Guy Pène du Bois murals upstairs. We also noted the old doors, the tap-room with its old tavern tables and chairs, many caricatures on the walls, and a note from Thomas Wolfe written on a page torn from his notebook. There was also an exhibition of the work of young living artists. When I came out of the shop, I felt that I had temporarily lost the character of a Chinese traveller and become an English antique hunter in a small way. Sophocles once wrote: "A true man should cherish remembrance if anywhere he reap a joy. It is kindness that still begets kindness. But whosoever suffers the memory of benefits to slip from him, that man can no more rank as noble." Though not aspiring to rank as noble, I shall not let the Jumble Shop slip from my mind.

I was in the Village again on several other occasions. I visited St. Luke's Chapel, the Mexican Gardens where Edgar Allan Poe lived, Jefferson Market and Fire Tower, and also houses along Washington Mews which are similar to those along Macdougal Alley, and on two occasions I had a meal at Chinese restaurants, 'Young China' and 'Bamboo Forest'. But the place I enjoyed most was the Balyea's Dickens Room, where Dickens had breakfasts of crumpets, marmalade and tea when he was in New York a hundred years before. Unfortunately it was only a tea shop in Dickens' time, otherwise he could have left records of his favourite dishes. He must have been a connoisseur of food judging by his mouth-watering descriptions of roast sucking pigs, with apples in their snouts; baked goose, suety plum puddings like speckled cannon balls, and cold game pies as big and round as barrel tops. But after living in England in recent years, one begins to wonder whether Dickens was not indulging his imagination.

Though many features of this Village are quite unlike England, somehow it did not feel strange. It even contains a Downing Street, in which, oddly enough, a Polish friend of mine, Mr. B. Leitgeber, occupies a flat—and actually at No. 10! When I went there for a drink with him, however, there was nobody outside the house like those policemen and sightseers

Little garden behind St. John's Church

watching the Prime Minister or other Cabinet Ministers coming to or going from No. 10 Downing Street, London.

Greenwich Village has a local paper called *The Villager*. Its sixteen pages surprised me when I thought of the meagre size of the English *national* papers in wartime and since. It records the Village happenings in detail, and I made a point of reading it to learn about current exhibitions and so on. The sculpture exhibits organized by The Village Art Center in St. John's Church Garden delighted me. Twenty-four sculptors showed their work and there were also some water-colours by a compatriot of mine who was in Shanghai at the time. I liked the co-operative spirit of the artists, who were helping each other in the arrangement and labelling of the exhibits. Presently I slipped away from the crowd to get a glimpse of the garden at the back of the church. It contained many odd little ornamental carvings which took my thoughts far from the center of the busiest city in the world.

I have only one regret about my visits to Greenwich Village and that is that I did not have the pleasure of meeting its famous Professor Seagull, whose name I thought fascinating. I heard too of another celebrity, known as Captain Whale, because, it was said, he had a pair of spouting eyes and a huge belly full of sea water or root-beer; his real name had been forgotten. As a sailor in his younger days, he had been to most parts of the world and collected many strange things. He had apparently endless tales to tell and was a good raconteur. I wanted very much to meet him and to hear if he had ever been to Canton, Shanghai or Peking and, if so, what he had to say about them. I haunted public bars in the Village but in vain, and I was eventually told that there was no such person, but that I really must meet Professor Seagull.

I had been fooled once and knew how easily one can be misled in New York, where one is never sure what will happen next. So I was rather wary about Professor Seagull. My friends and acquaintances in the Village assured me, however, that there was such a figure and that he was very much talked about. I was told his real name and many other details about him but I can only remember him as Professor Seagull because this sounded so interesting. Apparently he was a graduate of Harvard, spoke with a Harvard accent, was interested in eugenics, had done some specialised work in North Dakota, and measured thousands of heads of Indians, before coming to live in Manhattan. At first he took a job as a newspaper reporter and reviewed books, magazines and papers. Later he gave up reviewing to write a very important book of his own, which he called *An Oral History of Our Time*. He had been writing it for more than twenty years and had not yet finished it. He always carried a huge portfolio containing masses of manuscript and notes, and he read a great deal in the New York Public Library. With this background he could certainly be counted a person worth having in the Village. In addition to all this, however, his sayings, dress, manners and opinions contributed to his fame. He came from the well-to-do family of a doctor in

Massachusetts and his parents had left him some money which had rapidly disappeared. He was known to despise money. He never wore a proper suit; in winter he stuffed his shirt with newspaper. He slept on subway benches, got food and drink by reciting poems or delivering lectures or through the kindness of bartenders and friends. He managed to live in New York for weeks without a single dollar in his pocket and never appeared to worry that he was not making progress with his Oral History. Though his presence sometimes proved embarrassing at Village parties, very few took place without him, whether given by friend or enemy, and whether or not he had been invited. I found it most refreshing that such a thing should be possible in 'materialist' New York; and coming as I do from China, whose history has been adorned with such personalities, I wanted to meet him. Unfortunately, the parties I attended in the Village escaped his notice or he was occupied elsewhere.

Despite Professor Seagull's knowledge of art and letters, he has never been admitted to membership of any formal literary or artistic organization in the Village. The Raven Poetry Circle, which holds an exhibition in Washington Square each summer, considers his poems foolish, even childish. Once he was allowed to recite at the Circle one of his poems called 'My Religion' which begins "In winter I'm a Buddhist, And in summer I'm a nudist." Another time, on their nature-poetry night, he performed 'Seagull', a new type of poem without words. He simply screeched like a seagull while waving his arms up and down and hopping round the room. Presumably this imitation earned him his nickname. He is said to have spent hours watching gulls and claims to understand their language. His philosophy regarding world happenings and human entanglements consists of seagull screechings. To my mind he sounded like a figure from Taoist legend. In Confucius's Analects, one of our great sage's pupils, Kung-yeh Chang, is reported to have understood the language of birds. That was more than two thousand years ago. I wish I had known him too.

On my mentioning this regret of mine later to Paul and Stella Standard, they both exclaimed that Professor Seagull was the famous Joseph Ferdinand Gould and an acquaintance of theirs. "He is all kindness and cultivation," Paul said, "and gifted with a critical and historical sense unique in our time.

He knows only too well his own weaknesses, and can be realistic and humorous about them." I do not know why I had not mentioned him to them before. But nothing is too late for me, and now I shall look forward to meeting him through them when I next land in America.

Effect of sun on Coney Island

XIX

ON GEORGE WASHINGTON BRIDGE

IT takes time to walk across George Washington Bridge. With its approaches, it measures 12,430 feet. One needs time to think about it, too! The river span is 3,500 feet, the roadway 250 feet above the water, and it is the only bridge on the west side of Manhattan. The expanse of the Hudson River from Manhattan to the Palisades of New Jersey is not as great as the lower part of the Yangste River, but I should never have imagined it possible to span such a space with a bridge. Yet here was a bridge. The sight disturbed some deep feeling of reality in my mind. The very nature of a bridge was changed for me.

In the formative years of my boyhood a bridge was a simple affair, ranging from a bunch of tree-trunks roped together, to sturdy wooden structures elaborately ornamented with carvings. I saw stone bridges too, sometimes with only one arch, sometimes with as many as seventeen. In every case, a bridge was essentially something which *stepped* across an obstacle. George Washington Bridge cannot by any stretch of imagination be said to step across the Hudson. It spans the river in one soaring leap such as no fairytale giant could accomplish. "Not a bridge" was the thought it injected into my mind. "Something else—a new kind of structure for which a new word should be found."

I wish in no way to disparage this wonderful bridge, whose grand and simple structure is one of the great engineering achievements of the modern world. I only wish to describe its effect on me.

The bridges on the east side of Manhattan merge easily with the closely-packed buildings around them; but the arresting personality of George Washington Bridge cannot be missed from any angle from which it is in sight at all. Everything in its vicinity is dwarfed. I like it best from a good distance away; no other bridge reveals its magnitude and grandeur so well, yet so simply and even so gently, in the soft haze of distance. I had taken car-rides over it and steamer-rides under it, and it remained for me to walk across it.

One sunny afternoon near the end of May I caught an uptown bus to the beginning of the eastern approach to the bridge at 197th Street. Walking along the pavement, with cars passing to and fro in the middle, I did not feel I was on a bridge, for the roadway merged with the street in a continuous thoroughfare. Then, ahead of me, I saw an immense steel

Pattern in Steel

tower with another tower, foreshortened, behind it. Its height dizzied me and made me feel smaller than had the tallest skyscraper, though the actual height of the tower is but 635 feet, which is less than two-thirds of the Empire State Building. This was probably because I had never faced any of the skyscrapers as closely and squarely as I now faced this tower. I was the only pedestrian in sight.

About half way across the bridge, as I thought, I paused and leaned on the parapet. The great expanse of the river stretched far away to the sea. But on looking down I found that I was only just above Riverside Drive and not yet over the water at all. The highway is another gigantic creation, its twin roads designed for cars and lorries only. An endless chain of cars rolled swiftly in each direction. I had no feeling that the myriad vehicles were bound upon *different* missions. It seemed that these ribbons of cars must all be in some secret, hurrying towards some single universal bourne.

"There would be a much better view of the downtown skyscrapers if the air was clearer," said a voice behind me. The speaker was in uniform and appeared to be a member of the bridge guard. As such he would doubtless know the effect of different kinds of weather on the view. I was glad custom had not staled the sight for him.

Passing the guard's post I reached the first tower. It was all of steel, and the lowest member of the structure, seen from the inside, had the shape of the capital letter X. A notice said: 'People are warned not to throw articles of any kind from bridge, sidewalk or roadway.' If it was worth while to put up such a notice, there must sometimes be many walkers over the bridge. Peering through the X, I looked over the river bed to the horizon. Gradually the haze cleared and a number of slender, darkish vertical lines appeared in what looked like the remote distance—the faint images of the downtown sky-scrapers. Fitting so neatly into the middle of the triangular steel frame, they made a charming picture.

As I gazed round aimlessly and drowsily in the hot afternoon sun, my legs grew heavy. I had left the tower a good distance behind. The swift-running cars flashing past kept bringing me back to earth. I was not really sleepy, but in the spell of a dream. Both towers were now remote, and the buildings backing the eastern one and the rocky Palisades backing the western, were obscure. Though I knew I was walking slowly along a substantial sidewalk, I was more conscious of the hollow depth beneath. Presently there was a pause in the succession of cars and silence reigned for a moment. I suddenly felt that the reality around me—the towers, the Palisades, the buildings, even the cement-parapet and the sidewalk—had vanished, and I was standing in the air. I was in a kind of ecstasy, related in some way to my position on the bridge, for I realised that I had felt like this before when standing alone on Kew Bridge above the Thames while the thick English winter fog engulfed me. Only, there, the mutter of the Thames water running with the tide made me feel closer to the earth; the Hudson water was too far below to be perceptible to the ear.

The stream of cars beginning again behind me restored the feeling of solid matter beneath my feet and broke my dream, bringing a feeling of vague discontent. It is said that one lives and learns, and also that travel broadens the mind. But here was I, after fifteen years of travel and sight-seeing on the opposite side of the world from my home, still unable to appreciate adequately a great achievement of modern engineering. And not a great one only, but a beautiful: for I felt sure that with engineering knowledge I could have relished the beautiful economy with which the vast stresses and strains of the huge structure of Washington Bridge were maintained. But all I could do now was to recall mournfully the occasions during my youth when I had meditated on the decorative stone carvings along the parapets of ancient Chinese bridges and enjoyed the aesthetic skill with which those bridges had been sited. In the West, bridges are placed where it is most practical and convenient to place them. Old Chinese bridges were placed where they would look most effective in the landscape, or where, standing on them, the traveller would get the most beautiful views. It was the *individual* who, I was brought up to think, was the unit to be provided for. We did not concern ourselves with 'streams of traffic', 'numbers of passengers per hour', and such-like abstractions. Standing on the George Washington Bridge I felt invisible, as if the bridge had never been intended for me or any single soul. Modern ideologies generally affect me in the same way. Sometimes they seem to have praiseworthy ideals, but hardly ever do they place the individual first. I do not want to be self-assertive or eccentric— at least I think not, but one is rarely a judge of oneself—but I do deplore the encroachments of modern life upon the individual, the person, the 'simple soul which issues from the hand of God' (in Dante's phrase).

It may seem contradictory, after saying this, to affirm that I feel myself to belong now to the modern world and do not want to go back to an older civilization, with its many drawbacks. My desire is only that the great achievements of the Western world should not dwarf or disable the living units for whom, alone, they were created.

My head heavy with these thoughts, I craned over the

parapet to see a river steamer pass under the bridge. The passengers on the deck stared upwards, their faces like tiny blank pink discs, so far were they below me. The fact that the steamer could so easily pass under with mast and funnel erect came as a surprise to me. I was filled with contradictory sensations: of commanding size in relation to the steamer and its doll-like passengers; of infinitesimal proportions in relation to the vast bridge.

An old Chinese joke occurred to me, about a man in the province of Shantung who, having heard stories of huge bridges said to exist in Southern China, set out to see them and met on the way an inhabitant of Soochow, in Kiangsu Province, who had heard similarly marvellous accounts of the giant turnips grown in Shantung and was travelling in the opposite direction to see them. Why, asked the man from the South, weary yourself with this long long journey when I can *describe* to you the wonder you wish to see? The height of Soochow bridge, he said, is so great that on the third of June last year a man fell off the parapet and a year later his body had not reached the water. "That is high indeed," said the man from the North. "But I should not advise you to go all the way to Shantung to see the turnips there, for though they are enormous, the roots of the ones planted this year will be with you in Soochow by next year."

The recollection of the story made me smile and lifted the oppression from my mind. Moving on, I passed through the further tower of the bridge and came out at the Palisades. On one side the rock has been cut to accommodate docks, tunnels, terminals and ferry wharves; on the other, the grandeur of the untouched natural formation remains: between, the bridge joins a road which runs deep into the countryside. The rocky outlines had a familiar look to my eyes, for they resembled many a stretch of mountain verge along the Yangtse River. There were no boats over here, and, apart from the traffic on the bridge and road, little noise. Seagulls wheeled about, a slight breeze moved the trees growing among the rocks, and the water-surface looked as soft, smooth and shiny as white satin—like a huge silk scroll for some giant artist to paint on.

It was time to get back to Manhattan. Someone told me that I could catch a coach back at a certain point on the shore. With Chinese obstinacy I did not fancy the suggestion and preferred to make use of my legs again. As I walked I tried to remember lines of poetry about bridges by great Chinese poets, but my memory did not seem as good as it used to be when I was young. A few lines by an English poet, however, did rise to my mind, soothing me till I realised that they were hardly suitable for the bridge on which I was walking, with its well-paved surface and long expanse:

> Lo! the sun upsprings behind,
> Broad, red, radiant, half-reclined
> On the level quivering line
> Of the waters crystalline;
> And before that chasm of light,
> As within a furnace bright,
> Column, tower, and dome, and spire,
> Shine like obelisks of fire,
> Pointing with inconstant motion
> From the altar of dark ocean
> To the sapphire-tinted skies;
> As the flames of sacrifice
> From the marble shrines did rise,
> As to pierce the dome of gold
> Where Apollo spoke of old.

Thus sang Shelley in *Lines Written among the Euganean Hills* as he looked at sunrise over the city of Venice. Watching the sunset over the city of New York from George Washington Bridge I had the same feelings even if occasional words did not fit. I have already said that the skyscrapers of New York are not unlike the campaniles of Venice. The setting sun was now sending broad, red rays far and wide. Above, a few scraps of cloud had turned pink-gold, like graceful birds, particularly like those red-throated humming birds, or like elongated goldfish drifting motionless. The rich light made me catch my breath. Presently the formation of the clouds changed to golden strips and big red patches. It became an enormous fireside with all creation leaning towards its warmth. Both banks of the river turned black, and silhouetted images stood out against them. The distant skyscrapers revealed their slender structures elegantly without even the thinnest veil of evening mist. The day was melting. The scene breathed contentment, and yet it seemed as if Nature were mocking man. In this very man-made city, Nature's presence is seldom noticed, yet during my short stay I experienced a bigger down-pour of rain, a heavier fall of snow, and a stronger blast of wind than anywhere else! And now came this enchanting sunset. It was as if Nature were trying to show off before those who have tried to conquer her. Wealth, hospitality and friendliness there have always been in every big city of the world, but also loneliness and cynical coldness for forgotten individuals. I do not imagine New York is an exception, and her forgotten individuals may have endured greater loneliness and coldness than those of any other big city. But Nature's warmth is for all, as Longfellow sang:

> Yet whenever I cross the river
>   On its bridge with wooden piers,
> Like the odour of brine from the ocean
>   Comes the thought of other years.
>
> And I think how many thousands
>   Of care-encumbered men,
> Each bearing his burden of sorrow,
>   Have crossed the bridge since then.
>
> I see the long procession
>   Still passing to and fro,
> The young heart hot and restless,
>   And the old subdued and slow!
>
> And forever and forever,
>   As long as the river flows,
> As long as the heart has passions,
>   As long as life has woes;
>
> The moon and its broken reflexion
>   And its shadows shall appear,
> As the symbol of love in heaven,
>   And its wavering image here.

Re-crossing the Hudson river, I wondered what Longfellow would have had to say in my place. George Washington Bridge has no wooden piers and the long procession on its back passes by on mechanical legs, but the young heart must still be hot and restless, and the old subdued and slow. The moon is the symbol of love in heaven, but the sunset spreads Nature's warmth for all on earth.

Walt Whitman in his *Crossing Brooklyn Ferry* also describes a scene as intoxicating as the one I had before me:

Flow on, river! flow with the flood-tide, and ebb with the
    ebb-tide,
Frolic on, crested and scallop-edg'd waves!
Gorgeous clouds of sunset! drench with your splendor me,
    or men and women generations after me!

I was a man in the generations after Walt.
It was getting dark, but I could not bring myself to hurry.
A poem of my own began to fit itself together in my mind
as I drew to the eastern shore:

前橋戲無沈中語
戲者過數醉流我
過多是夕是連獨
此後誰陽步不步

Many people have crossed this bridge before me,
How many more will come to cross it after me!
But who is there now to soak himself in the beauty of the
    sunset?
I linger on, speechless and alone, on foot.

XX

IN HARLEM

Men rarely reach one hundred years,
Yet always worry over things for a thousand,

wrote Li P'o twelve hundred years ago. Do not his words
apply equally to life to-day? Very few of us ever achieve one
hundred years of life, yet most of us behave as if we expected
to live for a thousand. Perhaps people in New York do enjoy
longer life than people in China, if one makes the comparison
in terms of how much can be done in the same length of time.
In New York I found myself doing a year's work in a couple of
days and taking a month's pleasure in a few hours. When
I visited Harlem on the evening of Easter Monday, I did in
less than five hours more than I should have believed possible.

I had been in America for several weeks before I discovered
that the name Harlem was that of a part of Manhattan Island.
It conveyed nothing special to me, as I have not the habit of
attaching information to names. In fact, I had already silently
travelled through the district both by day and in the evening,
without realizing it. When I mentioned this casually to my new
acquaintances, they said that I ought to be careful. Harlem
then began to mean something to me. The name must surely
come from Haarlem in Holland, but although Dutch relics
are said to abound in New York, I saw none in Harlem. Perhaps
I did not sufficiently know what to look for. Many of the
houses have an almost uniform design. Shops and places of
entertainment are practically identical with those in other
parts of Manhattan, yet they struck me as different. On a
Sunday morning I saw many folk, young and old, wearing
what was obviously their best clothes, the men with fresh pink
or red roses in their buttonholes. On another occasion I saw
a long procession of men on their way to church, some in
tail-coats, again with roses in their buttonholes, and beautifully-
brushed black silk top hats. I liked those sights.

Mr. William Allen asked me to meet him in the hall of the
Grand Central Terminal in the evening of Easter Monday. I

mingled with the crowds of non-silent travellers and red-caps, and was just being pushed into the arms of one of the gentler sex wearing an umbrella-like headgear which waved almost like a fan to cool me, when Mr. Allen dashed up exclaiming how sorry he was to be late; and indeed the big market underneath the subway line near one end of Park Avenue, which he particularly wanted me to see, was closed when we got there. Mr. Allen was relieved when I told him I had visited this market the day before. There was not a soul to be seen outside and we had to rely for transport on our two pairs of legs. It was the

Rendezvous at Grand Central Station

quietest quarter I had encountered that day in New York. The twilight was throwing bluish-grey tints on the houses and streets, and I could not see clearly the places of interest Mr. Allen pointed out.

He was interested in everything exotic, so we entered the Royal Restaurant, at the north end of Fifth Avenue. I remembered having enjoyed Spanish cooking in a Spanish restaurant in Soho, London, but on those occasions I could read the menu and converse with the manager and waiters in English: here the menu was printed in Spanish and the waiter, with his squarish face, jet-black hair and tiny black moustache, spoke only Spanish. Mr. Allen began to talk to him and ordered the dishes. Before the food was ready, he told me about the

Q

quaint arrangements inside this restaurant. "Here is South America," he said, "here is Mexico, the Argentine, Spain. Why do people want to spend a lot of money *going* to Mexico or the Argentine when they have these countries right here?" He seemed genuinely distressed at what he considered the obtuseness of his fellow New Yorkers, and talked on like a waterfall. The only thing I asked was why the restaurant should be called Royal, but that he did not seem to know.

Our first course was called 'Mofongo Con Chicharrones', a delicious dish the main ingredient of which was crisp pig-skin. I had no idea that pig-skin was a delicacy elsewhere than in the southern part of China, where I had last tasted it. In south China it is the practice to roast the pig whole so that it comes out with a crisp brown skin. A few compatriots of mine, I have noticed, are a little touchy about the fun Charles Lamb pokes at the Chinese in his essay *On Roast Pig*, but I am myself inclined to think that there was truth in the story. The second dish was Arroz Con Calamares, a mixture of boiled rice and fried fresh cuttle-fish. A stew of dried cuttle-fish and fresh pork is considered a delicacy in China, but this was probably the first time I had eaten fresh cuttle-fish. Finally we had Orden de Platanos which consisted of fried bananas of a special fat variety. I used to eat lots of these when I stayed on Hainan Island in South China some twenty years ago, and was interested to find that, fried in lard, they had a most agreeable flavour. Someone slipped a nickel into the juke box, and our ears were filled with Spanish music. Everyone was affected. The waiter hummed and two girls at the bar followed suit, their bodies swaying. We had been the sole diners, but now the room seemed to become warm and full. My companion explained the music to me earnestly and was pleased that I listened to him more happily now after the meal.

Afterwards we went to the Teatro Hispano. A picture called '*Bobby Capo*', or some such name, was being shown and there was continuous movement among the audience. As the film was unintelligible to me, the intermittent outbursts of clapping, sharp whistles or roars of laughter gave me a series of mild shocks. I received periodical explanations from my friend. The whistling became sharper and the clapping louder when Enesto Tanco and Antonieta Lorca appeared on the stage, each with a stringed instrument and wearing the typical bright-coloured costumes of their country. They played and sang and danced together in the manner I remembered having seen in Hollywood films. Their liveliness and the flashes of colour impressed me, and I made a sketch of their poses as far as I could see them in the dark. They must have been favourites of the audience for they had to give two encores. Then more people came in and the house was so full that a good few had to stand. On the stage there now appeared a new figure whose name was Estela Reynolds. Elegantly erect in an evening frock of plain yellowish green she sang three songs

Scene in a Subway train

in Spanish, 'Alma Libre', 'Diez Anos' and 'Tango Uno'. We joined in the clapping, shouting and laughter at the end of each song. It was Estela Reynolds farewell night, and that was why the house was so unusually full. My companion was delighted that I appeared to be enjoying myself. I might have told him the tale, well known in China, of the blind man sitting with a number of his friends. When they laughed at something, he laughed too. Presently he was asked what he saw that made him laugh. "Well, friends," he answered, "surely you are all laughing at something laughable; you wouldn't be playing a trick on me."

We did not wait for the end of the programme. When we

came out it was very dark in the wide street, but the electric signs were hard and bright. Now and then I was directed to peep into one of the public bars, inside which the light was generally dim. Mr. Allen would exclaim: "Look, how artistic, mysterious and romantic!" In the days when the oil lamp was in common use, the electric lamp came as a thing of thrilling brightness: now, when brilliant electric light is universal, dimness inside a room is fashionable. In one or two bars I was particularly directed to notice girls wearing black sun-glasses of an almond shape and slightly slanting at the outer corners. I was amused to think that our Oriental eyes should have become fashionable here!

A taxicab took us to a house where a famous theatrical consultant lived. No one came to answer the door bell. Fortunately there was a light behind the basement window, which lit up all kinds of advertisements for me to see. I was not able to read the scattered newspaper cuttings as I have not the dexterity of a small boy in clinging to railings, but I could read a few admirably written words about the theatrical consultant and see a number of photographs. My companion became apologetic because I was not to have the pleasure of meeting the great man, and began to tell me something about him. He was once a 'red-cap' in the Grand Central Terminal and had occasionally worked as a film extra or stage hand. Then his gifts were recognised and he became an accomplished actor. Eventually he set up in business as a consultant, to train and supply certain types of character actors and actresses.

Before I had absorbed all this information I was guided down some steps to a brightly-lit door, leading to the night club called the Savoy. A few figures with red roses in their buttonholes stood just inside and I took a ticket from one of them before leaving my hat and coat in the cloak room. There were people of both sexes streaming up and down the two staircases by the entrance. The atmosphere was cheerful, but somehow I felt rather ill at ease, perhaps because I did not possess a face like the other visitors. The face of my companion looked pinker than ever. He warned me not to sit down unless I wished to dance. There was not time for me to explain that I could not dance anyhow. Most of the seats round the dance floor, as well as those in front of the bar and by the walls, were occupied. The light was as artistic, mysterious and romantic as my friend could wish. Youth and exuberance were the keynotes of the place, intensified by the quick music of the band and the shouts and jerky steps of the dancers. I felt as though I were being lifted up lightly and dropped down heavily on the floor again. Outwardly I was silently travelling as usual. To my surprise, when I got near the bar I noticed two or three fine figures of men in uniform with revolvers in holsters. We did not even have a drink because my companion knew that I would only take root beer or coca cola! I had seen much jitterbug dancing in films but this was the first time I had met it in real life. It was not unacceptable to my Chinese mind when I recalled songs of my country written three thousand years ago. Here, for example, is one that seemed to have been composed about the dance I was watching at that moment:

> Ef you think o' me,
> Ah'll lift mah petticoat
>   An' cross de ribber Ts'en.
> Ef you think not o' me,
> Well, ain't d'ere other men?
>   O, you silly boy!
>
> Ef you think 'o me,
> Ah'll lift mah petticoat
>   An' cross de ribber Wo.
> Ef you think not o' me,
> Well, ain't d'ere other guys?
>   O, you silly boy!

I suppose that anything that has happened to other races of mankind has had its place in the long history of China too. From our ancient records and from local folklore and remnants of dancing songs it seems possible that there was a kind of jitterbug dance and music in existence before Confucius' time two thousand five hundred years ago. I remember hearing similar exclamatory sounds among the guests at a musical party and dance held during some festival in my boyhood.

Confucius might be thought to have censured such songs and dances, but in fact he collected about three hundred popular songs into a *Book of Odes* which includes the one mentioned above. However, his teachings on ethics and morality gradually took deep root in the Chinese mind and many Confucianists exaggerated them, insisting, for instance, on the separation of the sexes in public. As a result popular folk music and dances lost their hold and in the end disappeared.

My companion remarked that we could still make for the Apollo, where the floor show was renowned as 'the most beautiful in the world'. I have never ceased to express my admiration for the audacity of New York taxi drivers. They seem to possess a kind of magic glue to keep my spine stuck fast to the back of the seat. In less than a minute I was told to get out. We walked a little distance in the dark towards the brightly-lit front of the Apollo, my companion explaining that it was better not to ride in the taxicab right to the entrance lest we be mistaken for millionaires. I knew that he was pulling my leg. Nevertheless, what a thoughtful fellow he was! Had he not, to save my precious dollars, warned me not to sit down at the Savoy? Just inside the main entrance, a young fellow was closing the doors and an older man in a blue uniform was sweeping the floor with a huge broom. His shining white teeth flashed in his dark face as he smilingly recommended us to come earlier tomorrow.

We had a little drink in a Chinese bar called Hua Ting before we parted. I thanked my companion profusely and urged him not to regret the theatrical consultant and the Apollo. Lying on my bed I felt myself glowing all over with the thought that I might for a moment have been taken for a millionaire. This kept me awake, and I finally got up to take a cold shower. But something had gone wrong with the tap and the water deluged on my head instead of sprinkling it. Even a momentary thought of being a millionaire was too much for me!

XXI

ALONG RIVERSIDE DRIVE

OF Riverside Drive I have many memories, but four stand out. After a glance at the Soldiers' and Sailors' Monument at 89th Street, I went down the steps leading to Riverside Park. Beneath the pedestal of the monument is a huge rock, most of its natural face untouched, with masses of trees and flowering shrubs all about. The winding steps follow the natural gaps in the rock. There were very few people about. It was early and rather windy. Two girls and then an elderly man appeared. I stopped every now and then to listen to the tossing and colliding of the leaves and twigs, always agreeable sounds to me, and now accompanied by the flapping of an American flag flying from the top of the monument. Suddenly a splash of colour flew past. It was a bright, pale blue. An American bluebird, I thought. Searching for another glimpse of it I lost it among the many other birds dipping and wheeling around me. The sun had suddenly gone behind a bank of cloud and the birds' plumages were indistinguishable. They flew low as if the air above were heavy. The wind was very strong, and the river was swollen to the point at which it seemed likely to overflow, and this made the Palisades on the farther shore seem closer. Thousands of leaves were torn off branches and whirled about among the birds. Then I noticed that all the birds had gone, with a better instinct for safety than my own. I moved to a sheltered corner of the rock, but a small tree nearby cracked so violently that I feared it might fall on me. The thick-trunked trees were less threatening but their long arms beat up and down like engines.

Peeping through the branches at the sky, I saw that the commotion there was even greater. Linked masses of clouds were rushing down the sky, not rolling but being propelled at great speed, to some fixed destination. Suddenly a single clear chirp reached my ears in a lull and I saw a sparrow on a branch not far from me, calmly swinging up and down with the branch as if saying: "Why worry? The wind will soon stop."

I was glad to find that the bird had taken refuge near me. Generally birds have little trust in man. Why did this tiny creature not fly away when I intruded on him? Perhaps he knew that I was in the same plight as he and would therefore not harm him.

After a while the sun came up in the sky again and the footpath was soon once more filled with people. Peace was restored to this plot of earth. "No squall ever lasts the whole morning," says Lao Tzu. And no war lasts for ever. It is

Ginkgo tree planted by Li Hung-chang

peace that we all seek, even in war. Perhaps if I had not experienced the blast over the Hudson River, I should not have had so strongly the contrasting feeling of peace.

On another day, after having lunch with a friend in the dining hall at Columbia University, I walked up the steps to Riverside Park and found myself not far from Grant's Tomb. The well-planned lawn and shrub beds in the foreground and the general spaciousness are admirable. I entered the mausoleum and examined the sarcophagi containing the bodies of the General and his wife. Then I stood on the doorstep and felt elated by the commanding view of the Hudson River. The trees were not high enough to shadow the tomb. I moved backwards to get a full view of it. To my surprise my back struck the iron-railing which encircled a small tree. It was a ginkgo tree. A bronze tablet recorded the following in Chinese and in English:

"This tree is planted at the side of the tomb of General U. S. Grant, Ex-President of the United States of America, for the purpose of commemorating his greatness, by Li Hung-chang, Guardian of the Prince, Grand Secretary of State, Earl of the First Order Yang Hu, Envoy Extraordinary and Minister Plenipotentiary of China, Vice-President of the Board of Censors, Kwang Hsu, 23rd year, 4th moon, May 1897."

This naturally appealed to me. I was amused at the resounding titles old Li Hung-chang gave himself. I had read about Li Hung-chang's friendship with General Grant while he was Chinese envoy to the United States. This ginkgo tree was planted by him not merely to express his personal affection for the General but to symbolise enduring friendship between America and China. The '*Ginkgo Biloba*' or maidenhair tree is said to have a past older than human intelligence and to be the only tree which still flourishes as it did when the earth was formed! In China it has long been planted as the Sacred Tree in the groves of our ancestors' temples and in monasteries. It is used as a symbol of longevity because it 'never' dies, and its kernels, with their shells, are given as birthday presents to convey best wishes for a long life. Li Hung-chang was wise to choose a ginkgo tree to plant near Grant's Tomb. A curious feature about the ginkgo is that it is a single-sex tree. It will not bear fruit or kernels unless another ginkgo of the opposite sex is nearby. According to the records, the ginkgo was introduced into England in 1754 and into the U.S.A. in 1784. It is said that the ginkgo trees in England are all female. I wondered what was the sex of the ginkgo tree which Li Hung-chang planted. Perhaps the international friendship it symbolised could bear fruit if a ginkgo of the opposite sex were to be planted beside it.

While I was thinking it began to rain. I have often expressed my fondness for rain, but it must be *English* rain—drizzling, misty rain. My experience of New York rain affected me differently. I soon had to leave the ginkgo tree and shelter under a pavilion. The rain came down as if resolved to drive away every living creature from the ground. The surface of the Hudson River seemed connected directly with the sky by myriads of silky strings like a huge harp. Nobody was in sight, and on a vague impulse I stretched my hands in the rain as if to play the instrument. The tune grew louder. Then the sun re-appeared, though the rain continued to fall as hard as ever. Grant's Tomb was lit by a single shaft of light. The flawless granite blocks shone like silver, while all the thick crystal shafts of rain merged into a shiny glass screen. The Tomb was like something in a dream, and a little poem formed itself in my mind:

在陵界桓江
雨寢寬無岸
中立卓遮獨
看好然眼盤

I linger alone on the riverside,
My eyes cover a vast unobstructed expanse.
Solitarily stands the mausoleum.
It is seen at its best in rain.

There are many big churches in New York City, but none of them stands out better than Riverside Church. Situated in 122nd Street, it has not, like so many other New York churches, a neighbouring skyscraper to overshadow it. Its tower, being the tallest building in this quarter, can be seen from a good distance. I made a special point of going inside it. In the spacious vestibule I found, to my surprise, two young ladies at a small table selling postcards. No clerical gowns were to be seen. A uniformed elderly man with a cap was taking visitors up in a lift at twenty-five cents a time. I went up. The lift did not take us right to the top. We had to climb a narrow metal staircase to pass the seventy-two bell carillon. Someone shouted: "This carillon is the largest in the world." What interested me was that the seventy-two bells were constructed by modern scientific methods and must be the newest piece of mechanical work in any church building. At the top I gazed far downtown to where three long, thin, blackish sticks, like incense sticks before

Riverside Park in snow

a shrine such as I used to see in Buddhist monasteries, represented the tallest skyscrapers. Their images darkened or faded in the movements of the morning mist.

As my hotel was not very far from Riverside Church, I visited it often. It was the outside which pleased me most. From the window of my hotel bedroom I could not see the sky, and one morning I came out to find that a heavy night fall of snow had whitened the whole of New York. It was still snowing. Teams of workers were clearing the road and piling the snow seven or eight feet high close to the pavement. The morning paper stated that it would cost the City Council $200,000 to clear the streets. It had never occurred to me that snow could be so costly to taxpayers. In the afternoon I went for a walk along the riverside to view the snow. The foot walk in Riverside Park was still covered, and I took a childish pleasure in the crunch of the snow beneath my feet and laughed when I slipped. The dark trunks of tall leafless trees made stark sketches on the white ground. Through gaps in the trees I caught glimpses of Riverside Church. The tower rose high above the tree tops. A group of startled pigeons flew up and circled just over the tree-tops, adding life to the picture. A snowscape can be a dead one—cold, grim and sad—if without the appearance or suggestion of living things. In front of this church the liveliness was considerable, and it increased towards dusk. Living conditions inside the limited space of apartment houses in New York seem to drive the occupants, especially the younger ones, out for walks whenever possible. What a blessing is Riverside Park for those who live near it!

Presently a gay and high-pitched voice and the barking of a dog arose. A little girl of about ten appeared, scolding and chasing her dachshund, which had jumped into some deep snow, burying its whole body so that only its tiny head looked out pathetically. It jumped out, but after every jump sank again in the snow. In the general whiteness the little girl found it difficult to trace her dog, which barked to help her. But then New York dogs always do seem to bark. English dogs, as one sees them in London parks, for some reason don't; it is as if they were self-consciously well-mannered.

Among the trees I lost the general outline of the church, so I moved to the low surrounding wall and then stepped back slowly to get a full view. It was not quite dark; the snow brightened everything. Overhead the trees made a huge black-velvet canopy under which people might pass to church. There was an enchanting light effect, neither gay nor solemn, but still and indescribably peaceful. There was romance too, of a kind which reminded me of those 'Shadow Plays'—a set of thick paper figures performing against a sheet of white linen in a wooden frame—which I used to see in China. There are no distinctions in the figures between old and young, pretty and ugly, fat and slim, subtle and crude. They make love; they part; they laugh; they shout; children follow them about; they come singly or in groups and go in like manner. It is their silhouetted gestures that count. The same sort of shadow-play was being performed in front of me now. Faces were invisible: and therefore differences of race, nationality and class were also invisible. I felt that I was seeing, in this shadow-play, a vision of humanity without its artificial divisions, and that this was a truer vision of life than the one of everyday in which each of us is an American or a Chinese, old or young, 'white' or 'yellow', upper class or working class.

Stepping backwards again, I collided with an elderly man who prevented us both from falling by seizing my arm tightly. "I tell you, I wish I could be one of those kids down there", he exclaimed. Outside the wall youngsters were tobogganing and snowballing and shouting, and their merriment infected us both. I soon went down the steps. The wide slope between the lower footpath and the wall was ideal for tobogganing. Often youngsters fell off their sledge on the way; some started too soon; one grown-up shared a sledge with a little girl, his considerable weight making his sledge faster than the others and often overturning it. When he fell it was a sight, and when he tried to walk up the slope it was a sight too. His laughter was as hearty as any of the youngsters'. The tobogganners made a scene which might have occurred on any snowy slope. But behind reared the stately lines of Riverside Church and that made it peculiar to New York. Without Riverside Church it would have been merely a merry occasion: with it, there was serenity and dignity. I made a painting of it afterwards.

It took me a little time to calm myself after reaching Fort Tryon Park by subway. The moon was clear and high in the sky. When I turned along a footpath and stopped near a big tree I found myself in a totally different world—a silvery dream world. No visitors came to see the Cloisters at night and the roads close by were now empty. The moonlight illuminated the tree-leaves, the little rocks and even the tiniest petals of some wild flowers. Their colours were not emphasised as they would have been by sunlight, but were toned down as if each had been newly washed. Their freshness exhaled an atmosphere of tranquillity and soothed my mind. I felt disinclined to move, for the stillness of the shadows of trees and rocks seemed to influence me to keep still as well. Shadows in the daytime have beauty but no secrecy. However, I went on the top of the Fort and enjoyed seeing the Cloisters under the moon. But I enjoyed even more the sight, later on, of the Fort as a whole with rocks and trees from a distant point near by the cloisters. I recorded the view in a painting entitled *Fort Tryon under the Moon.*

The Cloisters

XXII

IN THE BOWERY

VISITING Forest Hills one day to see some friends, I was taken after dinner to a nearby cinema where we saw a rather old picture called 'Sun-Bonnet Sue'. The heroine, Sue Casey, brought up by her rich aunt in the wealthiest quarter of the City, ran away to become a dancer in a Bowery café, owned and run by her father Matt Casey. When the aunt discovered this she arranged to have the café wrecked and thus retrieve Sue. But Sue came to hear of the plot and promptly left her aunt again, while the café, through the influence of the mayor's wife, formerly a dancer in a similar café, was restored. As we came out of the cinema my host and hostess apologised that the picture had not been better, but I had enjoyed it for I had noticed some scenes familiar to me. I must, I realised, already have been in the Bowery without knowing it; and I decided to make a tour of the place in my silent way.

A double-decker bus dropped me near Wanamaker's and I at once noticed Stuyvesant Street. In a glow of childish pride at the possession of a trifling piece of knowledge, I told myself that this must be the beginning of the Bowery, because Peter Stuyvesant, who wrote about New York in the 17th century, would have given the place its name. Whether my theory was right or not, I found nothing remarkable in Stuyvesant Street. Presently I came to a pair of huge stone lions, carved in conventional Chinese design, in front of the entrance to Wanamaker's department store. They filled me with nostalgia for my younger days in China, where in nearly every town and city there used to be a pair of such lions flanking the main entrance of the local yamen, the residence of the highest official in the place. Apart from their function as door-guardians, to which was attached some sort of mystical symbolism, they looked very decorative and gave an imposing appearance to those houses whose owners held high office. As a child I climbed with other youngsters on the lions in front of our local yamen, sat on their backs and looked proudly round. Each lion was on a high pedestal and it was not easy to get to the top. Some twenty years later I myself, as district governor and magistrate of Kiukiang, occupied that very yamen. But the stone lions were no longer there: when China became a Republic, they were considered symbolical of the old regime. I was too busy with my duties to find out what had happened to that particular pair. Perhaps they were before me now at the entrance to Wanamaker's!

Wanamaker's stands out in my mind from the many huge department stores in New York because of a story about the owner. A friend of his boyhood days presented himself one day and told a hard-luck story of being half-starved and turned out of his hotel room. Wanamaker was so moved that he took the man to his own restaurant and urged him to choose any food he fancied. He also gave the man money for his hotel bill and promised to give him a good job next morning. But the poor fellow never came. He had died of acute indigestion during the night. A sad story, but I venture to think that the man passed away *content*. I raised my hat to Wanamaker and bade farewell to the pair of stone lions.

Somewhere near Astor Place, I had been told, was the site of the first drinking place established for travellers between New York and Boston. It was well-known in the 17th century as Rebecca's House, when most of Manhattan Island was still marsh, rock and field. All travellers on the Boston Post Road stopped to rest here. It was established by a Dutchman and later run by his wife Rebecca, whose name contributed to its fame. Afterwards it came into the hands of an Englishman, John Clapp, who printed the first almanac in New York and also built the first hackney coach to his own design. Clapp is claimed to be the first person to have advertised a tavern. The wording he used is attractive: "a baiting place where gentlemen take leave of their friends and where a parting glass or two of generous wine

> If well applied makes the dull horses feel
> One spur in the head is worth two in the heel."

This has the same sort of poetic humour as I have seen on inn signs in my own country. In China the wording would still be true. But in New York there is no trace of Rebecca's

House; nor could I picture travellers on horses. Times have changed!

However, there was no point in dwelling on the past of New York and I proceeded to Bleecker Street, where a fruit and vegetable market was in full swing. Loud, but to me unintelligible, cries announced what was for sale. The atmosphere was no different from that of open markets in other parts of the world, further evidence that human life is much the same

Market near Bleecker Street

all over the globe. To my delight I noticed some new types of push-cart near the market. Before coming to New York I had imagined that everything in the city would be run by machinery. Imagination often contradicts reality, and in fact I have found many types of street-barrow, flower-cart, push-cart, hot-dog stand, peanut wheelbarrow, and a dozen other hand-propelled vehicles used for carrying things for sale. They interested me very much and I sketched them whenever I could. For me, they symbolize New York life in general better than skyscrapers and limousines.

I made a quick sketch of two ladies standing by an oyster

Sitting by the lake in Central Park

stall, one in a fur coat, the other holding a new pram in which her baby lay. Both were eating oysters from dishes on the stand, inside which the man who served could hardly be seen. Presently there appeared an unshaven young man wheeling an old broken pram, on the edge of which were a number of sticks with columns of pretzels on them. He did business with his customers as he went along. Two fellows who had each bought a packet of jumbo peanuts from a barrow, were walking towards

Oysters for all

me, throwing the nuts high in the air and catching them in their mouths as if in a competition. It was their *leisureliness* which, on this as on so many other occasions in New York, surprised me. Here, in this hive-like market, were even a few people who were loth to disturb the air at all, for they lay on the door-steps of small hotels that I passed. Su Tung-p'o (A.D. 1036-1101), the Sung poet and painter, tells a story of two poor fellows who were discussing what they would do if they had money. One of them said: "I have always wanted to eat and sleep whenever I liked. If I got rich, I should just eat,

R

and sleep, and then wake up to eat again." The other disagreed: "If I became rich," he said, "I should just go on eating, eating, eating. There would be no time for sleep." Those who slept round here may have belonged to the first type, or to a third type who would just go on sleeping, sleeping, sleeping, with no time for eating.

I knew I was definitely in the Bowery now, for I noticed a signboard on one of the steel pillars supporting the Elevated railway. I was between Kenmare Street and Delancey Street. The Elevated cast an interesting shadow-pattern of black and white on the road beneath. While I watched it, the white

How to eat peanuts

parts of the pattern began to jump about as if some pianist was darting his fingers along them. The only music, however, was the thunder of the train overhead. A moment later I realised I was standing near the exit staircase of an elevated station, for masses of people now came rushing down upon me and brushed me aside.

Presently I discerned loud laughter nearby, followed by a dismal wailing. An elderly fellow was singing with his eyes half-closed. He had apparently been thrown out of a pub. He could hardly stand, yet he attempted to move along, exhibiting that elaborate affectation of steadiness which one associates with Sir John Falstaff. Suddenly he lurched on to a push-cart, clutching at the pretzels. The owner dragged him off. While I was telling myself that I must help him, he came swaying towards me. Happily for me, the push-cart man intervened and gave him a shove in another direction. The push-cart was then rapidly wheeled away. I recalled the words of an ancient Egyptian: "Do not go into a beer tavern, for it is unpleasant to hear words reported as having come from your mouth when you do not remember that you said them." And then again : "If you fall down you may break your bones, but nobody will come to your help. Even your drunken friends will get to their feet and say, 'Throw out that drunkard'!" It is four thousand six hundred years since Prince Ptah-hotpe made that admonition, and the truth of it was being exhibited before my eyes.

The eating and drinking places, I noticed as I walked, were more distinctive than the shops, though the latter included a number of pawnbrokers, some dating back as far as 1800. My curiosity was aroused as to why the three gilt balls of the pawnbrokers' sign should here be arranged in line,

Pawn shops in the Bowery

whereas all over Europe, so far as I know, they are always arranged in a triangle.

A commotion near me drew my attention but I could see nothing in particular between the shoulders of the crowd. A brief but heated argument arose and subsided. Then I glimpsed a man paying seven cents—*seven cents!*—for what looked like a bright silk necktie. Had I not bought a similar one for thirty times that price the day before? The commotion, or rather the crowd composing it, suddenly dispersed, and I moved on into Canal Arcade.

I had already seen many shops dealing in second-hand clothes, but in Canal Arcade practically every shop was filled

Secondhand clothes carts

to overflowing with big bundles of such garments. One or two elderly men sitting on chairs outside the shops glanced at me as I passed, but clearly decided I did not look as if I belonged to their trade. On emerging at the other end of the Arcade, I saw three young fellows each pushing a sort of square box on wheels. I suspected these of containing more second-hand clothes. Dealing with second-hand, third-hand and even fourth-hand clothes must be a very big business in this part of the world. I was to learn that mass-produced new clothes, after being worn for a while, reach the hands of second-hand dealers, who clean and press them by modern machine methods so that they look almost new again. I suppose the same thing happens after the second using, and the third, and so on until the garment passes peacefully away.

From Orchard Street a babel reached my ears and I found

a solid line of wooden stalls and push-carts, barrel tops and boxes in the middle of the street, and many more on both sides of it. Coloured umbrellas were used as shelters from the bright sun, and the great crowd gave the scene the appearance of a slowly moving procession. Many of the people must have been mere spectators like me, but the rest seemed to be there for more definite purposes.

This was presumably the Ghetto quarter. Food and commodities, including second-hand goods, and clothes of every description, were on sale. The selling and bargaining methods were familiar to me from Petticoat Lane in London, but here there was more colour—picturesque figures wearing long black beards and black garments, holding either a pole strung with paper bags or a basket

Laundry push-cart

of oranges and other fruit for sale. All the hard-working vendors were very much on the alert ; indeed very much more keen than gay.

In a drugstore round the corner of Lafayette Street, I had a bite to eat. A dark-faced young man entered with a bundle of papers in his hand, smiling and looking happy. He showed the papers to the girl behind the counter and said that he had just composed some music. Then he began to hum and to drum with his fingers on the counter. "Quite good," commented the girl, who carried on her business at the same time as her conversation. Presently the young man left the drugstore without eating anything, and the girl remarked to me : "You never know—we may have a dark Frankie on the air one day". I joined in the burst of laughter from the other end of the counter, but it was, in fact, some time afterwards that it dawned on me that Frank Sinatra was the explanation of the joke. Silent Travellers are not quick at taking these points!

After lunch I had a good look at the empty, conventional, building of the Criminal Court and, directly opposite, a new building evidently erected recently to take the place of the other. Though their styles contrasted, there was a harmony between the two. The sun haze was dense enough to soften the sharp lines of the immense Municipal Building and New York Sun buildings in the distance. I began to make a sketch for a painting.

Afterwards I sat on a bench in front of the City Hall. None of the people moving about seemed in a hurry, perhaps because it was now near the end of the day and work was finishing.

Peanut seller

I had had my day in the Bowery and felt entitled to a rest. The old Court House, with the skyscraper of the Municipal Building above, looked content with *its* day's work. And when I got up to set off for a dinner engagement in mid-town, a flock of birds flew over the trees in front of the Hall, homing also.

I told my dinner host, a very energetic young American, what I had done that day. He thought it exceedingly funny! The Bowery, he affirmed, must be seen by night. I begged to differ. But he continued and argued that in New York every one preserves his energy for the night. And after dinner he proceeded to put me into a taxi to visit the Bowery again. I do not know where we went to, for everything looked alike. Nor can I say what café we entered, for I had not time to look at the sign before being rushed in. Someone standing by the door shook hands with my friend and then with me too. I began to take off my hat and coat, but no one offered to take them and my friend gave me a pat on the shoulder to move me on further. When we sat down at a table I noticed many men with their hats and coats still on; there were even some dancing in them.

I am a little hard of hearing in one ear, but now the other ear seemed to become deaf, for I was unable to hear anything my friend was saying to me—what with the clinking of glasses and bottles, the shouting, the singing, the laughing, and the band! Nowhere had I seen people laugh with their mouths so wide open, nor heard such loud voices, nor seen so many friendly happy faces. Yet, oddly, nowhere had I found it easier to be alone and quiet and able to relax! A pedlar with hot-dogs for sale came round. At one table a girl helped her boy-friend to some, at another table a man took one for his girl. Another pedlar selling peanuts and pretzels had a good drink himself after finishing his round. The atmosphere was unique. A singer whose figure only Rubens could have drawn was winning attention and laughter from a large part of the house, while another short and elderly female danced and sang in her own way, receiving applause from those round her. Here no one knew the words 'restraint' or 'restriction'. In many ways it was like a fancy dress gathering. Not only were the women's hats of many forms and shapes that I had not previously noticed in New York, but even the men's headgear was not uniform. It was not that any new shape of hat had been created, but that the ordinary-looking hats were set differently on their heads. Some had even decorated their hats with long feathers or sparkling ornaments in order to be different from the rest. It was obvious that all these people had come out for a good time.

Omar Khayyam said: "You know how little while we have to stay, and, once departed, may return no more." But his words were not appropriate to this place which had a red electric sign on the doorway saying 'Thank you, call again.' I was wondering if it was like this every night and if I might call again during my short stay. My friend got up to dance with someone, while my thoughts rose and whirled round, mingling with the smoke of cigarettes and cigars. I had felt the noise acutely when we first entered, but now it did not seem so loud. I remember hearing that a new type of soundproof ceiling had been put up by a chain of restaurants in order to meet the demands of their quiet customers, but that this had not proved successful because it made the customers feel lonesome and so the owner of the restaurants had to take them down again. Perhaps some people had come to this restaurant to cure their loneliness.

Many Chinese poets have loved a glass or two of liquor and many of their lines still bring a smile to our lips when we read them today. At that moment I recalled the fourth century poet Liu Lin, whose love for liquor was unrivalled. He used to go out for drinks, followed by two servants, one carrying a coffin and the other a spade and other digging tools. He had no thought of returning alive. Such an act would be impracticable in the modern age, especially on Manhattan Island where there is no space to dig a hole! Yet, there might be some among the crowd without thought of returning. What about myself, for instance? A Martini meant nothing to many New Yorkers but it meant a great deal to me, especially with something else on top of it. My eyes refused to focus and everything appeared double or treble and unusually beautiful. Where had my thoughts gone? . . .

The next morning I awakened in bed and wondered how and when I had come back the night before. Presumably my friend had seen to that. At least I had not returned on a stretcher! I was glad to have seen a little more of the Bowery anyhow.

Grape fruit seller

XXIII

ON THE HUDSON RIVER

THE sunny days of March and April can be very warm in New York, as I discovered. Nevertheless the steamer company does not run its full programme of river-trips until late May. I was able to take a trip round Manhattan Island, but

The Elevated at 125th Street

I could not wait for the one between New York City and Albany as my boat for England left three days before it started. However I hastened to book a ticket for the first run between New York City and Poughkeepsie. It was sunny and bright when I got to the landing stage at 125th Street. I was an hour ahead of the time scheduled for the steamer to arrive, so, while I waited, I watched the water washing against the stone bank beneath my feet, and then I gazed over to the other side of the river, where through the morning haze I could see faintly the iron structure of the Palisades Amusement Park and other buildings. Before me stretched myriads of tiny ripples, looking like piles of raw silk laid across to fill up the gap, and all golden from the reflection of the sun. I did not enquire why none of the seagulls who flutter about so much downtown had come to this part; nor did I puzzle over the unusual peacefulness at this junction of the river not far from the busiest centre of the busiest city in the world.

Presently other people began to arrive to fill the seats behind mine. Most of them were boys and girls in shorts and bright coloured dresses. Some carried tennis rackets, some bags of food and swimming suits and some had nothing at all, not even coats. A fight started between two boys, one, a dark-skinned boy, had been chewing bubble-gum which he had blown to a good size, when the other boy burst it, intentionally or unintentionally I do not know. The fight was a playful one and the onlookers gave loud encouragement to both sides. The boys must have belonged to the same school. The arrival of the steamer *Hendrick Hudson* stopped the fight and the younger passengers brushed me aside to get on board.

There were already a large number of people both on the open upper deck and on the lower one. They had joined the steamer at Battery Park. Almost everyone was near the rail. More were sitting on the right side than the left, for the steamer was moving closer to Riverside Drive and there were different buildings and landmarks to be pointed out. Talking went on incessantly, mingled with jokes and laughter. I did not know what it was all about. Suddenly a commotion was caused by a number of youngsters dashing upstairs to the open deck when the steamer was about to pass underneath George Washington Bridge. It was certainly an unusual sight and a sensation for anyone who had not passed underneath before. Conversation then centred on the Cloisters, and on the movable steel-bridge at the place where the Hudson branches off into Harlem River. After Yonkers, all the excitement died down and an unusual quietness reigned. Occasionally one or two youngsters walked round briskly or even ran; they did not disturb the prevailing stillness but rather added something to it. Some passengers began to read, but the majority showed signs of drowsiness and a good many were already sound asleep. The sun meanwhile had become brighter and hotter.

Summer must have already been far on its way for I could not detect any other colour but rich greens along the banks. I had by now managed to sit on a deckchair on the left of the top deck facing the seemingly unending Palisades. One section was thickly wooded, another was rocky. Two thick silvery white lines, some distance apart, came into sight and I took them to be waterfalls. As our steamer was rather far from the bank, I could not be sure of the real colour of the rocks, for they were tinted by the different shades of green all round and looked more or less purple in the sunny haze, reminding me very much of the famous Red Cliffs on the south bank of the Yangtse above Kiukiang. These were made famous by two beautiful essays written by the Sung scholar, poet and bamboo-painter, Su Tung-p'o (A.D. 1034-1095). In these he described two moonlight boating expeditions along the Red Cliffs with his friends. He revealed their enjoyment of the beautiful scenery and also traced the battle scars left during the dispute between Wu and Wei States in the third century. Not only have these essays since served as a model for our literary style, but 'Boating along the Red Cliffs under the moon' has been a favourite theme for many Chinese artists. Some twenty-five years ago I had the pleasure of boating along the Red Cliffs, not under the moon, but on a spring morning in a small junk, which moved along near the shore producing a hissing sound among the long weeds. The gleam of the cliffs in the sunshine and their reflection in the river tinted the junk, my clothes and my face as if we had all had a strong drink. Such sounds and colours are the inexhaustible gifts of Nature, a feast for me all along, while the unending flow of the Yangtse made me envy the eternity of time. It was a memorable trip.

This experience seemed to be repeating itself as I gazed at the Palisades while the steamer moved along slowly. The scene did not change much for a good while, for the Palisades extend for twelve miles, 350 to 550 feet high, and are more or less uniform in structure, particularly when seen from a distance. The sameness of the scene—the wide expanse of water, the evenly arranged Palisades on one side and the continuous bun-like formation of soft green hills on the other—made the steamer appear stationary. The atmosphere was remarkably restful. It was no wonder that most of the passengers on the upper deck had their heads covered with a handkerchief or a newspaper and slept peacefully. Those of us who were awake showed no inclination to move. Occasionally the faint chug-chug from the engine room and the clear flapping sound of the steamer's flag on the mast could be heard. The sun was bright and warm; the breeze fresh; and my thoughts roamed near and far. I thought of the contrast between this place and the streets of New York City not very far away. I thought of the days when Henry Hudson, whose name was later given to the river, came to this part of the world. I also wondered what the Palisades looked like to Verrazano who proceeded a short distance up the Hudson by boat in 1524. It was useless to ponder how they looked to the former Indian inhabitants; or to enquire how Washington Irving gazed at them during his last days at Sunnyside. Their general appearance cannot have changed, just as those Red Cliffs along the Yangtse have remained the same from the time of the battle in the third century up to the present day. I cannot think either that the trees and birds in these parts have undergone much change through the ages. The only change is in man, imposed by him and experienced by him. To Nature man must always have been a troublesome creature!

Gradually the Palisades were left behind and the river widened. I felt myself expand with the river. The gentle breeze unexpectedly changed into a strong wind. There was great activity on the water-surface, as the masses of wavelets scrambled over one another. There was, too, a sudden commotion among my fellow passengers. Our steamer began to turn. A voice shouted: 'Indian Point'. A number of passengers with their belongings began to walk down the steps to the landing stage. I got up to follow them until at the last moment someone asked me where my destination lay. Then I was turned back, for apparently Poughkeepsie was still a good way off. I remarked: "Poughkeepsie or Indian Point means the same thing to me, as I don't know either of them and only want to see what is up the Hudson River". This raised a laugh and someone said: "What a guy! He doesn't know his buck's worth!" I wonder if I will ever mend my ways and read something about my route before I start a journey.

After Indian Point had disappeared, a small steamer

similar to one of the tug-boats round Manhattan Island appeared in the distance on my right. It was the first moving boat I had seen since leaving New York City. I wondered why there were not more boats on the Hudson, as it seemed to me a highly navigable river. I wished I could have seen some of the huge white sails of the Yangtse junks.

But Mr. Henry C. Brown tells me in his book *The Story of Old New York* published by E. P. Dutton & Co., Inc.:

"As the population grew and the river played an ever-increasing role in the City's growth, it developed a type of boat peculiar to its needs—the Hudson River Sloop. . . . It was rather wide, had a rail running around the deck and a single mast stepped well forward with an enormous boom. It was roomy and was designed to carry both passengers and freight. It carried an immense spread of canvas. It resembled the familiar catboat of the harbour and bay, but differed slightly in the more forward step of the mast and, unlike the cat, it carried a foresail. Perhaps its great advantage was in the fact that it could be easily handled by two men. In a sudden squall, the sail was lowered from the peak or sheeted in altogether. Sometimes the force of the wind, if from the rear, was sufficient to send her along scudding under bare pole at a great rate. . . ."

He also says that before the days of Fulton the Hudson River sloop was a delightful mode of transportation, and very popular because it had spacious decks covered with awnings and comfortable chairs, and passed through beautiful country at a leisurely speed. At every lock or anchoring place there was always a small crowd gathered to look and listen as well as to sell fruit and flowers. The passenger could have time to go ashore and spend an hour looking over the little town with it half-white, half-red population. This is just what happens along the shores of the Yangtse when a junk anchors even in present-day China. But we have no half-white, half-red, only all yellow populations in the little towns. I can well visualise the sails of the Hudson River sloops gliding along the Palisades, and past Indian Point, Alas! man—man only—has forced changes on the present-day Hudson! Now Fulton's *Clermont* has vanished from the river in its turn too. But credit must be given to the men who have kept the shores of this river tidier and added more ornaments to it than we have to the Yangtse.

Presently the steamer made a turn to the left and another range of mountains came into view. Someone said that we had

now passed Peekskill Bay. On the left the distant peak of
Donderberg Mountain or 'Thunder Mount' became faintly
visible in the haze. On the right the river branched off
into Annsville Creek, but I was too late to see it as the steamer
kept moving in a north-westerly direction. I did not mind. My
eyes were gazing straight ahead. The river bed became narrower
while more and bigger hills appeared. A great commotion
began again on board, in which almost everybody seemed to
take part. Every possible space along the rail was occupied
and I joined the throng. Standing on my right was an elderly
man with a rather heavy white moustache—not a very familiar
facial ornament in New York. He stretched out his hand and
told me that on rounding the next bend we would see Bear
Mountain. I was jotting down some lines in my little sketch-
book to mark the contour of the mountains.

The steamer gradually slowed and at the same time, as if
by magnetism, the mountains on both sides drew closer
together. They towered above us higher and higher while
we on board seemed to sink lower and lower. In the end
we reached a point where the mountains were so near each
other as to be joined by a long metal bridge, which is Bear
Mountain Suspension Bridge. I had difficulty in stretching
my head over the railing sufficiently to see the top of the
mountain on my right. The steamer was tiny by comparison.

The elderly man went on to tell me that the mountains
on the right were Manito Mountains and further away on the
same side was Anthony's Nose. But Bear Mountain on the
left lay a little inland and could not be seen very well. Nothing
is more agreeable than receiving helpful information from a
friendly soul. I much prefer it to guide books.

Soon we anchored and most of the passengers streamed
ashore on their way to Bear Mountain Park. Having inquired
how long the steamer was stopping I followed them but did
not take the hillpath. The happy chatter and laughter of the
younger passengers echoed all round. I listened cheerfully and
waited until the sounds became quite faint in the distance
before I re-embarked. By the water's edge I noticed a few
weeping willows swaying in the gentle breeze and brushing
the dust into the river. There were birds singing in the trees
and fluttering around. But very few flowers could be seen and
summer seemed to be taking its shape more here than

elsewhere. There was an unusual coolness, for the high mountains on both sides hid the sun for much of the day. The mountain face became greener and greener and then dark green from top to bottom, its reflection in the river suggesting immeasurable depth. The whole scene was very peaceful indeed. I would have liked to stay here longer but it was not possible.

More than half the passengers had now left our steamer and I found it easier to move about. I overheard snatches of conversation. Someone was pointing out Anthony's Nose, which was named after the big nose of Anthony Corlear, Peter Stuyvesant's trumpeter, someone mentioning Sugar Loaf and someone telling with great pride the story of the bulbous Dutch goblin, the 'keeper of the mountains,' whose presence in this part of the river over a century ago was feared by the captains of river-craft. He usually wore a sugar-loaf hat and carried a speaking trumpet. If the captain of any river-craft did not lower his peak in deference to the goblin, he would blow his trumpet to pipe up a gust of wind and a heavy storm would rise to endanger the boat. He was once seen riding full tilt against Anthony's Nose. Another time a pastor began to exorcize him by singing the hymn of St. Nicholas, and he immediately threw himself in the air, rolled round like a big ball and vanished in a whirlwind. But the pastor's wife lost her nightcap, which was carried away by the mischievous goblin and was found hanging on the top of a church spire forty miles away on the following Sunday. This foul weather producer was often seen surrounded by a large group of mountain imps, in broad breeches and short doublets, performing acrobatics in the air and buzzing round Anthony's Nose like a flock of bees when the storm, thunder and rain reached their height. The passenger who was telling this story had a vivid way of imitating the movements of the goblin and his imp friends. His voice silenced all the other chatterers. He laughed at times and his listeners laughed too. I was happy to eavesdrop. I thought I had read this goblin story somewhere, and I found it later in *The World of Washington Irving* by Van Wyck Brooks.

Some old fortress-like buildings appeared high up the precipitous rocks on the left, with a lofty church spire in dark grey stone in the background. There were no other houses in sight. I had seen nothing similar along the Hudson so far, and I was reminded of some big English mansion or castle along the Thames. A voice came up from below announcing: 'West Point'. No one made any move to disembark, and the steamer glided on round several bends, always revealing a different scene.

The steamer made a slight turn to the left. The group of people who had just finished the storytelling were now busy pointing out various landmarks. One spectacled fellow remarked that a heavy iron chain was placed across the river somewhere nearby in April 1778, to obstruct the British

Girls singing on the boat to Poughkeepsie

ships during the revolution. How faithfully history repeats itself—if not in one country then in another! A heavy iron chain was placed by Wu State across the Yangtse river a little way below Kiukiang to obstruct the ships of Wei State in the third century.

The river became wider and wider. The sun, though still very bright, was not as warm as before and was tempered by a gentle breeze. There were a number of large cotton-wool clouds floating high above like balloons and changing shape all the while. The steamer had passed Fishskill Creek and soon approached Newburgh, but went on without making a call.

Presently the sky turned darker as if there were a shower imminent. On the left some hills stood out ruggedly as we passed. There was a bright red and white lighthouse near

Morning mist over the Palisades

the water and this must have been Danskammer Point, which,
I was told, was a favourite meeting place for the Indians. Far
ahead of me were masses of reeds nodding their heads in the
strong wind as if welcoming me. A large flock of wild geese
rose and circled over the reeds.

I sat down on a chair close to the central mast instead of
near the rail. The sun was once more shining brightly again,
as the clouds had vanished. The small white caps of the waves

The Church at Poughkeepsie

shining in the sun chased each other tirelessly. After gazing at
them a while my eyes began to close. Then I heard somebody
singing, and opening my eyes saw it was two young girls, both
about fourteen, sitting each with one hand touching the rail,
their long, loose hair streaming in the wind. Their voices were
low and attractive, and I found the song wonderfully soothing.
I never dreamed that it could be so quiet on board. The
music became clearer and purer as if commanding all to keep
still.

"Poughkeep-sie, Poughkeep-sie--e, last stop!" came a loud
trailing voice from below. Almost everyone came on to the

s

open deck. The steamer was steadily approaching Poughkeepsie Bridge, which like others on the lower Hudson is a metal suspension bridge.

The steamer was to stay for an hour or so at Poughkeepsie. I was one of the last to disembark, and many people had already gone off in horse-drawn carriages to see the sights of the town. Some had been met by car and others had gone on foot in various directions. I had no fixed objective. The big fellow with a dark face who had announced the arrival at each place on our trip came up and told me that I could walk through the tree-lined avenue to the main street. I followed his suggestion. I did not meet another soul even after I passed the railway station, where no one was in sight on the platform either. There was a strike on that day. I was surprised to find Poughkeepsie so quiet, but perhaps it is not always so. Presently I came to a stone church. I stepped inside the wooden gate to the churchyard and read 'Episcopal Church of the Holy Comforter' on the board under the porch. The church was locked so I could not go inside as I have been accustomed to do in my travels round the British countryside. I sat on the doorstep to rest. In the bright sunlight the lawn looked unbelievably green and shiny. A few dark bay trees were at one end of the church and some lighter sycamores at the other. I thought there must be a breeze blowing up as I saw some grass moving, but then I saw this was caused by an American robin, looking for food. I watched it standing erect and cocking its head first on one side and then on the other as if listening to the movement of a worm underneath the earth. Every now and then it hopped a few steps and dug for one.

I did not go into the town but returned straight to the steamer. It was not long before we were in the middle of the river again, now going down stream and apparently gaining speed. The mountains and hills on either side were flying backwards as if in a nature film. The wind helped to push us along. As we passed West Point it began to rain but stopped before Bear Mountain Bridge was in sight. All the passengers who had gone ashore here on the outward journey embarked again, and the noise on board was terrific. People were chasing round and round the deck, while gramophone records were played and dancing took place in the lounge. One card game led to a fight. It grew a little chilly on deck. After India Point more passengers arrived to swell the noise.

Although I have not been able to go up to Albany to have a look at the Catskill Mountains where Rip Van Winkle once slept, nor to study the many Dutch relics all along the Hudson Valley, I have at least had the pleasure of being taken to the heart of the Hudson. It was a perfect day.

Paper stand at the station to Weehawken

XXIV

AT INNISFREE

It was in August, 1938, that I first met the owner of Innisfree in London. He had then invited me to visit him at his home. Many years elapsed without my being able to accept, as I wished, so I was doubly pleased when soon after my arrival in New York the invitation was renewed in the following letter:

"My wife tried to communicate with you over the wire after dinner, but you were not in. A message was left for you to call us in the morning after nine o'clock. We wanted you to see the country as it is here by the lake in spring. The beauty is very impressive. We thought you could finish writing up here, staying three or four days. Maud, the maid, and her husband, Fred, would take care of you. From your *OXFORD* book, we learned how much you like to be alone, and therefore we planned, as we had to be in town by Monday afternoon, that Charles, the chauffeur, could call for you at your hotel and take you up here. Starting about five or a little after, you would be here for dinner. Later in the season you will again be our guest, we hope, when we are in residence. You will find the house open this time and we beg you to make yourself fully at home in it. This is the first time we have asked a guest to occupy the house alone—but you are a poet, painter, and essayist, for whom aloneness in such surroundings is a necessity. That is our thought, and there is no other. Charles will also take you up the hill to see some dogwoods there. By strolling around you will find a lot of bloom. You might use a boat and land at the island. The osprey was streaking silver over the lake early this morning. Humming-birds are building, and baby ducks are already out and seen occasionally. . . ."

How could I resist such a sympathetic and understanding invitation? I accepted with alacrity.

Innisfree is in New York State some ninety miles from Manhattan Island. As the weather was getting warmer and warmer at the beginning of May, my friend thought that I would enjoy the country as a change from the city. He even increased my indebtedness to him by proposing to accompany me himself after all, so that he could show me Washington Irving's house on our way. Irving's name sent my memory chasing back to my younger days in school when I had to read his *Sketch Book* after learning the English language for only a short time. The book was much too hard for me then. I shed tears in my efforts to understand the writing and wore out my dictionary in search of the many unknown words. Not until a much later date did I begin to enjoy reading the *Sketch Book*, and Rip Van Winkle then became a vivid, lovable character in my mind for always. Such a bitter-sweet memory of his book made me eager to see Irving's house on this trip. We set out after ten and followed Riverside Drive to Yonkers and beyond. The trees by the roadside were opening their green eyes and the morning mist hung beneath the boughs in the way which had become familiar to me in London's suburbs.

We were now on the highway, which was wide, smooth-surfaced and as straight and long as if it had no end. While driving along my friend told me a story of the origin of the two-way traffic system. A little country lady who came to town and found herself held up by traffic jams wrote to the authorities to ask why they did not let one lot of cars move on one way and another the other way. The authorities thought she 'had something': and since then the traffic problem has become much easier. "Just think of the development of our modern double highways out of so insignificant a letter," my friend remarked with a smile. I thought, however, that it had needed an alert authority to perceive the underlying truth in the country lady's letter.

Presently we reached Irvington, named after Irving who built a house called *Sunnyside* there and had been associated with the place in his childhood. We had a little difficulty in locating the place at first, but soon noticed a statue of Irving guarded by two characters from *Rip Van Winkle* in bas-relief. We entered a narrow, tree-lined lane but had to turn back because the big car could proceed no further. It must have been raining heavily a little while previously, for all the young yellowish-green leaves were glossy, while the unpaved road was rather muddy. My friend had only wanted me to see what Irving's country looked like and I said that I could make a special trip here myself later on.

At Tarrytown my attention was drawn to Kijkuit, the home of Mr. John D. Rockefeller, Jr. at Pocantico Hills, where

I believe many Chinese art treasures are kept. I wished I could have had the pleasure of seeing them. Philipse Castle near by was also pointed out to me. We got out of the car to have a look at Christ Church, where Irving worshipped, but we did not linger long. After passing Peekskill and Fishskill—the suffix being, I was told, of Dutch origin—we came to Millbrook in Duchess County. Leaving the main highway we turned into a side road. Some of the rocks have been left on both sides and one or two in the middle in their natural formation, overgrown with moss and grass. This pleasantly broke the monotony

An old Dutch church in Sleepy Hollow Cemetery

of the long straight track and made the scenery very inviting. The air became fresher, yet extraordinarily still, not even disturbed by the rapid movement of our car. Perhaps the stillness was intensified by the roar of the traffic which had been ringing in my ears only two hours ago. I knew what a store of enjoyment lay ahead for me in being with nature.

For a good while we were all alone. Here and there trees close to the road waved their long branches to welcome me. A number of birds busily flew about singly or in pairs along our way as if announcing that a guest had come. The distant hills were also aroused and began to move nearer me. The trees by the house looked as if eagerly waiting to receive me, but they all seemed to step back a little when our car came to a standstill. I got out and smiled around at them. What a big change it was from those piles of moulded steel, furnaced brick and carved cement in the city! I was very grateful to my friend for letting me share his joy. I drew a deep breath and felt greatly refreshed.

I was then shown to the room which was to be mine. It was called the 'English Room' and I felt that it had been chosen by my host with care as I was coming from England. I used to spend a month or so with a friend at Parcevall Hall in Yorkshire nearly every year and my room there became known as the 'Chinese Room'. I always think that to have good friends is one of the most worth-while things in the struggle of one's much-troubled journey on this earth. I am lucky to have been blessed with a number. In this room everything was arranged according to English taste and some of the furniture had been made in England. Two large windows looking out on the panorama of trees, hills, rocks and birds attracted me to stand and gaze.

Soon I came out into the entrance hall and stopped to admire an oil painting of a philosopher. Its brushwork and colour technique pleased me. A maid who appeared informed me that it had been painted by my friend. I smiled and said "I know". I knew that he had been a well-known artist in America and that many examples of his work hang in the Smithsonian Institution. I have also seen a few of his water-colours and have read one of his books. Yet he himself has never mentioned his work to me. "The happy man conceals his talents" says one of our proverbs, in this case truly so.

Most of the house was not yet open for use. But I was treated to a glimpse of the spacious hall. The height and width of it emerged after half the curtain of one window was drawn back to let the sunlight in. There were a large number of works of art, mainly Chinese bronzes, porcelains and jades, tastefully arranged. Presently we entered a small room to one side with many shelves specially designed for smaller objects of art. My friend took down a jade carving of a landscape and I gave him a rough translation of the poem written on it by the emperor Chien-lung. Upstairs in the study a big shelf contained books on art and philosophy. Many of them were taken down and piled on the desk among written notes. A new book must have been taking shape, though I made no enquiry about it.

Meanwhile lunch was ready. We sat at either end of the big plain oak table in a room rather like a verandah, with glass windows all round, facing the lake and the hills. On the floor were many kinds of hot-house flowers and small shrubs in pots; some, with fat, thick leaves, which particularly took my fancy, were from semi-tropical places in South America. While I satisfied my physical appetite, my mental capacity was filled too, and still there was more to learn about Innisfree. My friend said modestly that his own interest was now more or less confined to garden planning. I learnt that herons, ospreys,

Shad blossoms in a Chinese vase

deer, ducks, humming-birds, and kingfishers made their appearance round the lake in turn according to the seasons. Egyptian yellow lotus would display their glory there in summer. Some of the shad trees had already been in bloom and masses of dogwood were in bud on the hills beyond. I was indeed filled with expectation!

Later I went for a stroll with my friend in part of the garden. A number of ornamental statues were dotted about. One plant after another was pointed out to me on our way. We passed over a tiny bridge, under which flowed a narrow winding stream. Its gurgling and murmuring sound was very pleasant

to the ear. A few gardeners were busy weeding or attending
to the plants and flowers in order to be ready for the show
later in the season. Round a small rock garden were many
tiny fountains, spraying out water to help the growing plants.
On a little mound were two shad bushes in full bloom. I had
not seen any before and stepped nearer for a close look. The
straight stems were very thin and looked fragile. Each flower
had five tongue-shaped white petals. They looked similar
to the Chinese service-berry which grows abundantly in
Hupeh and Kiangsi provinces in Central China, though it
is a little taller and has a scent. There was a sort of bower on
the mound containing a number of seats. I gazed round from
there to get a general view of the place. Apologetically yet
with a kind smile my friend remarked that his doctor forbade
him to climb or to walk too long, thus reminding me of the
lift inside the house. When he told me that he was over eighty
years of age, I was dumb with amazement, but I gave him a
deep bow of respect. I had thought him much younger.
This youthful appearance must be due to his great love of
Nature which I hope he will enjoy for many more years to
come.

"The contentment of knowing content," says Lao Tzu,
"will ever be contented." Although I have not yet reached the
stage of contentment of knowing content concerning my work
in life, I was feeling quite content for the moment. My friend
left me after saying that I was to do what I liked. Indeed,
leisure did confer upon me many privileges. I went to have a
look at the many dogwood trees on both sides of the main
avenue leading to the entrance of the house. Their average
height was a little more than seven feet, and they had slender
trunks and many wide-spreading branches. From each graceful branch grew little twigs covered with greenish buds but
with very few leaves. They would not be in bloom yet awhile.
I had not seen these trees before, nor have I yet seen their
flowers but they must be a lovely sight when they are in full
bloom. A bird hopping somewhere produced vibration in one
little branch and this made me notice the stillness of the
rest of the trees. There was no wind, but an occasional breath
of air swept gently over the grass. I stepped forward to find
out what sort of bird it was, but it flew away. My eyes
followed it on the wing and saw it disappear into a

distant bush. The faint murmur of the tiny stream was to be heard at times. The sky was all azure except for a big handful of woolly clouds hung above the horizon. They appeared too idle to move. Whether the sun had shifted my attention to them by directing its rays there I could not tell. It was an open and expanding view, empty yet full, mystic but penetrating, placid and alive.

My contented feeling increased when I stood by the glass-door inside the house, gazing at the lake enclosed by hills and trees. From the doorstep at the back a large well-cut lawn stretched down to the water, exposing its fresh green to the sun. The surface of the lake was like a long sheet of blueish satin, unwrinkled and beautifully shaped to fit round the island and the foot of the hills. The trees were not yet all in leaf but were veiled in a purplish vapour indicating that spring had already come. Dark-green firs stood out against the purple hills, but the distant ones wore a paler garment. I detected at least one shad tree in full bloom looking like a small white cotton ball suspended by an invisible string and held in the hand of some heavenly creature playing with her pet dragon —the long, twisted shape of the lake, its surface ruffled into scales when a breath of wind blew across it. The ball was not being shaken, so the dragon lay there in complete comfort and contentment, its scales glittering and moving. Their movement put life into the scene without disturbing its tranquillity. Gradually the shiny scales changed from silver to gold, to bright red and violet and then mauve. The sun must have been setting, and I was facing a fairy-land on earth. By and by the golden scales lost their lustre and mingled more and more with the rest inside the approaching purple-black bedcover of enormous size which was being spread by Mother Nature. The little white cotton ball of the shad on the island had long vanished. The dragon might still be lying there or have flown away without my knowledge. I thought I was dreaming. Not until the maid came to call me for dinner did I seem to wake. Not the slightest movement had occurred, nor faintest noise sounded. My happy feeling over the dream-like scene made me smile as I thought of my congenial friend and also of the most inviting food!

Next morning when I woke something was puzzling my mind. It was a bird singing on a bough just outside the window.

一聲山鳥啼　幽夢忽喚醒
起來開竹扉　日上東峰頂
　　右元僧哮山中詩

黑鳥兩三自　地上下相將潑
羨水一噪春　晴篁畫領略自然

造物本仁惠　原無殘殺心
人言算近虎　此虎如可親

湖上春來似畫圖
亂峰圍繞水平鋪
松排山面千重翠
月點波心一顆珠
碧毯線頭抽早稻
青羅裙帶展新蒲
未能拋得杭州去
一半勾留是此湖
　　右白居易春題湖上詩

傳言山裡雀　待救來百花時
經日即為別　重來應有期

> A single note sung by a mountain bird
> Suddenly wakes me from a happy dream.
> I get up to open the bamboo-door:
> Lo! the sun is already high above the eastern peak!

So wrote our poet-monk Yin of the thirteenth century as if for me on this particular occasion. Sunbeams were shining on my face through the crack in the curtains. I hastened to wash and dress in order to respond to the call. When I went out, the bird itself had vanished but I liked to imagine that it was leading the chorus of song which greeted me on all sides. I returned the greeting with a broad smile, for the whole atmosphere was jubilant, refreshing and soothing. The clear morning air seemed to have dusted the dull look of sleep from the whole wide view and to have filled it with a radiant satisfaction livelier than that intoxicating contentment of yesterday.

I was soon called in to breakfast and given a message from my most understanding host, who wished me to make myself entirely at home, to enjoy my breakfast alone, and to wander where I liked. The breakfast table was set in the study of my hostess, who was detained in the city by her engagements. I again found myself facing the lake and hills, but from a new angle. The lake looked narrower, as if the hills on either side had moved nearer to each other. This effect was due to two tall trees standing right in the middle of the view, almost filling the gap between the hills. Their thin trunks and straight branches, particularly a long one stretching out to the left, produced a pattern on the surface of the lake like a piece of lattice work.

One wall of the study was close to the hill and a window in it revealed a huge rock with a rugged face at the bottom of the hill. I spied a hollow in which rain water had collected. Two birds looking like chaffinches and one American robin were enjoying a bath there in turn. Never before had I watched birds bathing at such close range. They were perfectly at ease, hopping away a little after taking their bath in the most carefree and natural manner. They ignored my presence or perhaps they could not see me inside the window. Some years ago I wrote a poem in a London park, which suited this moment very well:

> Two or three small birds are jumping up and down
> Together, splashing the water and chattering about the fine
>   spring day.
> I envy their penetrating understanding of Nature's beauty;
> Such a heavenly instinct cannot be expressed in pigments.

American Marmot

The birds were soon joined by a creature which I had not met before. It was rather like a small squirrel, but it had a brown fur coat with black stripes and did not have a bushy tail. I knew it must be the American marmot. Though the birds made no fuss over its presence, the marmot did not seem at ease, but perhaps it was just eager to satisfy its hunger. It darted under the stones and in and out of the holes to pick up any nut or suchlike left by the birds. Its mouth and whiskers moved incessantly to smell as well as to eat. I watched its precise movements and alert manner in these natural surroundings with great interest.

After breakfast I went down to the lake by the glass-door through which I had gazed at the scene the evening before. It did not take me long to cross the beautiful lawn for it was so soft and elastic that it seemed to bear me along without any effort on my part. Near its edge the lawn was dotted with clusters of daffodils in full bloom, dancing and nodding hilariously in the breeze, while a few small plain white butter-flies fluttered to and fro among them. It seemed that invisible wires must have attached the butterflies to the daffodils, for they constantly turned and flew back to their starting point.

A good many stones and rocks were scattered round the lake-shore. At first I thought they had always been there, but presently I realised that they had been placed there artistically by my host as garden ornaments. This reminded me of a little conversation I had had previously with my hostess. She told me that each time she extracted from her husband a promise not to bring any more rocks into the garden, a bigger one than ever appeared shortly after-wards. He had only smiled as he listened. I now understood that each of these rocks had a tale to tell. In China rocks are valued for their strange and curious shapes. They have been the principal ornaments in our gardens for centuries. Many famous Chinese gardens have acquired their name through their ornamental rocks, particularly in Soochow. Though these rocks are placed and arranged by human hands they fit mysteriously as if they were in the scene naturally. Rocks are the bones of the earth, so that a natural scene without them is like a human body without bones. Nature is always asym-metrical—asymmetry is in consequence the essence of Chinese art. As a nation the Chinese love Nature and try to identify their minds with her and live with her as she really is, rather than to imitate her or conquer her. In the rational sense the natural rocks in our gardens may be compared with the carved marble or ornamental sculptures in the gardens of the West. If the owner of Innisfree had planned this part of his garden with marble steps, railings, and terraces ornamented with statues or marble vases symmetrically arranged, no doubt it would have looked grand, commanding the whole view of Nature's features —the lake, hills, trees—as if they were all subordinated to it. And I might have sat here feeling like a tiny dot in a huge living embroidery, conscious of the mighty effort of the human mind to be victorious over Nature. However, as it was, I seemed to have come near the very bosom of Mother Nature in all her majestic yet benevolent friendliness.

I do not mean that no garden should contain sculptured marble ornaments, but that the selection of rocks and their arrangement in a garden is an art in itself. Rocks are as widely different from one another as human faces. Many of our old masters wrote essays about them and worked out artistic revelations in the natural formations, such as in the well-known *Treatise on Rocks* by Li Hsi Ch'ai, published in the fifteenth century. In this book many famous rocks and stones from different notable places all over China are discussed. In the few existing Sung masterpieces, and perhaps T'ang too, rocks are painted as subjects simply for the sake of their aesthetic shapes. We Chinese feel that nature is a storehouse upon which every kind of artistic talent can draw. The talent may reveal itself through all kinds of media, such as water-colour, oils, wood, stone or metal, but also through the selection of a rock. A beautiful piece of rock has been valued as highly as any work of art and they have often been collected by connoisseurs. Probably this art has not yet been practised outside China, but with the tendency in modern art towards abstract, surrealistic or non-objective expression, the study of beauty as revealed in rocks may become more widespread. Herbert Read once told me that Henry Moore, the English sculptor, often meditates before natural rocks, absorbing inspiration for his own creations. Here my host had long made use of his artistic mind's eye to select rocks and collect them for his garden. His choice and arrangement of them won my admiration.

My pleasure drew me, in turn, close to each of the rocks along the shore, and though no formality or ceremony was needed, for I was not being watched by a single soul, I greeted each one with a smile and sometimes with a friendly touch of the hand. Unexpectedly one rock assumed for me the shape of a tiger, approaching the water to drink. Had it been carved by a human hand, it might have displayed the human conception of a tiger and its ferocity would have disturbed the tranquil scene. As I gazed at it I wrote a little poem:

> One is told not to approach a tiger,
> But this one looks very friendly.
> Nature is at heart benevolent,
> Never designing cruelly!

Presently a few ripples stirred the satin surface of the lake on the left. I saw a big duck floating along with a number of her offspring. Even the little ones did not seem to wish to utter any cry. When they were not far from the tiger rock and me, the duck made a swift turn towards the island and her offspring followed. By and by the few ripples stirred by their gentle movement were no longer perceptible and their bodies blended into one black dot. Just at that moment a big shadow appeared in the water. Lifting my head I saw a huge blue heron drift

The Tiger rock and other rocks

past. At once it widened the scope of my gaze, bringing all the distant hills, lake, trees, island, and rocks into a composition for a picture. I stretched out my hand and patted the tiger rock as if to say "What do you think of it, old man?"

An unusual gate formed by a pile of rocks drew my steps. There I bumped against another rock with a shape like a human figure. A biggish bird, perhaps a raven, perched upon it, immediately took to flight. Annoyance at my clumsiness did not diminish my high spirits and the following old Chinese joke came into my mind:

A very short-sighted man lost his way on a journey in the country. Noticing a big rock on the roadside with a crow sitting on it, he mistook it for another man. He therefore asked the direction and as he received no immediate answer shouted louder and louder, until eventually he frightened the crow away. Thereupon he swore: "I asked you the way several times and you gave me no answer. Now your hat has been blown away, but naturally it is not my business to help you."

A narrow footpath wound among the trees between the lake and the hill. It did not seem to have been trodden by any human being for some time and my foot-prints stood out clearly on the damp soil. Occasionally I slipped a little but was prevented from falling by the rugged roots of the trees protruding from the surface of the earth. The sun did not penetrate here, but there were occasional dry spots. I had no plans but just moved and paused in turn, as my eye was pleased or my mind delighted. A few lofty pine trees had their twisted branches interlocked in interesting patterns. A great commotion arose at my approach, a flock of wild duck flying up and away over the tree tops to an island near the other side of the lake. When they circled round and returned to their original base, I was happy to realise that they were only displaying their aerial ballet for me to see.

My eyes were next attracted by the inverted image of the island on the water. Many trees looked so mysterious and magical that I wished I could go down among them. As that was impossible I turned back. The wildness of this part of the garden appealed to me.

Having arrived back at my starting point, I had a good look at a beautiful slender rock sticking out of the water near the shore. It might easily have been in a Soochow garden. Even its environment fitted, for between this rock and the wooden-fenced edge of the lake I noticed a few withered stalks and stems of the lotus leaves and flowers of the previous summer.

· Passing the lotus pond I walked on towards a hut where a few boats were kept. Somehow I did not feel prepared to row myself out to the thickly-wooded island as I had intended a few moments ago. So on and on I wandered. Tall pines rose above the other trees. Masses of brown and yellow leaves left over from the winter were piled several inches deep and rustled under my feet.

I was now facing the island from a new angle. Most of the

lake was hidden behind it. The house of Innisfree had become a decorative structure in the centre of the distant hill. With the island in the foreground and the lake in between, it was like a landscape painting by one of our old masters. Three small shad bushes with their clusters of white flowers gleamed in the sun. Though there were doubtless many interesting things to be found on the island, I felt I had lingered long enough and reluctantly retraced my steps without making the attempt to reach it.

Shrine for Kuan Yin

On my way back along the main path, I noticed another path made of stones of different sizes leading up to the house. I went up it step by step and it was a joy to me to walk on these stones, as unevenly placed as if they were there in their original positions. After climbing a little way I came upon a beautifully carved white stone statue of Kuan-Yin, the Chinese Goddess of Mercy, set in a niche like a natural shrine. In front of this stone image were a number of tall straight trees with thick trunks. The air was so still and the sun so unusually bright, that not even a single shadow of a twig was blurred. I was back in my own country, standing meditating inside the main hall of a Buddhist Monastery high up Lu mountain on a fine day. The

T

tall trees were big wooden pillars. Some one was praying too, or else a monk was beating the Mo-yü, or wooden-fish, a kind of Buddhist musical instrument, for I heard a succession of clear notes somewhere close to me. I looked round and at first could see no sign of anyone, but eventually I spotted a woodpecker high above, busily pecking at a tree trunk for insects and other food. Then I saw another woodpecker. First one would peck, then the other, producing a continual tapping noise, and the notes sounded very much like those of the Mo-yü. Nothing could have suited the scene better. It carried me right out of the western world into the eastern hemisphere. The half-opened eyes of Kuan Yin and her gentle smile showed complete approval of my immobility. My friend had again shown his perfect discretion in putting here this peaceful Goddess instead of a muscular, dynamic and vigorous sculpture of a human figure or animal. Bathing in the warm but not too hot sun of early May, I sat here for a while in solitude. It came to me that 'Yun-chin' or 'Footpath of the clouds' would be a suitable name for this rocky part of the garden and I decided to write the Chinese character for my friend later on.

Before entering the house, I noticed two little stone lions of Chinese origin on either side of the threshold, as the door-guards in our sense, I presumed. At last I was back inside thinking how pleasant life would be if every human being could manage to spend one hour or even half an hour a day in companionship with nature. Those who are day and night between walls of cement and steel under unhealthy electric light must inevitably become exhausted with words, figures and documents, so that they turn into irritable, quarrelsome, greedy and warlike beings. They estrange themselves from nature. So, if any universal rule could be set up, I wish it might be one to compel every human being, particularly businessmen, indust-rialists, deadly-minded materialists and pig-headed statesmen and politicians, to come out of their cells and spend a little time with nature each day. Perhaps then—only then —peace would enter all ordinary homes, towns and cities.

My cheerful countenance drew a smile from my friend at lunch. He did not enquire much about what I had been doing and I said very little. Later when I was again facing the lake, there came into my mind the following poem by our T'ang poet, Po Chu-yi:

The Lake at Innisfree

The presence of spring has turned the lake into a picture:
Many rugged peaks surround it and its water surface spreads
    evenly.
Groups of pines are dotted on the hill-face in emerald,
    layer after layer;
The reflection of the moon in the water looks like a pearl.
Young crops lift their heads, woven into a green carpet.
New leaves of the high weeds stick out like ribbon's ends
    round an azure skirt.
I cannot leave Hanchow and go away;
Half of the reason is that this lake makes me want to linger.

For the same reason I did not want to leave Innisfree. But
I look forward to my next visit, knowing that I have many
more things to see there and many more happy moments to
enjoy. My gratitude to my friend expressed itself in a little
poem :

> After only one day we have to part;
> But I hope to have time to come again.
> I leave my words with the mountain birds:
> "Await me until all the flowers bloom!"

Dogwood in a Chinese Vase

XXV

TSAI CHIEN, NEW YORK

Tsai-chien is the Chinese equivalent of 'Au revoir'. It means 'See again'. In villages or small towns, where friends meet every day, the phrase used is 'Ming Tien Chien', 'See you tomorrow'. A compatriot of mine had been only a few days in London, when he and I went to a tea-party. Before leaving, my friend thanked the host and said 'Ming Tien Chien', afterwards translating it literally into English. At the time our host did not seem to notice the expression particularly,

but the next day a telegram came to my friend saying: "Unable to see you today, previously engaged". My friend was greatly surprised, having no recollection that a meeting had been suggested. I had to explain that his literal translation had given rise to the telegram and that the incident was an example of how English people weigh words. I cannot truthfully say 'Ming Tien Chien' to New York in these days of travelling difficulties, yet I hope to see it again some day!

I felt surprised the first time I heard a sweet voice say "Darlings, good-bye," and a moment later the same voice exclaiming "Thank goodness, they've gone". I am used to it now. It happens in China, in London, and I expect in New York too. We all often express ourselves contrary to our true thoughts and quite naturally accept such behaviour from each other. Can anyone truly claim never to have committed a single offence against right conduct? Perhaps it is not seriously wrong to bid a passionate farewell to someone whom one does not particularly want to meet again. Wrong doing on a big scale will finally be tried by fallible human laws, but a small wrong is allowed to pass unnoticed. To my mind there is a charm in this contradiction. We smile self-indulgently when we detect some contradiction in our own life and ought to submit to being laughed at when somebody else notices it. I must admit that I have often enough felt in two minds when saying 'Tsai chien'.

Nevertheless, I must make it clear that when I say 'Tsai chien, New York' there is no conflict in my mind. In the first place, New York is a place, not a person. Whether one wants to see a friend again or not is often a matter of hidden trouble. But it does not affect a place if one visitor among millions expresses a wish to see it again, though the inhabitants may be up in arms at once if one expresses no sadness at bidding them farewell. Everyone likes others to share his love—unless it is that of his sweetheart! However, there is something different about the inhabitants of Manhattan. During my stay in New York, I was continually reminded that a New Yorker only really knows the neighbourhood he sleeps in, no matter where his activities may take him. I think therefore that I can safely say 'Tsai chien, New York,' for the inhabitants of Brooklyn will interpret it to mean that I want to come and see Richmond again and so on. As I am a Chinese, no doubt I shall only be suspected of wanting to visit Chinatown again, if for no other reason than to sample some special Chinese delicacies to offset English rations. But it is not as simple as that. I have various reasons for wanting to see New York again.

As I have mentioned in one of my other books, even a small bird leaves claw-marks in the snow, and I too like to record my footprints on the places I have trod, though the inhabitants may not care at all. There is this difference between the bird and me, that whereas it does not bother to

look at its claw-marks on the snow, I am a man who, while
not fussy over many things, is quite touchy about his own
footprints. I not only make records and sketches of them but
also compare those made at a given place at various stages of
my negligible life. Dr. Samuel Johnson wrote in his *Life of
Addison:*

"History may be formed from permanent monuments and records;
but lives can only be written from personal knowledge, which is
growing every day less, and in a short time is lost for ever. What is
known can seldom be immediately told; and when it might be
told, it is no longer known. The delicate features of the mind, the
nice discriminations of character, and the minute peculiarities of
conduct, are soon obliterated; and it is surely better that caprice,
obstinacy, frolic, and folly, however they might delight in the description, should be silently forgotten, than that, by wanton
merriment and unseasonable detection, a pang should be given to
a widow, a daughter, a brother, or a friend."

I am in no position to write a history of New York, nor am
I sketching a biography of any particular character. Yet I do
like to give myself a pang or two now and then. I can only do
so when I record and make a fuss over my own footprints. New
York gave me more pangs than any other place I have been
to, for I never knew what I would do from day to day.

I have always felt more or less sure that the things and
buildings I have come to know in other places would look
almost the same if I should return. I do not have this certainty
about New York. One's reaction to a place when one is young
is of course different from one's reaction as one grows older,
but as a rule the general appearance and structure of a place
remain unchanged. This can hardly be said of New York. When
I first went to Park Avenue I noticed a solid old building,
many storeys high, and in what seemed like a few days it had
vanished to make way for a new skyscraper. I realise that I
shall be sure to see big changes however soon I return to New
York. Many people are inclined to lament the changing face
of an old place, but I accept some changes as inevitable.

Before I sailed for New York, I read such descriptions of
it as I could find. I was unable to follow much of O. Henry's
Baghdad of the Atlantic as I do not know Baghdad except
through the Arabian Nights. Van Wyck Brooks' description of
the cornfields on Nassau Street and of the Dutch-built houses

and fishermen's inns of New York in the seventeenth century captured my imagination; while the following extract from Edward Dicey's book *Six Months in the Federal States*, published in 1863, aroused mixed feelings in me about changes:

"Past Sandy Hook Fort, where the stars and stripes were floating gaily; through the winding Narrows: close beneath the wooded banks of Staten Island, where villas of wood, villas of stone, villas with Doric porticoes, villas with Italian campaniles, Swiss cottages, and Grecian mansions seemed to succeed each other in a never-ending panorama; we floated onwards, towards the long black line which marked the city of New York. . . . An old-fashioned English hackney-coach carried me to my destination, through dull, English-looking streets, with English names; and the driver cheated me at the end of my fare, with genuine London exorbitance. . . . There is a picture-gallery; there are a few public buildings, which are supposed to possess architectural merits; and there is the Croton Aqueduct, interesting to engineers. Still, with all deference to my New York friends, I hardly think that a European traveller need go far out of his way to visit any of these curiosities. . . . New York is not a show-place, and, architecturally, possesses but little claim to distinction. The Island of Manhattan, on which New York is placed, is very like the shape of a sole. . . . The general effect of the 'Empire City' is to me disappointing. Simple magnitude is never very striking to anyone accustomed to London; and, except in magnitude, there is not much to impress you. . . . There is no symmetry or harmony about the streets, so that it lacks grandeur, without having irregularity enough to be picturesque. . . . Fifth Avenue is symmetrical enough; but its semi-detached stone mansions, handsome as they are, have not sufficient height to justify its American name of the Street of Palaces; while its monotony is dreadful. . . . The poorer streets, towards the banks of the Island, have no architectural pretensions; and their prototype, the famous Bowery, bears the strongest family resemblance to the Walworth Road or Mile-end Gate. . . .

There is a popular delusion in England, that New York is a sort of ginger-bread-and-gilt city; and that, contrasted with an English town, there is a want of solidity about the whole place, materially as well as morally. On the contrary, I was never in a town where, externally at any rate, show was so much sacrificed to solid comfort. The ferries, the cars, the street rail roads, and the houses, are all so arranged as to give one substantial comfort, without external decoration. It is, indeed, indoors that the charm of New York is found. . . . The rooms are so light and lofty; the passages are so well warmed; the doors slide backwards in their grooves, so easily and yet so tightly; the chairs are so luxurious; the beds are so elastic, and the linen so clean, and, let me add, the living so excellent, that I would never wish for better quarters, or for a more hospitable welcome, than I have found in many private houses of

New York. . . . The quiet and order of the city are in themselves remarkable. There is an air of unsecured security about New York I never saw equalled out of England. . . . The people seem instinctively to keep themselves in order. . . . Anybody may stop his cart or carriage where he likes; and I have seen Wall Street in its busiest hours blocked up by a stoppage caused by some brewer's dray, which chose to stand still at the side of the narrow street. . . . There were few balls or large parties, and the opera was not regularly open, partly because public feeling was averse to much gaiety; partly, and still more, because the wealthy classes had retrenched all superfluous expenditure with a really wonderful unanimity. . . . But I know that, on a bright winter day, when the whole population

Every kind of impossibility is daily becoming possible

seemed to be driving out in sleighs to the great skating carnivals at the Central Park, I have seldom seen a brighter or gayer-looking city than that of New York."

Edward Dicey came to New York some eighty years ago, at the time of the American Civil War, and his book records the impressions of an English journalist of that period. I admire his capacity for generalisation; my mind has never let me see things in such a big way. What I have seen and recorded in words and pictures here centres round my own footprints. I remember reading that Lord Byron once wrote: "Thou art in London—in that pleasant place where every kind of mischief's daily brewing". Though being in no position to say things about New York such as Lord Byron could about London, somehow I feel I could perhaps remark in not dissimilar way: "Thou art in New York—in that pleasant place where every kind of impossibility is daily becoming possible". What a lot more I should be able to see if I found myself in New York again.

There is an old American saying about New York: 'It is a nice place to visit, but I wouldn't want to live there, because there is that little thing called MONEY." Nevertheless, I look forward to my next visit when the 'little thing' becomes available to me again.

Tsai Chien, New York!

Inside Pennsylvania Station

An afternoon storm over Times Square